10=
NET

Religion in America

A History

OF THE

Councils of Baltimore

1791-1884

Peter Guilday

ARNO PRESS & THE NEW YORK TIMES

New York 1969

A HISTORY OF THE COUNCILS
OF BALTIMORE

(1791–1884)

A HISTORY OF THE
COUNCILS OF BALTIMORE

(1791–1884)

BY

PETER GUILDAY

NEW YORK
THE MACMILLAN COMPANY
1932

Nihil obstat
ARTHUR J. SCANLON, S. T. D.
Censor Librorum.

Imprimatur
✠ PATRICK CARDINAL HAYES
Archbishop, New York.
January 16, 1932.

SET UP BY BROWN BROTHERS LINOTYPERS
PRINTED IN THE UNITED STATES OF AMERICA
BY THE FERRIS PRINTING COMPANY

PREFACE

WHEN the Code of Canon Law became the universal legislation of the Church in 1918, an important practical question arose concerning its effect upon the body of law contained in the decrees of our Baltimore Councils. It is commonly stated by canonists that the Code can be best understood when viewed in the perspective of the Church's general legislation and of the special laws promulgated by the hierarchy of each nation. The increasing number of commentaries on the Code is making this fact clearer. So far as the Church in the United States is concerned, apart from several commentaries, the doctoral dissertations issued by the School of Canon Law at the Catholic University of America, Washington, D. C., have dealt to some extent with the transition of the Baltimore legislation to the general law of the Church as prescribed by the Code.

The object of this short historical sketch does not include the history of this gradual transition since 1918 to the present; its purpose is to bring into a consecutive narrative the development of our canonical legislation as embodied in the conciliar acts and decrees of the Baltimore assemblies. Eleven of these have been held at Baltimore between 1791 and 1884, and, being national in scope and jurisdiction, their enactments have been a chief influence upon all synodal or conciliar assemblies held in other dioceses and provinces. In fact, the principal office of other councils and synods has been to make known and to execute the Baltimore decrees, and beyond this they have not ventured save in rare and mostly minor instances.

The development of our canonical legislation from the days when, with a small group of priests around him, Bishop John Carroll promulgated the first disciplinary code for the Church in the United States (1791), to that magnificent assembly, a century later (1884), when a hierarchy of over seventy archbishops and bishops met under the presidency of Archbishop James Gibbons, will ever be one of the most interesting chapters in Church law. It is the story of this development which is attempted in these pages. To have gone beyond the printed *Acta et Decreta* of the Baltimore Councils into the archival sources which reveal the minds of our legislators, would have carried the work beyond reasonable bounds. A simple chronological narrative corresponded best to the purpose of the writer.

The writer offers sincere thanks to a member of the Faculty of the School of Canon Law of the Catholic University of America, to Mr. Thomas F. Meehan of the editorial board of *America*, and to the Most Reverend Thomas J. Shahan, D.D., Rector Emeritus of the Catholic University of America, for their coöperation in reading and criticizing the manuscript.

It is fitting that this short contribution to our canonical history should be dedicated through their American Provincial to that body of priests who began the work of higher clerical education in the United States at the very time Dr. Carroll called his priests together in 1791, and who have assisted our prelates in the work of all the Councils from 1829 to 1884.

To the priests, living and dead, of the Society of Saint Sulpice, this is another unforgettable debt of honor due them from the Church in our country.

PETER GUILDAY.

December 20, 1931
Catholic University of America

CONTENTS

PART IV. THE PLENARY COUNCILS OF BALTIMORE

PART V. SUMMARY OF THE CONCILIAR LEGISLATION
         OF BALTIMORE (1791-1884)

A HISTORY OF THE COUNCILS
OF BALTIMORE

(1791–1884)

INTRODUCTION

"THE trials, the labors, the hopes and the consolations of the Spouse of Christ are distinctly and authoritatively expressed in the synods and councils which have been held in provinces and countries, or in world-gatherings by the bishops of the Church of God." [1]

These words of the Father of American Catholic history sum up the purpose of this historical sketch.

The subject matter of Church history, whether of a general nature or of a particular country or province, is now so extensive in scope that it is impossible to encompass it completely and thoroughly from all points of view. In its widest sense such a history should contain everything that had ever taken place in the life of the Church, without regard to time or place limits. For this reason, as well as for the fact that the history of the Catholic Church, however limited, is the truest history of mankind, since it embraces the story of man's progress toward his eternal goal, historians are accustomed to distinguish between its external and internal aspects. External Church history treats of the visible development of the Church—the propagation of the faith and missionary endeavor; the relations between the Church and political governments; the influence of Christian ideals upon public morals and social institutions; and the effect of the Faith on literature, art, science and even on material progress. Internal Church history embraces all those problems which arise from questions of hierarchical order and jurisdiction;

[1] Shea, J. G., "The Coming Plenary Council of Baltimore," *American Catholic Quarterly Review*, IX (1884), 340.

1

from doctrine and doctrinal development; from Christian discipline, worship, and liturgical rites; from Christian socio-religious customs and morals; and from the devotional life of Catholics.[2]

The progress of the Church in the United States since the consecration of our first bishop, John Carroll, in 1790 up to the present has been so tremendous that its external history alone is beyond the grasp of any one student. No one writer can keep pace with this external growth; and we have seen multiplied within the past half-century since the death of John Gilmary Shea (1892) a host of biographical sketches of bishops, priests, and laity, an ever-increasing number of corporative histories of religious Orders, Congregations and Communities, a large number of diocesan and provincial histories and a multitude of parochial histories. Such historical activity is innate in the Catholic heart which must ever desire to see perpetuated through these volumes, large and small, the outward signs of that inward vitality which is the basic reason for our exceptional progress in this country during the past one hundred and fifty years.[3]

To a large extent, owing to the limited sources at the command of our historical centers, this literature has been forced to neglect the inner life of the Church and of churchmen in this country. We need to know more about the internal growth and progress of the constitutional government of the Church, more about the rise and solution of disciplinary questions within the fold, more about the problems peculiar to our own Church in the United States, as well as the problems impinging on the doctrinal aspects of American life and action.

Hence, the purpose of this book is to approach the history of this internal development from the official records which have

[2] Guilday, *Introduction to Church History* (St. Louis, Mo., 1925), 33-35.
[3] So large has been the output of Catholic historical literature in the United States that even a guide or bibliographical list is the work of a group of researchers. Cf. Guilday, "Recent Studies in American Catholic History, 1892-1930," *American Ecclesiastical Review*, May, 1931, 528-546.

been handed on to posterity by those spiritual leaders who, in obedience to the desire of the Holy See, legislated in synodal and conciliar assemblies for the preservation of our Faith and for the harmony of our discipline with that of the universal Church.

The canon law of the Church is the Gospel of Christ in action. The adaptation of this common law of the Gospel both in the letter and in the spirit, with the exceptions permitted by the Holy See on account of local conditions, is the innermost history of Catholic discipline in the United States. All those assemblies of a synodal or conciliar nature which the diocesan bishop alone, or the bishops of a province, or again the hierarchy of a country call together, are so many channels from the fountains of ecclesiastical jurisprudence within the sacred keeping of the Church, ruled by the Sovereign Pontiff, the Bishop and Pope of Rome, the Vicar of Christ on earth.

The Fathers of the Second Plenary Council of Baltimore defined the chief duty of these conciliar assemblies as not merely to provide for a faithful adherence to the general laws of the Church whether in œcumenical councils or by pontifical constitutions, but also to correct abuses and to guard the doctrines of our holy Faith against the machinations of innovators.[4] "Their principal object, however, is to regulate discipline, whether by the correction of abuses, or the establishment of such rules of conduct as circumstances may require."[5]

Although the terms *synod* and *council* are interchangeable, the word *council* has come to be used: first, for the general or œcumenical assemblies of all the bishops in union with the Holy See and under the presidency of the Pope, who alone has the

[4] *Conc. Plen. Balt. II*, no. 57.
[5] *Pastoral Letter* of 1866, in *National Pastorals of the American Hierarchy*, ed. Guilday (Washington, 1923), 199. *Cf. Cath. Encycl., s. v.* "Discipline," v, 30: "Ecclesiastical discipline is the aggregate of laws and directions given by the Church to the faithful for their conduct both private and public. This is discipline in its widest acceptation, and includes natural and divine as well as positive laws, and faith, worship, and morals; in a word, all that affects the conduct of Christians."

right to convoke them; [6] secondly, for plenary or national assemblies of all the bishops of a nation under the presidency of the senior metropolitan or of an apostolic delegate appointed for that purpose by the Holy See, without whose permission they cannot be called; and thirdly, for provincial assemblies of the bishops of a province under the metropolitan who presides over the council. The Council of Trent ordered the convocation of provincial councils every three years. [7]

The convocation of a diocesan synod, or an assembly of all those clerics of the diocese who have the right or privilege of attendance, belongs to the bishop of the diocese. In a synod the bishop is the sole lawgiver. Previous conferences usually take place with groups or committees of prudent ecclesiastics, skilled in the law of the Church. The Council of Trent decreed that diocesan synods be held once a year. [8]

By means of plenary or national councils legislation is drafted and promulgated, with the approval of the Holy See, for the Church in the entire nation; by means of provincial councils a province (or, as is commonly, though inaccurately, called, an archdiocese) with like approval receives its legislative decrees and enactments from the hierarchy of that territorial jurisdiction; and by means of the decrees promulgated by the bishop in a local synod the administration of the diocese is regulated.

There need not necessarily be any filiation between these three classes of assemblies. For example, the first meeting of the clergy under Bishop Carroll (1791), whose ecclesiastical jurisdiction embraced the whole territory of the United States at that time, antedated the First Provincial Council (1829) by thirty-eight years; and this First Provincial Council preceded by twenty-three years the First Plenary or National Council of 1852.

[6] On the interesting historical question of the number of œcumenical councils, see Hefele-Leclercq, *Histoire des Conciles* (Paris, 1907), I, 78-91.

[7] Sess. xxiv. c 2. *de Ref.* The Code of 1918 prescribes that provincial councils be convoked at least every twenty years.

[8] The Code of 1918 prescribes such assemblies at least every ten years.

On the problems taken up for discussion and solution, the canon law of the Church provides that in national or plenary councils as well as in provincial assemblies and diocesan synods only those questions can be dealt with legitimately which concern the spread of the Faith, the discipline of Christian morals, the correction of abuses, or the solution of controverted points of discipline. The whole purpose of the council or synod is to create a uniform system of Church legislation in the diocese, province, or nation.[9]

In actual missionary work, the diocesan synod is of practical value in maintaining discipline at a high level and in perfect conformity with the ecclesiastical legislation of the universal Church. It was for this reason, among others, that the Council of Trent (1545-1563) confirmed the decrees of the Fourth Lateran Council (1215), insisting upon annual assemblies of the diocesan clergy for this purpose. However, this decree was not to be interpreted as recognizing the annual synod as a necessary means of spiritual progress in the diocese. It has been stated that probably in no diocese in the world from the time of the Tridentine decree to the Code of 1918 have annual diocesan synods been regularly held.[10]

In the United States, for example, where the Church was one diocese from 1791 to 1808, and one province from 1808 to 1846, annual assemblies were not necessary and would indeed have been impracticable, owing to the great distances, to the difficulty of travel, to the fewness of the clergy, and to the paucity of problems confronting the nascent American Church. It was only after dioceses began to multiply between 1808 and 1829 that some of our prelates believed national councils necessary for the purpose of creating this uniform legislation; even then, the necessity of these national assemblies was not generally accepted.

[9] Cf. Rev. C. Augustine, O.S.B., *Commentary on the New Code of Canon Law* (St. Louis, 1919), II, 305.
[10] Cf. Smith, "On Diocesan Synods," in *Brownson's Quarterly Review,* July, 1875, 314-333.

To understand the *Acta et Decreta,* one must be familiar to some extent with the procedure of the synod or council. The ceremonies to be observed in provincial councils and diocesan synods in this country are given in detail in the *Ceremonial for the Use of the Catholic Churches in the United States of America,*[11] which was compiled by Bishop Rosati of St. Louis at the request of the First Provincial Council of Baltimore of 1829. The *Ceremonial* received the approval of Pope Gregory XVI in 1841 and was formally adopted by the First Plenary Council of Baltimore in 1852. In 1883, under the direction of Archbishop Corrigan of New York, there appeared a little volume, from the pen of the late Archbishop Messmer, entitled *Praxis Synodalis: Manuale Synodi Dioecesanae ac Provincialis Celebrandae,* based upon the *Praxis Celebrandae Synodi Dioecesanae* by Gavantus, and compiled for the practical work of our American Councils in the future as well as to describe the method followed in the assemblies up to that time.

Since of the eleven meetings of a national character held in Baltimore between 1791 and 1884 the first only was strictly speaking a synod, the ceremonies of the provincial council alone need be described in a general way.

Under the canonical procedure in vogue previous to 1918, the conciliary method was as follows: before the opening of the council, letters of convocation are sent to all the bishops of the province and to all others who have the right to attend either as consultants or as prelates with a deliberative voice. On three Sundays before the council opens, the convocation is published in all the churches of the province and the prayers of the faithful asked for its success. It is customary for the collect *De Spiritu Sancto* to be ordered by the bishops of each suffragan See as an *oratio imperata* until the conclusion of the Council. The metropolitan church is to be adorned as for the greater festivals, and on the evening before the council opens the bells are to be

---

[11] Based on the *Caeremoniale Episcoporum* and the *Pontificale Romanum* (Tit. *Ordo ad Synodum*).

rung. The custom in the United States has been for the archbishop's throne to be placed at the altar itself, and the thrones of the bishops on either side of the sanctuary in order of seniority of consecration. The rest of the clergy, in order of dignity and priority of ordination, occupy the remaining portion of the sanctuary. What are known as pre-synodal meetings may be held, with the archbishop as chairman, for the purpose of arranging the congregations and sessions as well as for compiling the *agenda* of the council and the selection of conciliar officials.

The formal meetings held during the council are of three kinds. There is first the *private congregations* in which are present only the archbishop and his suffragans together with the secretaries of the council; these are usually held in the morning in the archbishop's house. In these *private congregations* all questions which the prelates may decide to discuss with the larger group of theologians, officials and consultants are decided upon, and in each case, as with the formal declaration of decrees, the decision rests upon a majority vote. It is the rule to open these *private congregations* with the prayer *Veni, Sancte Spiritus* and to end them with the *Sub tuum praesidium*. The secretaries are not present at those parts of the meeting in which the creation of new Sees and the nomination of bishops are discussed.

The *public congregations* are held each afternoon and the assembly is made up of the prelates, the theologians of the archbishops and bishops, the heads of religious Orders and Congregations, all the officers of the council, and in some cases of specially invited guests. Each clergyman present has the right to speak once on each subject, and again the decision rests upon a majority vote. Naturally, with so many ecclesiastics in attendance, these *public congregations* are surrounded with a wealth of ceremony which gives them the character of the ritual of greater festivals.

Three solemn *sessions* are held during the council. The first is the solemn opening of the council the first day. A procession of all the ecclesiastics participating in the council takes place, moving from the archbishop's house to the cathedral sanctuary. The prelates and bishops are vested as for the more solemn ceremonies; prescribed hymns and psalms are sung and recited, and solemn Pontifical Mass of the Holy Ghost is celebrated by the archbishop. At the end of the Mass, a sermon, chiefly intended for the people, is preached; and then the council is formally opened with suitable prayers, the Litany of the Saints, and the *Veni, Creator Spiritus.* After all have taken their places, the archbishop speaks in Latin on the purpose of the council and formally asks those present if it be their will to begin the deliberations of the assembly. Consent given, the archbishop declares the council opened. The list of those who have a right to be present, either by virtue of convocation or invitation, is then read, and also the list of the conciliar officials. After the names are read, the prelates present elect them by vote. In the seven Baltimore Provincial Councils, these officials have been Promoters, Secretaries, Masters of Ceremonies and Chanters. In the three Plenary Councils which followed, Notaries, Judges, and other officials were elected.

All bishops who have not taken part in a previous council then make the profession of faith as in the Roman Pontifical.

A second solemn *session* with special ceremonies is held during the council and solemn Pontifical Mass is celebrated for the happy repose of the souls of the bishops and clergy who have passed away since the last council; a suitable panegyric is given on the deceased prelates.

The third solemn *session* is held on the closing day of the council. Solemn Pontifical Mass is celebrated, and after the last Gospel a sermon is given. The secretary of the council then reads the decrees passed in the private congregations, and the promoter asks that these decrees be formally promulgated. The archbishop then proposes them to the judgment of the prelates, who reply individually that their promulgation is agreed upon, and the solemn declaration of the same is made by the archbishop, who then signs the decrees as do also the bishops in order of seniority. The *acclamationes* follow, the *Te Deum* is sung, the *Pax* is given by the archbishop to each of the bishops, and the *session* is closed with special prayers and the solemn blessing of the archbishop.[12]

The Church in the United States up to the present has had but eleven assemblies of a conciliar kind: the National Synod of 1791 under Bishop Carroll, to which may be added as a supplementary code of legislation the Agreement of the Meeting of 1810; the seven Provincial Councils of Baltimore from 1829 to 1849; and the three National Councils of 1852, 1866, and 1884. The *Acta et Decreta* of these councils together with the *Pastoral Letters* which were issued at their close "contain not only the history of the Catholic Faith in this country from the establishment of the hierarchy down to the present time, but they offer a prudent and sagacious commentary upon the events of the past and upon the influences which have at various epochs affected the Catholic life of our beloved country." [13] These *Acta et Decreta* have all been published (in Latin); they form the basis for a history of canonical legislation and contain the guiding principles of an adequate interpretation of the progress of ecclesiastical discipline in the United States since the creation of the American hierarchy.

The printed decrees of these eleven assemblies from 1791 to 1884 are not, however, the only documentary sources of what may be called up to 1918 our national canon law. All along these years there were promulgated for the discipline of the Church in this country, over and above these conciliar enactments, decrees from the Sovereign Pontiffs who have ruled over the Church since 1791, Instructions from various Congrega-

[12] *Ceremonial for the Use of the Catholic Churches in the United States of America, published by order of the First Council of Baltimore with the approbation of the Holy See.* 3rd ed. (Baltimore, 1885), 462-479.
[13] *National Pastorals of the American Hierarchy (1792-1919)*, ed. Guilday, Washington, D. C., 1923. *Cf.* MacCaffrey, *History of the Catholic Church in the Nineteenth Century* (St. Louis, 1910), II, 291-309.

tions of the Roman Curia, and in particular Instructions and Decrees from the Sacred Congregation de Propaganda Fide which governed our Church during its first or missionary period, from 1622 until 1908, when by the decree *Sapienti Consilio* the American Church was placed under the general administration of the Holy See.

Writing in the *Dublin Review* for July, 1875, on the "Origin, History and Nature of Diocesan Synods," Rev. Dr. S. B. Smith, then one of the prominent canonists of the American Church, explains the general decline of synods and councils within a century after the Council of Trent. Even so profound a work, he writes, as the classic *De Synodo Dioecesana* of Pope Benedict XIV (1740-1758), which has been styled one of the most important modern works in canon law, was unable to revive the popularity of these conciliar assemblies. The Synod of Pistoja in 1786 brought some discredit on these meetings of the hierarchy, and the long period of political and religious unrest in Europe from 1789 to 1815 gave little opportunity for the bishops to hold these meetings.

In contrast to this state of affairs, from the very beginning of our hierarchical form of Church government, synods and councils have prospered and thrived in the United States. No hindrances of a political or religious nature have stood in the way of these assemblies in our country, and it is believed that their frequency here has had the effect, especially in English-speaking countries, of stimulating their frequency abroad.

No accurate list of the diocesan synods from 1810, when Bishops Flaget, Egan and Cheverus took possession of their Sees as suffragans to Baltimore, or of provincial councils, since the last of these national assemblies was held at Baltimore in 1849, has been compiled. Shea printed an *Essay on the Bibliography of the Councils, Synods, and Statutes of the Catholic Church in the United States,*[14] but the list is incomplete. Probably, he has

[14] New York, 1890, 16 pp.

not missed any important diocesan synod or provincial council in the second, third and fourth volumes of his *History of the Catholic Church in the United States,* which ends with the Second Plenary Council of 1866; but the only sure way to compile an exact list is to appeal to the members of the present hierarchy. This the writer did in the autumn of 1929. Not all the chanceries were able to send this information. Some stated frankly that there was no means of knowing for a certainty all the diocesan synods that had been held. With the exception of a few dioceses, the number of these synods is smaller than would be expected.

On the Sunday before the opening of the Second Plenary Council of Baltimore, Archbishop Martin J. Spalding of Baltimore, the Apostolic Delegate of the Council, preached on councils in general but there is no reference to the progress of conciliar legislation in the sermon.[15] In his *Elements of Ecclesiastical Law,*[16] Dr. Smith has several succinct paragraphs on the *History of Canon Law in the United States;* but they are of little help except as having been provocative of an interesting question regarding the Holy See's approval of the decrees of the Second Plenary Council of Baltimore. A short sketch: *The Councils of Baltimore,* by Rev. Hugh P. McElrone, will be found in the *Memorial Volume: A History of the Third Plenary Council of Baltimore, November 9-December 7, 1884.*[17] This sketch, however, is a revision of articles in the *Catholic Mirror* of Baltimore, and displays little insight into the legislation of our councils. At this same council, Archbishop Ryan repeated in a sermon the ideas of Archbishop Spalding eighteen years before. There is one sketch which contains the outline for a general history of our national Catholic conciliar legislation—the article entitled "The Coming Plenary Council of Baltimore,"

[15] *Sermons delivered during the Second Plenary Council of Baltimore, October 7-21, 1866.* Baltimore, 1866.
[16] New York, 1881, 73-76.
[17] Baltimore, 1885, 29-45.

by John Gilmary Shea in the *American Catholic Quarterly Review* for April, 1884,[18] to which should be added his masterly essay: "The Progress of the Church in the United States from the First Provincial Council to the Third Plenary Council." [19] The *Concilia Provincialia Baltimori habita ab anno 1829 usque ad annum 1849* [20] is an official publication containing the *Statuta* of 1791 and the *Acta et Decreta* of the seven Provincial Councils of Baltimore (1829, 1833, 1837, 1840, 1843, 1846, and 1849). These will be found also in the *Acta et Decreta S. Conc. Recentiorum: Collectio Lacensis*.[21] In 1852, another edition was published containing in addition the *Acta et Decreta* of the First Plenary Council of Baltimore of 1852. Likewise, official publications appeared for the Plenary Councils of 1866 and 1884—*Concilii Plenarii Baltimorensis II., in Ecclesia Metropolitana Baltimorensi a die VII ad diem XXI Octobris, A. D. MDCCCLXVI habita, et a Sede Apostolica recogniti, Acta et Decreta*,[22] and *Acta et Decreta Concilii Plenarii Baltimorensis Tertii, A. D. MDCCCLXXXIV*.[23] These, then, are the official texts for the study of our national conciliar legislation, and they form the *Corpus Juris* of the ecclesiastical law of the land.

It is but natural to expect in the current periodical Catholic literature of the years between the First Provincial Council and the Third Plenary Council of Baltimore (1829-1884), many references, articles, and editorials on these assemblies. Strictly speaking, we had no Catholic press in the United States before the establishment of the *United States Catholic Miscellany* by Bishop England of Charleston in 1822, and in its pages up to Dr. England's death (1842) we find precious data on all the councils to that time. The Council of 1829 was responsible for the *Metropolitan* of Baltimore, founded in 1830, as our first Catholic monthly magazine under the editorship of Dr. Pise. It lasted only a year, but was followed by several newspapers: the

---

[18] VII, 340-357.
[19] *Ibid.*, 471-497.
[20] Baltimore, 1850, 2d ed., 1851.
[21] Freiburg, 1875.
[22] 2d ed., revised, Baltimore, 1868.
[23] Baltimore, 1886.

Catholic Telegraph of Cincinnati (1831), the *Catholic Herald* of Philadelphia (1833), the *Boston Pilot* (1836), and the *Freeman's Journal* of New York (1840).[24] The *Metropolitan* of Baltimore was succeeded in 1842 by the *Religious Cabinet*, which in turn was followed by the *United States Catholic Magazine* (1843-1848); then came the *Baltimore Catholic Mirror* (1849), to be supplemented in 1853 by the *Metropolitan* which lasted until 1859. By the time the Second and Third Plenary Councils were held, the American Catholic press possessed several outstanding periodicals, in which are chronicled the ceremonies of these great assemblies as well as summaries of their legislative acts.

For all the Baltimore Councils (down to and including that of 1866), the best source we possess is the four-volume *History of the Catholic Church in the United States* by John G. Shea.[25] The National Synod of 1791 has been treated in the *Life and Times of John Carroll*,[26] with new materials unknown to Shea, by the present writer; and the Councils of 1829, with its important historical antecedents, of 1833, of 1837, and of 1840, have been described from fresh documentary material by the same writer in his *Life and Times of John England*.[27]

The Second Plenary Council of Baltimore (1866) apparently aroused considerable historical interest. Apart from the published *Acta et Decreta* of the Council, an important source for the history of canon law in this country is Dr. Smith's *Notes on*

[24] Rev. Dr. Paul J. Foik, C.S.C., *Pioneer Catholic Journalism* (New York, 1930, United States Catholic Historical Society, *Monograph Series,* XI). A recent survey of the question is Baumgartner, *Catholic Journalism: a Study of Its Development in the United States, 1789-1930* (New York, 1931). The Third Plenary Council earnestly desired that there be one Catholic newspaper for each province (*ibid.,* 35-37).

[25] New York, 1886-1892. The final pages of his great work were those treating the Council of 1866. Guilday, *John Gilmary Shea, Father of American Catholic History (1824-1892),* United States Catholic Historical Society, *Historical Records and Studies* (July, 1926), 1-171. A brief history of the Baltimore Councils is in the *Balt. Cath. Mirror* (xxxv, October-November, 1884).

[26] New York, 1922, II, 419-446.

[27] New York, 1927, II, 68-132, 243-269, 377-404, 502-529.

*the Second Plenary Council of Baltimore.*²⁸ Immediately after
the Council (1866) there was published in Baltimore the *Sermons, etc.,* already mentioned, and there appeared also a little
brochure—*The Council in Baltimore: A Picture of American
Life,* by A. Niedermayer, translated by Rev. G. C. Perine.²⁹ For
the Third Plenary Council of Baltimore, there is a compilation
doubtless by Rev. Hugh P. McElrone, the *Memorial Volume,*
cited above. Apart from these secondary sources there are many
biographical sketches of the prelates who participated in these
eleven assemblies. In an article *The Catholic Church in the
United States (1870-1920),* the present writer has attempted
(with the guidance of the late Cardinal Gibbons) to show the
effect of the legislation of the Third Plenary Council of Baltimore up to the promulgation of the new Code (1884-1918).³⁰
To these bibliographical notes should be added the two excellent articles on the Provincial and Plenary Councils of Baltimore by Rev. W. H. Fanning, in the *Catholic Encyclopedia.*³¹
Other works and articles cognate to the subject are cited in the
references.

²⁸ New York, 1874.   ³⁰ *Cath. Hist. Review,* January, 1921.
²⁹ Baltimore, 1914.   ³¹ II, 235-241.

PART I

HISTORICAL BACKGROUND
(TO 1784)

CHAPTER I

THE PRE-COLUMBIAN CHURCH (to 1492)

THERE are several convenient chronological divisions to a treatment of the historical origins of canonical legislation in what is now the United States. The chief dividing line is the year 1791, when Bishop John Carroll convened the First National Synod of Baltimore. The period prior to 1791 has an historical background which includes the Brendan Legend and the story of ecclesiastical jurisdiction in the far-off Church of Gardar (c. 1124-1492), as well as in that part of the present territory of the United States once presided over by Spanish (or Mexican) and French (or Canadian) bishops. Of more immediate value to this background is the history of the jurisdiction of the London Church over the English-American colonies from the founding of Maryland to the Suppression of the Society of Jesus (1634-1773). After the year 1791 the logical divisions of the treatise are: the creation of ecclesiastical jurisdiction during the régime of John Carroll as prefect-apostolic, bishop and archbishop (1784-1815); the seven Provincial Councils held by his successors in Baltimore (1829-1849); and the three Plenary Councils of 1852, 1866, and 1884.

How much credence is to be placed in the celebrated voyage of St. Brendan and his followers in the sixth century to the "Land of Delight" or Greater Ireland (probably the Chesapeake Bay region), as it became known to later writers, is still a matter of high conjecture. Obviously, the settlement of St. Brendan from the viewpoint of ecclesiastical life and discipline has no historical bearing on our subject; although the *Navigatio Brendani* enjoyed such a marvelous popularity in medieval

17

times that the legend, if legend it is, should not be overlooked in any history of the Church in the New World.[1] Five centuries later, however, we come to a fully established Church organization in the Diocese of Gardar in Greenland. The earliest account of Gardar is in the *Gesta Hammaburgensis Ecclesiae Pontificum,* compiled by Adam of Bremen (1043-1072), and in other Icelandic and Norse sagas of the following century.[2] In none of the extant sources, however, will any reference to synodal legislation in Gardar between 1124 and 1377 be found. Evidently, the Church there was guided by the legislation of its metropolitan See, Trondhjem, established by the English pope, Adrian IV (Nicholas Breakspeare),[3] to which See the Gardar bishops were expressly ordered by Adrian IV to be subject.[4]

[1] Many prominent writers of the last century (Beamish, O'Hanlon, Gaffarel, MacCarthy, and others) who claim for the Irish the honor of first discovering America, base their studies upon the *Navigatio.* For a scholarly presentation and a critical bibliography of the problem, *cf.* Dunn, "The Brendan Problem," *Catholic Historical Review,* VI (1921), 395-477. The popularity of the *Navigatio* can be seen in Hardy, *Descriptive Catalogue of Materials relating to the History of Great Britain and Ireland* (London, 1862), I, 159.

[2] For a description of these, *cf.* Meinburg, "The Norse Church in Medieval America," *Catholic Historical Review,* XI (1925), 179-216. A detailed description of life in Greenland at the time will be found in Larson's edition of *The King's Mirror* (New York, 1917) and in his article "The Church in North America (Greenland) in the Middle Ages," *Catholic Historical Review,* V, 175-193. Some of the documents from the Vatican Archives bearing directly on the Church in Greenland, were published by John C. Heywood in 1893 (*Documenta selecta e Tabulario Secreto Vaticano*), and were reprinted with translations in the *Catholic Historical Review,* III (1917), 210-227. Cardinal Ehrle has analyzed these documents in his article "Der historische Gehalt der päpstlichen Abtheilung auf der Weltausstellung von Chicago," in *Stimmen aus Maria-Laach,* 46 (1894), 367-394. *Cf.* also, "The Medieval American Church," by O'Gorman, *Catholic University Bulletin,* I (1895), 415-427. Meinburg givts the list of the Gardar bishops (*l.c.,* 196-214). Another treatise on the Gardar Church is in De Roo, *History of America before Columbus* (2 vols., 1910). The extensive bibliographies in De Costa, *Pre-Columbian Discovery of America* (Albany, 1890) and Fischer, *Discoveries of the Norsemen in America* (St. Louis, 1903) reveal the wide extent of study and research on the Norse Church in America. Reeves, *The Finding of Wineland the Good* (London, 1890) is the classic on the subject.

[3] Eubel, *Hierarchia Catholica Medii Aevi* (Münster, 1898), I, 270.

[4] "Urbem Nidrosiensen (Trondhjem) ejusdem provinciæ perpetuam metropolim ordinavit et ei Grenelandiæ episcopatus tanquam sue metropoli perpetuis temporibus constituit subjacere et . . . obedire." Innocent III to Archbishop-elect Thorer of Trondhjem, February 13, 1206 (*Cath. Hist. Review,* III, 214).

Omitting all conjectures and uncertain names, the following Bishops of Gardar are historically certain: Arnold (*c.* 1124-1150), John I (1150-1187), John II (1188-1209), Helgo (1212-1230), ·Nicholas (1234-*c.* 1240), Olaf (1246-1280), Thored (1288-1314), Arne (*c.* 1314-1349), and Alf (1365-1377). At this last date (1377), a decline apparently began; and, although other bishops were appointed by the Holy See, few of them came to Gardar and they are not known. Practically the only historical fact proving the existence of the bonds of jurisdiction between Norway and Greenland during the Middle Ages is the legislation regarding Peter's Pence.

More than ordinary historical interest is attached to the fact that the last of the documents we possess on the See of Gardar is the appointment by Alexander VI, probably in the year 1492, of Matthias Knutsson, a Danish Benedictine, to Gardar. The letter of appointment is a striking historical document. Alexander VI states that he has been informed that "no resident bishop or priest has ruled the Church there for some eighty years past. . . . It is said that the people of that land have no other relic of the Christian religion than a corporal, which they exhibit once a year, upon which the Body of Christ was consecrated by the last priest who was resident there one hundred years ago." [5] It is not known whether Bishop Knutsson had the opportunity of going to Gardar. In 1519, at the request of King Christian of Denmark, Leo X sent a Franciscan, Vincent Petersson Kampe, to restore Catholic life and jurisdiction in Greenland, but the introduction of the Lutheran heresy into the Scandinavian countries swept the Norwegian hierarchy out of existence, and "then silence and oblivion fell upon Greenland." [6]

[5] *Cath. Hist. Review,* III, 226. *Cf.* Jelic, "L'évangelisation de l'Amérique avant Colomb," *Compte-rendu du Congrès . . . des Catholiques* (Paris, 1891), V, 183.

[6] O'Gorman, *Roman Catholics,* IX in the *American Church History Series* (New York, 1897), 11.

CHAPTER II

THE RISE OF THE HIERARCHY IN NEW SPAIN
(1493-1545)

THE Catholic Faith was first brought into the present territory of the United States by the priests who accompanied the early discoverers and colonizers of that vast expanse known as New Spain. For convenience' sake we can divide this activity into four geographical centers: the West Indies; "Florida," which meant all the territory from Key West to the St. Lawrence; the present southwestern section of the United States, or what was to become the States of Texas, Oklahoma, Kansas, Nebraska, Wyoming, Utah, Nevada, Colorado, New Mexico, and Arizona; and the present state of California.

The coöperation extended by Spanish Franciscans and Dominicans to the project of Columbus is well known. Father Juan Perez, O.F.M., the confessor of Queen Isabella, Father Antonio de Marchena, O.F.M., and Father Diego de Deza, O.P., who later became Archbishop of Seville, are names inseparably linked with the discovery of America.[1] The interest shown by these priests, two of whom held important Church offices, was highly instrumental in Columbus' success, and it seems strange that no priest accompanied the three vessels with their one hundred and twenty men on the journey westward in August to October, 1492.[2] Before setting out, Columbus and the officers

[1] Cf. McCarthy, C. H., Columbus and His Predecessors (Phila., 1912), 110-115; Mandonnet, Les Dominicains et la Découverte de l'Amérique (Paris, 1893); Dillon, "Dominican Influence in the Discovery of America," Records, Amer. Cath. Hist. Soc., XLI, 193-229.
[2] Cf. E. Ward Loughran, "Did a Priest accompany Columbus in 1492?", Cath. Hist. Review, XVI, 164-174, where the latest documentary evidence on the question will be found.

and crew of the little fleet received the Sacraments of Penance
and Holy Eucharist, it is said, from Father Perez. But whether
there was any official ecclesiastical recognition of the venture is
uncertain. The return voyage after the discovery of 1492 was
completed on March 15, 1493, when Columbus cast anchor in
the harbor of Palos.

The news of the great discovery was sent to Pope Alexander
VI, himself a Spaniard. There can be little doubt that the problem of ecclesiastical jurisdiction in the new territory was a
mooted question in the Roman Curia during the summer of
1493. The relations between the sovereigns of Castile and the
papacy were of such a nature that between 1482 and 1508 the
increase in ecclesiastical authority of the king is very marked.
In 1482 Pope Sixtus agreed to nominate to Castilian Sees only
those acceptable to Ferdinand.[3] Two years later Pope Innocent
VII granted to the same king the *jus patronatus* of all the benefices in the territories that had been or were to be conquered
from the Moors. Pastor writes:

On the 3rd and 4th of May, 1493, Alexander VI put his signa-
ture to three highly important documents. The first, dated 3rd May,
confers on Spain an exclusive right of possession over all the islands
and countries now discovered by Columbus and all future discoveries of his, on condition of propagating the Christian Faith in
them, and provided such lands are not already occupied by a Christian power. . . . The second, dated the same day, described these
rights in detail; while the third, dated 4th May, defined the limits
of what we should now call the spheres of influences of Spain and
Portugal.[4]

While these grants were of a political nature, easily under-
standable in the spirit of the times, it is fair to conclude that
the strictly missionary aspect of the Spanish discoveries was not
overlooked by the sovereign pontiff. In the preparations for

[3] Pastor, *History of the Popes,* IV, 397.
[4] *Ibid.,* VI, 160.

Columbus' second voyage, both Ferdinand and Isabella and Alexander took pains to provide missionary priests for the evangelization of the native races. Their choice of a leader for the band of preachers shows with what care the selection was made. A friend of St. Francis of Paula, the Benedictine Bernard Boyl, was the first apostle of the New World. In the brief of 25th June, 1493, Alexander VI conferred upon this distinguished and in every way most competent man and his twelve companions, all the powers and privileges which they needed for their holy enterprise. Amongst his companions may be mentioned the celebrated Bartholomeo Las Casas, Fray Jorge, Commander of Knights of Santiago, and Pedro de Arenas, who is supposed to have said the first Mass ever celebrated on the newly discovered islands.[5]

In Boyl's bull of appointment [6] it is evident that the jurisdiction granted to the first American vicar-apostolic did not depend, as is commonly stated, upon the metropolitan See of Seville, but directly upon the Holy See. The *Pius fidelium* of Alexander VI

[5] Pastor, VI, 163. There has been considerable discussion over the identity of Buil, Boil, or Boyl, who was the first vicar-apostolic of the New World. There are some writers who hold that there were two ecclesiastics of this name: the first, a Benedictine; the second, a Franciscan. This theory is based upon the fact that the original bull of appointment, brought to light from the Vatican Archives by Roselly, was directed to *dilecto filio Bernardo Boil, frati Ordinis Minorum,* while the Bernard Boyl, or Buil, who came out to Hispaniola with twelve priests in 1493, was a Benedictine. Part of the original bull of June 25, 1493, is reproduced in facsimile in the *Catholic Encyclopedia* (II, 414). In his "Establishment of the First Vicarate of America, A.D., 1493," published in the *Records* of the American Catholic Historical Society (VII, 1896, 141-154), Heuser reaches the conclusion that Ferdinand, by virtue of the pontifical privileges already granted him, deliberately availed himself of the similarity of the two names to substitute that of his favorite, Boyl, the Benedictine, for that of the saintly Bernard Boil, Provincial of the Spanish Franciscans. Hernaez (*Colección de Bulas etc.,* II, 1069) calls Boyl the Apostolic-Delegate of the Holy See in the New World and states that he was first a Benedictine monk of Montserrat and later a Franciscan Minim. Father Fita in the *Boletino de la Real Academia de la Historia* of Madrid (XIX-XX, 1891-1892) "has the merit of being the first to give a clear account of Boyl's life" (Pastor, VI, 163 note). *Cf.* also Streit, *Bibliotheca Missionum: II. Amerikanische Missionsliteratur* (Aachen, 1924), 5-6. For the latest discussion of the documents on this question, *cf.* E. Ward Loughran, "The First Vicar-Apostolic of the New World," *Eccles. Rev.,* LXXXII (Jan. 1930), 1-13. The *Relación* of Pedro de Arenas was discovered by Father F. Fita, S.J., in the National Library at Madrid and published in the *Boletin de la Real Academia de la Historia* (XVIII, 551-554), in 1891. *Cf.* Streit, *op. cit.,* II, 1-2.

[6] Published in Latin and English by Heuser, *l.c.,* 147-154.

contains more than the ordinary faculties accompanying episcopal jurisdiction, and the bull is a good norm by which to judge the large-minded grasp upon the discovery possessed by the Spanish pope. Had Bishop Boyl's mission been successful, the canonical aspect of the concessions and privileges would furnish an interesting page in our Catholic history.

Of the difficulties which arose between Columbus and the vicar-apostolic we are not concerned. Boyl returned to Spain in 1494, and whatever jurisdiction he had apparently ceased. After Boyl's return to Spain he was lost to sight, and it is not certain whether Ferdinand asked for the appointment of a successor in the Vicariate of Hispaniola. There is extant a letter from the king to the Spanish ambassador at Rome, Garcilasso de la Vega, asking for similar privileges for another friar who was destined to take Boyl's place, since "el dicho fray boyl es venido aqui de las yslas doliente." [7] It is unfortunate that Bishop Boyl was not made of sterner stuff; the scanty facts on this salient episode in the history of canonical legislation in America are not heartening.

The next seventeen years (1494-1511) saw the little flock in Haiti and Cuba without a shepherd, owing to the difficulties the Holy See faced in reaching a compromise with the Spanish crown over the question of ecclesiastical titles and benefices.

Some priests remained in the islands; others came out to labor there, acting no doubt upon the faculties granted to them by their superiors. Pastor says that the number of religious and converted Indians increased so quickly in Hispaniola (Haiti) that in 1501 negotiations were begun in Rome for the establishment of a hierarchy there. [8] The actual establishment was not made at once, owing to problems which continued to keep the pope and the Spanish sovereigns apart. The first step apparently was the Bull *Illius fulciti* on November 15, 1504, signed by

[7] Cf. Fita, "Fray Bernardo Buil y el Monasterio de Monserate," *Boletin de la Real Academia de la Historia*, XIX (1892), 199. Ferdinand wrote in a similar strain to Fonseca, President of the Council of the Indies (Fita, *l.c.*, 201). Cf. O'Hara, "Fonseca," *Cath. Hist. Review*, III (1919), 131-150.
[8] *Ibid.*, VI, 169.

Julius II, erecting the ecclesiastical Province of Hispaniola, with three Sees: the metropolitan See of Hyaguata, and its two suffragans, Magua and Bayuna (or Bainúa).[9]

Altercations of a politico-canonical nature at once arose. There were differences of opinion over the sites of the three Sees and especially over the question of the tithes which the three bishops were to enjoy for the upkeep of religious services. Ferdinand refused to make any concessions and the hierarchical establishment was in consequence postponed for seven years.

The increasing number of missionaries heightened the realization that a central ecclesiastical jurisdiction was necessary for the proper regulation of Catholic life in the islands. Each missionary received his faculties either from his own superior or bishop in Spain, and this far-off jurisdiction was all that could be counted upon to stabilize the nascent Catholic life in the colony.[10] Ryan writes:

Nothing could be done without yielding to Ferdinand's demand that the bishops should not share in the revenues mentioned. This policy was dictated by considerations more practical than a tenacious adherence to traditional abstract rights. Without implying that the crown misappropriated such revenues, we may see how loath it would be to suffer the introduction of such a practice which might grow into a serious difficulty. . . . Even the interests of Christianity were not suffered to prevail in such a case, and the danger no less than the hopelessness of successful opposition in so important a matter led the pope to agree that the new bishops should receive no share in the precious revenues.[11]

[9] The Apostolic Letter appointing Fray Garcia de Padilla, a Franciscan, to the See of Bayuna (November 16, 1504) is given in Hernaez, *Colección de Bulas y otros Documentos etc.* (Brussels, 1878), II, 708. Hernaez does not give the *Illius fulciti* of 1504, and names the other Sees as Lares de Guahaba and Concepción de la Vega (*Ibid.,* II, 707).

[10] Cf. Shea, *Catholic Church in the United States,* I, 11.

[11] "Diocesan Organization in the Spanish Colonies," *Cath. Hist. Review,* II (1917), 153-154. On November 16, 1501, Alexander VI granted to the Spanish sovereigns all colonial tithes for the reason that these sums were to be used especially in the conversion of the natives. Cf. Cuevas, *Historia de la Iglesia en Mexico* (El Paso, 1928), II, 46, and Solórzano, *Politica Indiana* (Mexico, 1736), IV, I. On the legality of the papal concession and the authenticity of the bull, cf. Cuevas, *op. cit.,* 47-48.

The *Illius fulciti* of 1504 has exceptional interest for the canonical historian since the Holy See created the new American Province independent of the Metropolitan of Seville, up to 1545 the acknowledged source of Spanish-American Church jurisdiction. The selection of the three Sees was geographically a mistake, and the uncompromising attitude of Ferdinand regarding tithes rendered the action of the Holy See nugatory.

Another compromise was attempted by the bull *Universalis ecclesiae regimini* of July 28, 1508, in which Julius II granted to Ferdinand and Joanna the right of appointment to all benefices in the colonies. The Holy See reserved the right of approval, but this followed as a matter of course. The consequence was that no bishop might be appointed and sent to New Spain without the express consent of the Spanish sovereigns.[12]

Probably in all Church history no greater privilege was ever conferred upon a monarch than the *Real Patronato* of the Spanish crown.[13] No chapel, oratory, mission, church, convent, monastery, or other ecclesiastical institution might be erected without the permission of the king as general patronato, or of his viceroy as vice-patronato.

The Province of Hyguata (*Aguacensis*) was formally suppressed by the Holy See on August 8, 1511; and three other Sees, as suffragans to the metropolitan of Seville, were erected: San Domingo and Concepción de la Vega in Hispaniola, and San Juan in Porto Rico. The bishops named in the Bull of 1504 were reappointed to these Sees, and Bishop Manso (translated from Magua to San Juan) arrived in his diocese in 1513—the first permanent bishop in the New World since the extinction of the Diocese of Gardar in Greenland. A fourth diocese, that of Baracoa in Cuba, was erected in 1518, and four years later

---

[12] Solórzano says that this bull "constituted our kings . . . Vicars of the Roman Pontiff," *Politica Indiana*, II, IV, c. ii; *cf*. Engelhardt, *Missions and Missionaries of California*, II, 672. The *Universalis ecclesiæ regimini* is in Hernaez, *op. cit.*, I, 24-25.

[13] Of the abuses which arose in consequence, *cf*. Engelhardt, *op. cit.*, 672-674; Icazbalceta, *Don Fray Juan de Zumárraga* (Mexico, 1881), 128-129.

(1522) this diocese was suppressed to give way to that of Santiago de Cuba, which, being the nearest See, may be considered as possessing immediate jurisdiction over the Church in "Florida."[14] During the next two decades (1522-1542) the progress of the Church in New Spain was remarkable, and episcopal Sees were erected wherever the number of the faithful and of the clergy warranted them.[15]

Between 1511 and 1545, in which latter year the Spanish colonial dependencies were divided into three ecclesiastical provinces, the number of bishoprics rapidly increased. In the vice-royalty of New Spain (created April 17, 1535), comprising all the mainland north of Panama, the West Indies and the present State of Venezuela, there were erected the following dioceses: San Domingo (1511), Concepción de la Vega (1511), San Juan (1511), Baracoa (1518), transferred to Santiago de Cuba in 1522, Yucatan (Diocese of Carolana, 1518), Tlaxcala (1525). Rio de las Palmas (1527), Mexico City (1530), Honduras (Diocese of Comayagua, 1531), León (Nicaragua, 1531), Coro (Venezuela, 1531), Santiago (Guatemala, 1534), Oaxaca (1535), Michoacan (1536), and Chiapas (1538).

On January 31, 1545, Paul III, at the solicitation of the emperor (Charles V), created three provinces in the Spanish colonial church, thus giving it a canonical status independent from Seville. These three provinces were: Mexico City, as the ecclesiastical center of the vice-royalty of New Spain; Lima, for the vice-royalty of Peru; and San Domingo, for the islands and "Florida."

[14] On the question of the appointment of Father Juan Juarez (Suarez), cf. Engelhardt, "Florida's First Bishop," *Cath. Hist. Review*, IV, 480-485.
[15] None of the available sources (Gams, Hernaez, or Mendieta (*Historia Ecclesiastica Indiana*, 1875), gives a perfect chronological list of these early dioceses. Cuevas, *Historia, etc.*, I, c. XII (*Erecciónes de las Diocesis Primitivas*) has not treated the rise of the Spanish-American hierarchy with sufficient clearness. Cf. "The Origin of Ecclesiastical Jurisdiction in New Spain," Sister M. Kathleen Walsh, O.P., *Records*, Amer. Cath. Hist. Society, XLIII (June, 1931), 101-154.

The Archbishop of Mexico City was the highest ecclesiastical authority in New Spain during those years which intervened between 1545 and 1853 when the final settlement of the boundary line between the United States and Mexico was decided upon. Some of the suffragan Sees of Mexico held jurisdiction over the southwestern part of the present United States until the end of the War with Mexico in 1848. Principally, these were: the Diocese of Guadalajara, erected in 1548; Durango, erected in 1620; Monterey (Linares), in 1777; and Sonora, in 1779.

In the period before the completion of the acquisition of Texas and California and the Spanish Southwest (1859), the provincial councils of Mexico City and the synods of those dioceses whose territory stretched northward into the western and central parts of the present United States legislated for this section. Four provincial councils were held in Mexico City during this period; two under Archbishop Alonso de Montúfar (the second archbishop) in 1555 and 1565-1566; one under the third archbishop, Pedro Moya y Conteras, in 1585; and one under the twenty-fourth archbishop, Francisco Antonio de Lorenzana, in 1770.[16] Of the four provincial councils in our period, the third, in 1585, was the most important, since its statutes furnished the norm for ecclesiastical discipline in New Spain for the next two centuries.[17] The legislation of these synods, duly approved by the Holy See, was in full vigor in Texas, New Mexico, Arizona and California when those parts were acquired by the United States.[18]

While we have the record of episcopal visitations by Spanish

[16] The next provincial council was held in 1896.
[17] Cuevas in his *Historia de la Iglesia en Mexico* (II, 90-115 . . . *Los tres primeros Concilios Mexicanos*) treats these assemblies. See Mansi, xxxiv, 1015-1228, also bibliogr. Mansi, 36 bis, 318. *Cf.* Aguirre, *Collectio conciliorum Hispaniæ* (1694). Archbishop Lorenzana, one of the greatest prelates of his day, published in 1769-1770, the acts and decrees of the first three provincial councils (*Concilios Provinciales, I, II, III, de Mexico*). The Acts of the Council of 1770 were not approved by Rome and were not promulgated.
[18] Shea, "The Coming Plenary Council of Baltimore," *American Catholic Quarterly Review,* IX (1884), 342.

and Mexican bishops into Florida, New Mexico, Arizona, Texas, and California, the scanty sources we possess do not allow us to conclude that any special legislation left a permanent juridic impression as a result of their surveys. The visitation of 1725 made by Bishop Benedict Crespi in New Mexico and Texas is known because of the difficulty he found in having his episcopal authority recognized by missionaries in those parts. Bishop Martin de Elizacaechea made a visitation in New Mexico in 1737. In 1760 Bishop Tamarón visited New Mexico. Again in 1833 and 1845 we find the Bishop of Durango making similar visitations. Episcopal visitations of Texas were made by the Bishops of Guadalajara in 1759 and in 1805.

There are no available sources to show that the bishops of these Sees suffragan to Mexico City, whose territories once contained our southwest and California, held diocesan synods. The ecclesiastical legislation which prevailed, however, left little if any influence upon the early synodal enactments of the dioceses created out of this once immense Spanish domain. In the transitional period were created: the Prefecture-Apostolic of Texas (1839), the Diocese of both Californias (1840); the Vicariate-Apostolic of Texas (1841) which became the Diocese of Galveston (1847); the Vicariate-Apostolic of New Mexico (1850) which became the Vicariate-Apostolic of Indian Territory (1851); and the Archdiocese of San Francisco (1853).

CHAPTER III

THE JURISDICTION OF QUEBEC (1658-1784)

THE hierarchy of New France began with the consecration on December 8, 1658, of François de Montmorency Laval as vicar-apostolic of that vast territory which once extended from Quebec to New Orleans.[1] From his arrival at Quebec in 1659 until the resignation of Bishop Briand one hundred and twenty-five years later (1784), eight bishops exercised directly or indirectly jurisdiction over the Church in this part of the present United States. All through this century and a quarter of episcopal rule politico-religious affairs in France and in Canada created confusing situations between civil and ecclesiastical superiors, with the result that from the viewpoint of Church organization, the history of episcopal jurisdiction in New France is as meager as that of New Spain.

Bishop Laval had at first to assert his independence from the pretensions of the Archbishop of Rouen, and this conflict of jurisdiction was ended only when Quebec was created an episcopal See by Clement X in 1674. The new diocese embraced practically all North America except the English colonies on the Atlantic seaboard and New Spain. Ten years later, wishing to resign the burden of the See, Jean-Baptiste de Saint-Vallier was chosen as Laval's successor. Pending the arrival of his bulls, Saint-Vallier left for Canada in 1685, and three years later was consecrated at Paris as the second Bishop of Quebec. It was during his episcopate (1688-1727) that the first four Synods of Quebec (1690, 1694, 1698, and 1700) were held, the only

[1] A picturesque and well-documented history of the old French-Canadian Church in New France is Bishop Schlarman, *From Quebec to New Orleans* (Belleville, Ill., 1929).

29

synods in fact during the régime of the Quebec See over the
Mississippi Valley.[2] Saint-Vallier went to France in 1700 in the
interests of his diocese and on his way back was captured by the
English and detained in honorable captivity in London from
1704 to 1709, Quebec being governed by vicars-general in his
absence. In 1705 he applied to King Louis XIV for a coadjutor, and eventually in 1713 De Mornay was consecrated for that
post. Saint-Vallier's purpose was to station his coadjutor in
Louisiana in order to rule the Church in that province. De
Mornay apparently had no desire to make the journey across the
Atlantic and as Vicar-General of Louisiana sent religious of his
own Order (Capuchins) to the new settlement of New Orleans.
The result was a rough division of the Province of Louisiana,
with the Seminary priests in charge of the missions of Upper
Louisiana and the Capuchins and later the Jesuits over the missions of Lower Louisiana. On May 16, 1722, with the consent
of Bishop Saint-Vallier, the Province of Louisiana was divided
into three ecclesiastical jurisdictions. The first district, extending to the west of the Mississippi from the Gulf of Mexico to
the mouth of the Wabash, was confided to the Capuchins whose
superior, residing at New Orleans, was a vicar-general of the
Bishop of Quebec. The second district extended over all the
territory north of the Ohio River and was placed in charge of
the Jesuits whose superior was likewise a vicar-general. The
third district included all the territory east of the Mississippi
and was confided to the Carmelites whose superior as vicar-
general resided at Mobile.[3] The trials and difficulties which
these religious Orders and their superiors encountered from this
date until the great political change in government by the Treaty

[2] Cf. Gosselin, L'Eglise du Canada: Ière partie (Mgr. de Saint-Vallier),
Quebec, 1911, 1-472; Dilhet-Browne, Etat de l'Eglise etc. (Washington,
D. C., 1922), 152-159.
[3] Cf. Vogel, The Capuchins in French Louisiana (1722-1766), (Washington, D. C., 1929), 22-39; Biever, The Jesuits in New Orleans and the Mississippi Valley (New Orleans, 1924), 17-30. For a dissimilar view to that
of Dr. Vogel, cf. Kenney, Michael, S.J., Catholic Culture in Alabama (New
York, 1931).

of Paris in 1763—a date which coincides with the Suppression of the Society of Jesus in Louisiana—need not be treated here, except to stress the fact that the methods followed by the See of Quebec were not conducive to ease of jurisdiction in the Valley. Saint-Vallier died December 26, 1727; and since his successor, Bishop de Mornay, was still unwilling to go to Quebec, a vicar-general was named in 1729 in the person of Bishop Dosquet who had been consecrated Bishop of Sanos and Vicar-Apostolic of a portion of India. Bishop Dosquet went to Canada in 1729 and remained there until 1732, when he returned to France in order to persuade De Mornay to take up the burden.[4] After De Mornay's resignation (1733), Dosquet became the fourth Bishop of Quebec, but two years later ill-health forced him to return to France and his resignation was accepted in 1739. His successor, Bishop Lauberivière was consecrated on August 10, 1739, and died a few days after reaching Quebec on August 20, 1740.[5] The fifth Bishop of Quebec, De Pontbriand, was consecrated on April 9, 1741, and died on June 8, 1760. His successor, Bishop Briand of American Revolutionary War fame was consecrated in Paris, March 16, 1766, and resigned in 1784.

The jurisdiction of Quebec over the Province of Louisiana, never clearly defined geographically, may be described in the terms of the territory east and west of the Mississippi. Down to 1762-1763, the whole of the territory, east and west, was subject to the Vicariate-Apostolic of Canada (1615-1674) and to the diocesan rule of Quebec (1674-1763). In 1762-1763, at the close of the Seven Years' War, France ceded all the territory west of the Mississippi (together with New Orleans) to Spain, and automatically the western portion of the province became part of the nearest Spanish See, that of Santiago de Cuba, a suffragan of San Domingo. All the territory east of the Mississippi

---

[4] "An Episode in Quebec-Louisiana History," by P. W. Browne, in *Illinois Catholic Historical Review* (now *Mid-America*), XII (April, 1930), 296-305.

[5] At the time of his consecration there were three Bishops of Quebec living—de Mornay who had resigned, Dosquet who had also resigned, and Lauberivière.

(including Florida) became, as a result of the treaty, part of the English colonial dominion, and presumably was under whatever jurisdiction governed the priests and people after the Suppression of the Jesuits (1773) and the beginning of American independence (1783). This eastern section of the former French Province will follow from 1763 to 1789 the fortunes of the Church of the thirteen colonies and original States. What that jurisdiction was during these years will be seen in the following chapter.

It is with the western portion of the Louisiana Province that so much confusion in the matter of ecclesiastical jurisdiction arises from this date (1763) until the Jefferson Purchase (1803) and the appointment of Bishop John Carroll as administrator of the newly acquired territory (1805).[6] The Spanish (Cuban) ecclesiastical authorities began slowly to take possession of the territory west of the Mississippi. In 1772 the Bishop of Santiago sent four Spanish Capuchins to New Orleans to take possession, but they met with opposition from some French members of the Order led by Father Dagobert. To relieve the situation the Bishop of Santiago recommended the appointment of an auxiliary who should live in New Orleans. Father Cyril of Barcelona was accordingly consecrated as Bishop of Tricali and auxiliary in 1781, and made New Orleans his episcopal See. Bishop Cyril's jurisdiction extended over Louisiana and after 1783, when East and West Florida were returned by England to Spain, over the Floridas as well. The problem of episcopal jurisdiction over Florida was not entirely settled, however, until 1787 when the Holy See divided the Diocese of Santiago de Cuba and erected the Diocese of Havana-Louisiana-the Floridas. Later in 1793, by royal decree, Louisiana and the Floridas were created into a separate diocese; and Joseph de Trespalacios, then Bishop of Porto Rico, was appointed to the new See, Bishop Cyril remaining as his auxiliary.

[6] Cf. Kellogg, L., "French in the Mississippi Valley: A Résumé," in *Mississippi Valley Historical Review* (June, 1931), 3-22.

That same year, however, the latter was recalled by the Spanish crown, and Louis Peñalver y Cárdenas was appointed to the Diocese of Louisiana-the Floridas, with his episcopal See at New Orleans, where he arrived in 1795 and remained until 1801 when he was made Archbishop of Guatemala. His régime of six years in Louisiana was signalized by a notable attempt to bring juridic order into his diocese through an *Instrucción para el govierno de los Parrocos de Diocesi de la Luisiana.*[7]

The *Instrucción* was to serve as a norm for the clergy until such time as a diocesan synod might be held. The topics dealt with are: clerical life and discipline, observance of the rights of the Spanish crown in ecclesiastical affairs, parish boundaries, the obligation of celebrating Mass *pro populo,* Lenten regulations, reception of the Sacraments, laws on marriage, the keeping of parochial registers (two sets were to be kept, one for whites, the other for Negroes, mulattoes and Indians) in the Spanish language, the ringing of the *Angelus,* exposition of the Blessed Sacrament, Catholic elementary education, the conversion of the Indians, the trustee system, and the teaching of the catechism of Christian Doctrine—"We command them [*the parish priests*] in their exhortations to combat atheism, materialism, deism, the errors of the Protestants [*los espiritus fuertes*] who in this diocese assail Christian dogma and morality in their ravings [*con sus delirios*]." Finally, since all the duties of the parish priest could not be set forth in the *Instrucción,* "in all other matters where they do not prescribe they are as laid down in the Synod of Cuba."

Bishop Peñalver might have succeeded in rehabilitating ecclesiastical jurisdiction had there been sufficient time to study thoroughly the conditions of his diocese, then undoubtedly one of the largest in the Catholic world. But with the retrocession by Spain of the Province of Louisiana to France through the secret Treaty of San Ildefonso (October 1, 1800), a further

---

[7] The *Instrucción* is printed with a translation (J. G. Shea) in the *United States Catholic Historical Magazine,* II (1887), 417-443.

period of confusion arose in the history of its ecclesiastical jurisdiction. Before his departure for Guatemala, Bishop Peñalver
appointed two Irish priests of the diocese—Fathers Thomas Has-
sett and Patrick Walsh—as vicars-general for the interim. The
political status of Louisiana was unsettled and Church discipline
suffered in consequence. Two years later, on December 20,
1803, the Jefferson Purchase was completed and the next year
the Territory of Orleans was organized under Governor Clai-
borne. Bishop John Carroll assumed episcopal jurisdiction over
the newly acquired territory by virtue of a letter from the Sacred
Congregation de Propaganda Fide, September 20, 1805. After
some official correspondence with President Madison, Bishop
Carroll appointed a vicar-general for the Territory of Orleans,
Father John Olivier. The Holy See wished to place an adminis-
trator-apostolic over this new part of the American Church, and
eventually in 1812, Father William Du Bourg accepted the post.
After Jackson's victory at New Orleans (January 8, 1815), Du
Bourg went to Rome and was consecrated Bishop of Louisiana
on September 24 of that year.[8]

Internal disorders did not cease during the five years of
Bishop Du Bourg's absence from New Orleans (1815-1820),
but bravely striving to bring peace to the diocese he made a
visitation of the churches and held a diocesan synod in 1820 and
"was greatly encouraged by the zeal and deportment of the
priests who attended it." [9] After the cession of Florida by
Spain to the United States in 1819, Bishop Du Bourg extended
his jurisdiction over that part of his diocese, although blocked
to some extent by the arbitrary action of the Bishop of Santiago
de Cuba who declined to recognize his authority. Between 1820
and 1826, when Du Bourg resigned, several ineffectual moves
were made by Propaganda to straighten out the tangled jurisdic-

[8] Guilday, *Life and Times of John Carroll*, c. xxxiv (*Archbishop Carroll's
Extra-Diocesan Jurisdiction*).

[9] Shea, *op. cit.*, III, 372. The principal figure of these years (1804-1826)
—Father Antonio de Sedella, O.M.Cap., has recently been the subject of a
study by Antonio de Castillo, *La Luisiana Española y el Padre Sedella* (San
Juan, P. R., 1929), which casts a new and more favorable light upon
Sedella's part in the trustee troubles in New Orleans.

tion of our Southeast. Finally with the definite placing of Bishop Rosati over the See of St. Louis (1827), the creation of the See of Mobile in 1829 under Bishop Portier, and the election of Bishop de Neckere to the Diocese of New Orleans in 1829 regular ecclesiastical order began. Bishop de Neckere's diocesan synod in February, 1832, may well be taken as the beginning of a new era in Church life in this long distracted section of this once vast colonial possession of France and Spain.[10]

By this time practically all the ecclesiastical customs created by the legislation of Quebec or of the Cuban See had passed away. The legislation of the four diocesan synods of Quebec (1690, 1694, 1698, and 1700), as has been said, was too general in some respects and too local in others to leave any lasting impression on a Church which had passed through so many civil changes and disturbances.

An outstanding difference between the French and Spanish politico-religious systems was the attitude of the home government toward the exercise of episcopal jurisdiction in their colonies. One has but to compare the rapid and effective growth of hierarchical control in the Spanish colonies with the dreary hindrances created by the Paris officials, many of whom were Gallican in thought and action.[11] Even Laval's consecration in 1658 must be viewed as a triumph of the Holy See over the stifling Gallican policy of the Archbishop of Rouen. The reign of Louis XIV (1643-1715) was not conducive to that free and untrammeled development of the French colonial Church which might have been made by officials of a wider and more Catholic vision. That story, however, does not enter into the purpose of this chapter.[12]

[10] *United States Catholic Miscellany,* XI (1832), p. 342.

[11] "The Spanish colonial empire lasted three centuries, a period nearly as long as that of the sway of imperial Rome over Western Europe. During these ten generations the language, the religion, the culture, and the political institutions of Castile were transplanted over an area twenty times as large as that of the parent state. What Rome did for Spain, Spain in turn did for Spanish America": Bourne, *Spain in America* (New York, 1904), 202.

[12] Although somewhat unsympathetic toward the Church, Riddell, *The*

To sum up: from the available sources it seems that Quebec had never entered very heartily into the problem of ecclesiastical legislation for this immense colonial possession of France. Even though the number of the faithful was small at that time in this section,[13] it is evident that the Bishop of Quebec could exercise little personal influence at so great a distance. The most active of these prelates, Bishop de Saint-Vallier (1688-1727), resisted all attempts at subdividing his jurisdiction by the creation of vicariates-apostolic or suffragan Sees. In fact, he believed that ecclesiastical life and discipline could be best maintained by a centralized administration at Quebec.[14] So far, the colonial period of the Spanish and French jurisdiction over these parts of the present United States where formerly Spanish, Mexican, French and Canadian bishops ruled has not revealed much information on the problem of the possible influence such legislation might have had on our First National Synod in 1791. This may be due, as regards the Spanish-Mexican Church, to the inaccessibility of source material. The literature on the Church in New Spain is a large one; but the books and collections are rare or scarce and only to be found here and there in Mexican libraries, as Father Cuevas points out in his history of the Mexican Church. The French influence was even less, for the reason that, apart from centers like Detroit, Kaskaskia, Cahokia, and New Orleans, there were few Catholics in the territory governed from Quebec. These little French congregations were swallowed up in the drive toward the West which set in immediately after the American War of Independence.

Rise of Ecclesiastical Control in Quebec (New York, 1916) and Cahall, *The Sovereign Council of New France* (New York, 1913) have treated the question in detail. Gosselin's two volumes, *L'Eglise du Canada* (Quebec, 1928) give a more impartial view of the question.

[13] As late as 1766, for instance, there were only 1400 families or about 5600 souls in the territory, the majority living within the present State of Louisiana.

[14] The division of the Valley into three vicar-generalates (1722) simply stabilized a system of sub-delegated power which had been in existence during the previous period. *Mandements des Evêques de Québec*, Ière partie, (Quebec, 1911), 103-104.

CHAPTER IV

THE LONDON JURISDICTION (1634-1783)

OUR disappointment at not finding any appreciable influence upon our national conciliar legislation from Spanish ecclesiastical jurisdiction which lasted over three centuries (1522-1853), or from French ecclesiastical jurisdiction which lasted from 1657 until 1803, will be augmented by the jejune details we find in the history of ecclesiastical jurisdiction in the English colonies from 1634 to 1783.

To understand the juridic situation of the Catholic Church in the English colonies, emphasis must be placed upon the disturbed status of the Church in England to which Catholics here would canonically be subject in matters of discipline and hierarchical jurisdiction from 1634 to 1783. Briefly, the situation may be described as follows: with the extinction of the Catholic hierarchy in England between 1559 and 1585, the Church in that country as "a visible, public hierarchic body with its ancient rules, courts, privileges, and jurisdiction" ceased to exist.[1] Dr. William Allen, first president of Douay College (1569) and later Cardinal, was considered during the last twenty years of his life (1575-1594) as the head of the English Catholics. In 1581 Allen was made "Prefect of the English Mission" by Gregory XIII, and after his elevation to the Sacred College of Cardinals (August 17, 1587) by Gregory XIV, Cardinal Allen was, it is claimed, appointed Protector of England—an office

---

[1] Pollen, *The English Catholics in the Reign of Elizabeth* (London, 1920), 35. *Cf.* Phillips, *The Extinction of the Ancient Hierarchy* (London, 1905); Ward, B., *The English Secular Clergy* (London, 1910). The question has been treated in detail in the *Life of John Carroll* (New York, 1922), cc. IV-V.

37

which was continued irregularly until the restoration of the hierarchy in 1850. There is no doubt that unfortunate blunders were made in the management of the remnants of the English Church from 1585 until 1685. We need not go into the subject of the appeals made by the English Catholics for a bishop to guide them or into the influences which kept the Holy See from re-creating the proper juridic status of the English Church.[2]

The uncertain jurisdiction of Cardinal Allen was apparently shared with that of the papal nuncio of Brussels. After Allen's death (1594), an equally uncertain and highly colored title to jurisdiction was placed by the Holy See in the hands of the Archpriests—Blackwell, Birkhead and Harrison—from 1598 to 1623. These superiors only added to the juridic confusion of the Church in England. The shadowy forms of the two titular Bishops of Chalcedon—William Bishop (1623-1624) and Richard Smith (1625-1655)—who were Vicars-Apostolic of All England, scarcely caused a ripple in the apathetic stream of English Catholic life. The years which followed Bishop Smith's flight to Paris and his death (1631-1655) are without doubt the most mysterious of all in the period; for whatever jurisdiction there was in England was held by a Dean and Chapter, who had charge of Smith's division of the Church in England into seven vicar-generalates, twenty-three archdeaneries, and a number of rural deaneries. Several appeals reached Rome during these extraordinary years for a bishop, but the Holy See did not find it opportune to comply until James II came to the throne.[3] John Leyburne was then appointed Vicar-Apostolic of All England (1685). In 1688, England was divided into four Vicariates—Northern, Midland, Western and London—and this system prevailed until 1840, when the number was increased to eight.

Our immediate interest lies in the canonical status of the

---

[2] Cf. Ullathorne, *History of the Restoration of the Catholic Hierarchy in England* (London, 1871); Ward, *op. cit.*, 32-52.
[3] Pollen, *The Archpriest Controversy* (London, 1916).

period from 1634 to 1773; that is, from the founding of the
Catholic colonial province of Maryland by the Calverts to the
Suppression of the Society of Jesus a century and a half later.
Presumably, during this period jurisdiction over the Catholic
Church in the English American colonies was exercised by:
(1634-1655) Bishop Richard Smith, then in exile in Paris;
(1655-1685) the Dean and Chapter; (1685-1784) the London Vicars-Apostolic: Bishops Leyburne (1685-1702), Giffard
(1703-1734), Petre (1734-1758), Challoner (1758-1781),
and Talbot (1781-1784).

The first historical data for the question of jurisdiction over
English Catholics coming out to the New World belong to that
period antedating the colonization of Maryland (1578-1634)
when several attempts were made to create a refuge in the English colonies for the persecuted Catholics.[4] But since these
voyages were unsuccessful, they can be passed over without
comment. It was in 1633-1634 that the Catholic pilgrims began
and completed their successful landfall in Maryland. Two Jesuit
priests, Father Andrew White and Father John Altham-Grav-
enor, accompanied the *Ark* and the *Dove*. What jurisdiction did
they possess? Who conferred that jurisdiction? And how was
their jurisdiction exercised in Maryland itself? These questions
seem almost impossible of answer. Hughes has made an attempt
to answer these problems in the first volume of the *Text* of his
*History of the Society of Jesus in North America, Colonial and
Federal*. The facts given are few. We learn that the Jesuits
going out to Maryland were given faculties usually granted to
the missionaries in the Indies, and apparently the jurisdiction in
this *tabella* came to them from the General of the Jesuits
through the English Provincials of the Society. But the reader
will search vainly for any example of a resort to higher authority
on matters which involve a superior jurisdiction.

---

[4] *Cf.* Powers, "The Beginnings of English Catholic Emigration to the New
World (1578-1634)," in *Records* of the American Catholic Historical
Society, XL (1929), 1-37.

The second period from 1685 on, when presumably the jurisdiction of the London Vicariate may be supposed to have extended over all the colonial possessions of England, to the Suppression of the Jesuits in Maryland in 1773, has a singularly curious history.

From 1634 to 1696, when Pope Innocent XII attempted by a special decree—*Alias a particulari*—to bring order into the juridic status of the English Church, there is no evidence for the exercise of any canonical rights over the colonies by ecclesiastical superiors in England. The problem of canonical control does not seem to have arisen before 1715, when, as a result of a marriage case presented by Father Killick, S.J., the Superior in Maryland, to the English Jesuit Provincial, Father Parker, in which letter no allusion is made to Bishop Giffard then Vicar-Apostolic of the London District, not only the Provincial, but Propaganda and apparently the Holy See, were unable to decide where the proper jurisdiction lay.

In itself this marriage case, which concerns the impediment *disparitas cultus*, has no pertinent value for our problem; except this, that for what was perhaps the first time the Maryland Church appealed to higher ecclesiastical authority to settle a case of canonical jurisdiction. Father Thomas Hughes, S.J., deals with this marriage case with considerable skill and explains that the Jesuit Superiors had the power of dispensing in such cases as far back as 1585.[5]

The result of Killick's appeal to the English Provincial was that Father Robert Beeston, then Provincial in England, personally accompanied the American Father Attwood on a visit to Bishop Giffard, the Vicar-Apostolic of the London District, and as a result Father Attwood was given such power as was necessary to dispense in these cases. This apparently is the first tangible evidence of the exercise of jurisdiction by the London Vicariate over the Church in the English colonies. The impor-

[5] "A Maryland Marriage Case," *American Ecclesiastical Review*, XXIII (1902), 521-536.

tant point is that the London Vicar-Apostolic acted upon the supposition that his jurisdiction extended to Maryland. This as we shall see was erroneous. In an article, "The London Vicariate Apostolic and the West Indies, 1685-1819," Father Hughes throws new light on the reason why the London Vicariate should have considered the territory under its spiritual care.[6] There was, first of all, the *Alias a particulari* of 1696, which decree sanctioned for England the jurisdiction of the vicars-apostolic over all regulars, including the Society of Jesus, in such matters as faculties for hearing confessions, administering the Sacraments, and other functions of the *cura animarum*.[7] How the extension of this decree, made for England, was now a practice carried over to America and the West Indies cannot be discovered in any extant document. Evidently the status of ecclesiastical jurisdiction in the colonies was not stabilized, for some years later we find one of the American Jesuits writing to Father Richard Plowden, the English Provincial: "It will be hard to find under which Vicar-Apostolic Maryland is. London, too far; Quebec are [*sic*] foreigners. June 1715." [8]

Six years later, November 21, 1721, Bishop Giffard granted to Father Thomas Parker the privilege of giving plenary indulgences in *articulo mortis*. Father Robert Beeston communicated this privilege to Father Mansell, then Superior of the Maryland Mission. The same vicar-apostolic was asked (December 21, 1722), by two Fathers, Francis Ashton (Powell) and Robert Hill, Provincial, to sanction a regulation proposed for the observance of holy days, "on behalf of the Mission of Maryland for the ease and quiet of poor Catholics of that Mission." Bishop Giffard heartily commended the petition in a note of approval. Later (November 28, 1723) Fathers Hill and Attwood received from Bishop Giffard a number of faculties for all the mission-

---

[6] *Dublin Review*, CXXIV (1914), 67-93.
[7] It is to be noted that this Brief of October 5, 1696, is a ratification of Propaganda's decree of August 6, 1695, and that it abrogated the privileges of the regulars granted by the *Plantata* of Urban VIII.
[8] Cited by Hughes, *l.c.*, 69.

aries in Maryland, for fast days, holy days, indulgences, and matrimonial dispensations. These privileges were to be in force until actually revoked by him or his successors. He likewise confirmed, ratified, and gave, in case of any deficiency, power and jurisdiction to all the missioners, who were then in Maryland, for the exercise of these functions.[9] We notice, therefore, that under the provincialship of Father Robert Beeston these recognitions of the jurisdiction of the London Vicariate began. It would clarify the situation if we knew whether Father Beeston acted on his own initiative or whether the influence which caused this change of method came from the London Vicariate or from the General in Rome.

Other cases of recognition of jurisdiction of the London Vicariate followed up to 1730. On December 10, 1723, the Vicar-General, Father Barker, gave faculties to a Maryland missionary, Father Case, who applied for the same. In reply to two questions regarding the Divine Office, Father Barker told the American missionaries that they had a right to all the privileges enjoyed by the priests of the London District—"his reason was because we were part of, and belonging to, the London District." [10] Two years later, on March 17, 1725, the English Provincial, Father Thomas Lawson, wrote to Father George Thorold, the Maryland Superior, reaffirming all the faculties conferred on his (Thorold's) predecessors: "As to the faculties you have from me," Lawson writes, "I can't give you so clear an answer," and he suggested that if any doubts arose they might be sent to London "to be examined here," [11] Finally, on November 20, 1730, Bishop Giffard actually sent to Father Thorold a compendium of faculties under thirteen heads. They dealt with the power of absolving from heresy, of dispensing in the second degree of consanguinity and affinity for three cases only, and with cases of urgent necessity, and were to be in force for five years.

[9] Hughes, *l.c.*, 69.   [10] Hughes, *l.c.*, 70.   [11] Guilday, *Carroll*, I, 140.

No formal document from Rome exists in the extant ecclesi-astical archives (*e.g.*, Westminster, Stonyhurst, Maryland-New York Province) granting Bishop Giffard this juridic right, yet Burton says: "It is not likely that Bishop Giffard would sud-denly have begun to exercise faculties in these remote lands without the sanction of Propaganda in some shape." [12] Bishop Giffard's response to the various applications made to him by the American missionaries created what Father Hughes calls jurisdiction by devolution from a negation; and thus, he says, the Jesuits in Maryland "brought this jurisdiction, which was looking for a home, to the door of the London Vicariate-Apos-tolic who thus became the Ordinary for America." These cor-dial relations had the practical result, therefore, of installing Bishop Giffard "by common consent and mutual complaisance as the episcopal authority over Maryland." [13] In 1734 Bishop Benjamin Petre succeeded Bishop Giffard as Vicar-Apostolic of the London District; and apparently the same cordial relations continued, although the exercise of jurisdiction was, strictly speaking, irregular according to canon law. With the election of Dr. Challoner as coadjutor to Bishop Petre in 1741, the active exercise of jurisdiction over the American colonies passed into the latter's hands; and one of the first projects he proposed was to relieve the London Vicariate of the burden of the English missions across the seas on the mainland and in the West Indies. In 1742 or 1743 Bishop Petre suggested to the English Provin-cial, Father Charles Shireburn, a plan to name the Maryland Jesuit Superior Vicar-General of the London District. Nothing came of this proposal, probably because the General was averse

[12] *Life of Challoner* (London, 1909), II, 125.
[13] Hughes, *History of the Jesuits etc.*, Text II, 588-589. In his article, already cited (*Dublin Review*, XCCIV (1914), 71-73,), Father Hughes writes: "It is clear that this extension has assumed in practical life the char-acter of accepted tradition, and no one thought of calling it in question. But the right and title of such enlargement of jurisdiction, if difficult to explain on its own account, became more so when confronted with certain documents, both ecclesiastical and civil, of the time."

to any exception of the Jesuit rule regarding ecclesiastical dignities.[14] The decree of 1745, confirming the *Alias a particulari* of Innocent XII, obliged all religious (including the Jesuits) to obtain faculties from their respective Ordinaries or vicars-apostolic. A further decree from the Holy See (August 23, 1748) stated that "it would not be lawful for anyone to exercise any faculties in their districts except those received from the bishops." The English bishops then confirmed all existing faculties in their vicariates.

This decree was not accepted with alacrity. Opposition in England was shown by the Franciscans, Carmelites, and Benedictines. The English Jesuits, and in consequence those in the American colonies since they depended on the English Provincial, requested a delay until they had communicated with their superiors in Rome. The Brief *Apostolicum Ministerium* of May 30, 1753, issued by Pope Benedict XIV, was a "final" settlement of the question of jurisdiction in English ecclesiastical life. Known better under the name of the *Regulae observandae in Anglicanis Missionibus,* Pope Benedict's decree was virtually a Constitution of the Clergy in England down to the restoration of the hierarchy of 1850.[15] Dr. Challoner's interest in the Maryland Mission dates from 1743. In 1746, in a report sent to Propaganda by Bishops Petre and Challoner, on the state of the London Vicariate, the American missions are expressly mentioned as part of their jurisdiction. In 1753, probably as the result of negotiations with Propaganda, a report was drawn up

[14] In an article on "Confirmation in the Old Colonies," *American Ecclesiastical Review,* XXVIII (1903), 23-56, Father Hughes refers to a footnote to be found in John Grassi's *Memorie sulla Compagnia di Gesù, restabilita negli Stati Uniti,* where we are told that the author (Grassi) saw in the sacristy of St. Thomas' Church at Port Tobacco, a patent granting extraordinary faculties (including that of administering the Sacrament of Confirmation) to the Jesuit superiors, and concluded that the Vicar-Apostolic may have appointed one of the resident missionaries for this purpose. We know this faculty had been conferred upon the Jesuit missioners in various parts of the world by Pope Benedict XIV in a series of pontifical briefs between 1751 and 1753, and it would have been in order for Bishop Petre to secure these extraordinary powers for the Maryland superiors.
[15] Guilday, *Carroll,* I, 142.

for the Sacred Congregation, dated February 15 of that year, about the American missions in general, containing this significant statement:

> Whence the said priests received their faculties the present writer can give no information. He believes, however, that they get them from the Vicars-Apostolic of London; and he thinks he heard before that the Sacred Congregation had assigned this charge to the said Vicar. . . . As to the English Provinces on the mainland, the greatest number of Catholics are in Maryland, where the English Jesuit Fathers have a numerous mission. . . . It is supposed that the missionaries of this province are under the care of a Prefect appointed by the Provincial of the Jesuits in England.[16]

We have then a quasi-starting place for the history of ecclesiastical jurisdiction in the American colonies in the year 1753. It is evident that the two Vicars-Apostolic of London (Drs. Petre and Challoner) considered the American colonies as part of their District and under their episcopal jurisdiction. This is proven by their efforts in 1743 to rid themselves of the burden of the colonies. Likewise it is clear that Propaganda was uncertain whether the colonies were part of the London District. The American Jesuits had, since Dr. Giffard's day (1703-1734), shown a marked and growing tendency to appeal directly to the London Vicar-Apostolic. A further complication arises in 1756, when Bishop Challoner began a struggle of twenty-five years to have a vicar-apostolic appointed somewhere in the English colonies, either in the West Indies or in Maryland, because the faithful there "were destitute of the Sacrament of Confirmation." In his report, September 14, 1756, to the English Clergy Agent at Rome, Challoner stated that "all our settlements in America have been deemed subject in spirituals to the ecclesiastical Superiors here, and this has been time out of mind, even I believe, from the time of the Archpriests. I know not the origin of this, nor have ever met with the original grant." When this information was laid before Propaganda an immediate

[16] Cited, *ibid.*, I, 143.

search was made in the Archives for the origin of this presumed episcopal authority over the colonies, and it was found that no document in the Archives gave to the London District any jurisdiction over the colonies. The consequence was that in 1757, Bishop Petre's faculties were formally extended by Propaganda to the colonies *ad sexennium*.

Meanwhile a change occurred. In 1756, the last phase of the hundred years' war for the political control of the North American continent began, and General Wolfe's capture of Quebec in 1759 won Canada for England. Spain, too, added to the victor's winnings by ceding the peninsula of Florida and some of the West Indies to England. "In consequence to this increase in British territory," Burton writes, "Bishop Challoner had now to consider whether under the terms of his faculties he was or was not responsible for the spiritual well-being of Canada and other new possessions." [17] In 1763, Challoner endeavored to ascertain from Propaganda what his jurisdiction as to spirituals was in these new acquisitions. Propaganda replied (July 9, 1763), stating that the matter was so important that fresh information would have to be obtained before a decision could be rendered. In Bishop Challoner's reply, dated London, August 2, 1763, we learn that:

It is to be desired that provision should be made for so many thousand Catholics as are to be found in Maryland and Pennsylvania, that they may receive the Sacrament of Confirmation, of the benefit of which they are utterly deprived. Now that Canada and Florida are brought under the English sway, the Holy Apostolic See could easily effect this, a Bishop or a Vicar-Apostolic being established at Quebec or elsewhere, with the consent of our court, by delegating jurisdiction to him throughout all the other English colonies and islands in America. This would be far from displeasing to us, and would redound greatly to the advantage of those colonies.

[17] *Challoner*, II, 132. There was no bishop in Quebec at the time. Bishop Pontbriand died in 1760, and his successor, Bishop Briand was not consecrated until 1766.

Challoner's plan was the appointment of a bishop or a vicar-apostolic, to be located beyond the Proclamation Line of 1763, so as to be under the protection of the British Government, his purpose being to rid himself of America entirely. The colonies were of no appreciable value to the London Vicar-Apostolic, and he would have been far above the average of his time had he continued to feel an interest in a group ("beyond the seas") which brought him nothing but difficulty. Propaganda's reply (December 24, 1764), gave Challoner the necessary faculties, but deferred the appointment of a separate vicariate to the future. The situation remained in this *status quo* down to the outbreak of the American Revolution and continued until Carroll's appointment as prefect in 1784.

The treaty of Paris (1763) which ended the century-long conflict between England and France for the possession of what is now the United States (east of the Mississippi) and Canada, changed the extent of Bishop Challoner's jurisdiction of the mainland. He had presumably under his charge Nova Scotia, Canada, Florida, New England, New Jersey, Pennsylvania, Maryland, Virginia, Carolina and Georgia. "Ultimately, it was arranged that with the exception of Canada which remained under its own ordinary, the Bishop of Quebec, the Vicar-Apostolic of the London District was to have jurisdiction over all territory ceded to England by the Treaty of Paris." [18]

The question of a vicar-apostolic for Maryland is mentioned in other letters of a later date from Challoner, but nothing definite was done from this time until Carroll's appointment in 1784. During this period (1765-1784), many of the official duties of the London District were left by Challoner in the hands of his coadjutor, Bishop James Talbot, the brother of the fourteenth Earl of Shrewsbury. Once the War of Independence began, Challoner and Talbot, both patriotic Englishmen, ceased relations with the Catholic clergy and laity of the Ameri-

[18] Burton, *op. cit.*, II, 138.

can colonies. Two incidents of historic note which occurred during this time were the *Laity's Remonstrance* of 1765 to Challoner against the appointment of an American bishop—a remonstrance which Challoner misjudged—and the Suppression of the Jesuits in the colonies in 1773. Probably these two facts cannot be separated, but at any rate they served to postpone for another decade the creation of hierarchical jurisdiction in the American Church. Bishop Challoner is not altogether without blame in the matter, and it is insufficient to explain the absence of delegated authority as due to the alleged attitude of members of the Society of Jesus toward episcopal rule. A resident bishop in Maryland or Philadelphia was out of the question at the time.[19] Equally so was the proposal, after Bishop Briand's consecration in 1766, to place all the Catholics in colonial England (Canada and all the present United States east of the Mississippi) under the rule of Quebec. At the same time, however, it must be admitted that none of the London Vicars-Apostolic can be credited with more than a casual interest in the American Church.

We have no record of any synods in the London District during the years the American Catholics were presumably under the charge of its Vicars-Apostolic (1685-1757) or during the years when that jurisdiction was acknowledged by Propaganda (1757-1784). All that was done to create and sustain canonical regulations for the progress of the Faith in Maryland, New York, Pennsylvania, and Virginia—the range of missionary effort during this time—was done by the little group of priests of the Society of Jesus who had made untold sacrifices for a century and a half, only in the end to see themselves discredited by the Holy See, disbanded by their Chief Shepherd, and practically abandoned by the London Vicars-Apostolic, Challoner and Talbot. In the whole history of ecclesiastical jurisdiction there is

[19] "The Beginnings of the Hierarchy in the United States," by T. J. Campbell, S.J., *Historical Records and Studies,* I (1895), 251-277.

scarcely anything parallel to their situation. In the history of English jurisdiction over the Church in this country, there is little, if any, connection between the years prior to Carroll's appointment as Prefect-Apostolic in 1784 and the years following which were to witness the rise of the present hierarchy.

PART II

THE JURISDICTION OF JOHN CARROLL

(1784–1815)

CHAPTER V

THE PREFECTURE-APOSTOLIC OF THE UNITED STATES (1784-1789)

THE opposition by the Maryland laity to the creation of an American bishopric for the Church in the English colonies (1765) was interpreted by Bishop Challoner as having been inspired by the Maryland Jesuits. Challoner evidently knew nothing of the intense feeling, even in Anglican circles, against "prelacy" in the colonies, nor of the strong anti-Catholic bias aroused by the French and Indian War. Between the end of the war and the Suppression of the Jesuits occurred in 1770 the curious and impossible plan of placing the Catholics of the "lower colonies" under Bishop Briand of Quebec, the only bishop north of the Rio Grande. The Suppression of the Jesuits (1773) and the Revolutionary War (1775-1781) not only added further confusion to Catholic life in the rising Republic but also postponed until peace was secure the creation of a firm Church administration in the United States.

After the Suppression, the ex-Jesuits continued to live as secular priests under their former superior, Father John Lewis. There is no definite trace of any official act involving jurisdiction on his part from 1773 until Carroll's appointment.

During the Revolutionary War, nothing was done, nothing could be done, to regulate ecclesiastical jurisdiction in conformity with Church law. Correspondence with Europe was practically closed from 1775 to 1783, and the only fact that has definite historical value in these years is the knowledge which came to the Maryland group of the affiliation in 1778 of the remnants of the English Province of the Society with the unsup-

53

pressed Jesuit Province of Russia. This was to bear fruit later in the United States.

Burton, however, insists upon the fact that, theoretically at least, Dr. Challoner and Dr. Talbot were the Ordinaries for the clergy and the laity here during these years of political rebellion and independence.

> It is indeed a strange and curious fact to remember [he writes], but it is none the less true, that, during the rest of Bishop Challoner's life, his jurisdiction over his American priests and people remained the only remnant of authority in the hands of an Englishman that was still recognized in America. King and Parliament and Ministry had lost their power, but this feeble old man, living his retired life in an obscure London street, still continued to issue his faculties and dispensations for the benefit of his Catholic children in Maryland and Pennsylvania.[1]

During these ten years of inaction, when the American Church was practically speaking without a head recognized by Rome, Father John Carroll, who had returned to Maryland in 1774, gradually became recognized as the leader of the American clergy. He understood, while deploring the indolence and apathy of his fellow priests on the question of jurisdiction, that it was a condition caused by the methods employed in the Suppression itself; and no member of the great Order to which he belonged felt the blow which had fallen upon them more keenly than he. Carroll realized, however, that if the American Church was to have a proper canonical rule the time was urgent. Father Lewis was too old to reorganize ecclesiastical affairs. Besides, the older priests did not appreciate fully the fact that the former colonial order of things had passed away forever in the new Republic and that an entirely new life had set in for Church and State.

The initial step in reorganizing the jurisdiction of the American Church was taken by Father Carroll in 1782 in his proposal that deputies be appointed from what was known as the North-

[1] *Challoner*, II, 118.

ern, Middle, and Southern Districts for a general meeting of the clergy. Father John Lewis sent out such a convocation, and on June 27, 1783, six deputies of the American clergy met at Whitemarsh in a first General Chapter to consider the question of providing a temporary constitution for the Church here. The result of this first assembly, which concluded its infrequent sessions on October 11, 1784, was to place the requisite authority in the hands of Father Lewis as Superior of the American Missions. This was a logical measure for the legal protection of the former Jesuit properties. In November, 1783, a committee of five was appointed to petition the Holy See to confirm Father Lewis in the superiorship.

That all the American priests were not ready to accept the jurisdiction of an ordinary bishop is evident from the memorial of another committee appointed on October 11, 1784, to inform the Holy See that the presence of a bishop in the new Republic was unnecessary and would probably be resented by the heads of the provisional government of the United States. This petition was drawn up and sent to Rome the following December. Meanwhile, on June 9, 1784, the Holy See had appointed Father John Carroll Prefect-Apostolic of the Church here. The news of this appointment reached him on August 20, 1784, in a letter from his friend, Father Thorpe, then living in Rome. Since the letter was not official, it was not officially received by the Chapter then in session. Again, on September 18, 1784, he received the news from Father Charles Plowden, then chaplain at Lulworth, in a letter dated July 3, 1784. The news was verified in a letter from the French *chargé d'affaires* in New York, Barbé de Marbois, dated October 27, 1784, and finally on November 26, 1784, the official documents sent by Cardinal Antonelli, Prefect of Propaganda, reached him at his mother's home in Rock Creek.

John Carroll was now "head of the missions in the provinces of the new Republic of the United States of North America"— to use the phrase in the official decree of appointment.

This was a prudent step for Rome to take. The people of the United States were the people of the English colonies, and the dominant politico-religious attitude was one opposed to "prelacy." [2] The development of the Catholic Church here was a feeble one owing to the penal laws in existence in all the colonies at the time of the Revolution—laws which either curtailed freedom of worship or the freedom of the franchise or both. The territory was large. Congregations were scattered, most of them living in autonomous rule. A prefecture-apostolic is usually the first step toward the canonical organization of the Church in a new missionary field. The two chief powers of the prefect-apostolic, and the two the American Church needed most at the time, were those of appointing pastors and assistants and of conferring the Sacrament of Confirmation. [3]

The Church in the United States was thus for the first time brought formally under the jurisdiction of the Sacred Congregation of Propaganda Fide and with Father John Carroll as prefect-apostolic the beginnings were laid during the next five years for the establishment of the Bishopric of Baltimore. In the official letter of appointment, he was informed that it was the intention of the Holy See to create a vicariate-apostolic as soon as conditions here were fully known in Rome.

Father Carroll was highly reluctant to accept the post, and probably what influenced him in his hestitation was the extent of his dependence on the jurisdiction of Propaganda. [4] That he accepted the prefectship was due in a large measure to the unsat-

[2] Cross, however, in his *Anglican Episcopate and the American Colonies* (New York, 1902), is of the opinion that fear of prelacy died with American independence.

[3] The same day (June 9, 1784), Cardinal Antonelli, informed Bishop Talbot that his American jurisdiction had come to an end. *Cf.* Guilday, *Carroll*, I, 204.

[4] Shea has summed up the effect of this letter in the following paragraph: "The action of the Holy See had given the Catholics in the United States a separate organization; but among priests and people who had just emerged from the oppressed condition so long maintained by the penal laws, the temporary tenure of the Prefect, his absolute dependence on the Propaganda, and the extremely limited powers given him, were the source of much uneasiness." *Op. cit.*, II, 245.

isfactory condition of Church organization under Father Lewis and to the insistence of leaders among the clergy, especially Fathers Molyneux and Farmer. The practical value of his appointment is difficult to estimate. He was charged by Propaganda to give no faculties to any priest coming into the country except by the express permission of the Sacred Congregation and to take no decisive step toward reorganizing the Church here without the same permission. In Carroll's eyes these two "cramping clauses" in his faculties practically nullified his jurisdiction.

His formal acceptance is dated February 27, 1785, in the first Report ever sent from America to Rome on the condition of the Church here. In his reply, Cardinal Antonelli wrote (July 23, 1785) regretting the inclusion of the "cramping clauses" and sent him a new formula of faculties which gave Carroll free jurisdiction over the clergy coming into the United States and assuring him that Propaganda's purpose was not to hinder but to assist in all aspects of Church reorganization. Carroll's task was undoubtedly the hardest which has ever faced an American ecclesiastical superior. The field of his labors was immense in extent, and his jurisdiction was the only bond uniting the new Republic to the Holy See.

The necessity of canonical legislation for the purpose of controlling at the outset certain elements of disorder in his prefecture is evident in Carroll's Report of 1785. The Report itself displays the cautious and observant superior who is endeavoring to learn all that can be known on the state of the Church in the United States; and although no regulations of any kind were issued by Carroll during these five years, it is evident from the legislation of 1791 that he came to the First National Synod fully prepared to suggest laws and regulations for the steadying of ecclesiastical authority and for the betterment of conditions between that authority and the priests and people. It was a critical time in the nascent American Church, and these five years of his prefectship proved beyond cavil the necessity of episcopal jurisdiction over the Church in the new Republic. With the meager means at his disposal, Carroll endeavored to bring to uniform regularity Church life in the nation. The three ecclesiastical Districts—Northern, Middle and Southern—of the thirteen original States were retained; and during these years, he was not unmindful of the vast territory beyond the Alleghanies which had become part of the Republic by the Treaty of Paris of 1783. Father Peter Huet de la Valinière, a Canadian sympathizer during the American Revolution, was sent in 1785 to Kaskaskia; and later, Father Paul de St. Pierre, a Carmelite, was given faculties for the Illinois country.

Troubles arose first in New York City and in Philadelphia over recalcitrant priests and laity, but Carroll's reconstruction plans went on apace in spite of such egregious meddlers as Father Poterie in Boston and the ungrateful Father Patrick Smith of Dublin. He won the affection of his priests, and Propaganda's fear that the creation of a bishopric with episcopal power in the hands of a former Jesuit would result in an attempt to rehabilitate the Society in the United States was lessened. At a second General Chapter of the Clergy, held at Whitemarsh in 1786, it was definitely agreed that "a diocesan Bishop alone" could adequately control those responsible for the opposition which had arisen over the control of Church property. Other problems—the supply of the clergy, the education of priests and people, the relations of clergy and laity, and the creation of a strong juridic power in the general administration of the Church here—could only be met by one invested with episcopal authority. The Holy See had decided about this time (May, 1788) to proceed with the creation of a bishopric for the United States and it was generally admitted that John Carroll would be chosen.

The Holy See permitted, as a singular favor, the American priests to select their own bishop, and Carroll was elected in May, 1789. The choice of the clergy was confirmed by Pius VI, and on November 6, 1789, the Brief *Ex hac apostolicae* was issued creating the new See of Baltimore and naming John Carroll its Ordinary, giving him jurisdiction over the Church in the United States which meant all the territory east of the Mississippi River except the Floridas, which had been receded to Spain by England in 1783. "These five years of Carroll's prefectship were as critical in their own way to the Church as was the uncertainty which ruled the political life of the nation between the Treaty of Paris in 1783, and Washington's election to the Presidency in 1789. It is a singular, not to say providential, coincidence that Washington and Carroll came to their offices at the same time. Washington was inaugurated April 30, 1789; Carroll was consecrated August 15, 1790, and our political organization was fully fashioned in the very year that our church organization was perfected." [5]

At this distance it is not difficult to recognize the outstanding problems which had arisen during Carroll's prefectship. Chief among these was that of trusteeism, and closely connected with it was another of more serious mien—unworthy priests and rebellious laity; and it will be these two vexatious problems which will disturb the peace of his episcopate as well as that of the suffragans of Baltimore during the next half-century.

[5] Guilday, *Carroll*, I, 230; *id., Eulogy on George Washington . . . by John Carroll* (New York, 1931), i-xxiv.

CHAPTER VI

THE FIRST NATIONAL SYNOD (1791)

WITH Bishop Carroll's consecration at Lulworth Castle the first stone in the edifice of episcopal jurisdiction over the American Church was laid. From the canonical standpoint, however, a more extraordinary event must be acknowledged in the permission granted by the Holy See to the little band of priests here to select their own bishop. This solitary instance in our history could not have occurred at a more propitious moment, and it did much to allay the fears of the disbanded Society of Jesus on the question of Roman jurisdiction and of their property rights in the Maryland and Pennsylvania mission centers.

Bishop Carroll's five years' study of our domestic problems (1784-1789) prepared him thoroughly for the exercise of juridic authority over the Church in the new Republic. Several problems called for immediate settlement; but it is evident from his correspondence even before his consecration that he considered as most important to the peace and prosperity of Catholic life here the immediate appointment of a coadjutor. Ten years were to pass before this was an accomplished fact. Meanwhile, further study of our Church problems was made by Dr. Carroll in personal visits to Philadelphia, New York and Boston, and before a year had passed he was able to assemble his clergy in the First National Synod of his diocese. The legislation of the Synod of 1791 and its application to the increasing number of parishes can be better estimated if we see first the means taken to create a permanent hierarchy in the country.

For twenty years (1790-1810) Bishop Carroll was to rule

practically alone the whole Church in the United States. The problems awaiting him on his return to Baltimore (December 7, 1790) were complex and varied. First was the pressing necessity for priests for the growing missions. Convinced that a native clergy would best serve the interests of the American Church, he welcomed the coming of the Sulpician Fathers who reached Baltimore in July, 1791. A fortnight later they began their heroic labors in St. Mary's Seminary, now under their direction for over a century and a quarter. Out of the tragic fate which had befallen the Church in France came what Carroll called this "singular blessing"; for, the establishment of the Baltimore Seminary he considered "a new and extraordinary spectacle for the people of this country," and his hopes were based upon the remarkable piety, the long teaching experience and the profound culture of the Sulpicians who had out of their own treasury founded this house of learning for the future priests of America. Within a week after the opening of St. Mary's Seminary, the project of founding a college at Georgetown was realized, and the doors of this venerable institution were opened to receive young men who would be trained by the century-old pedagogical methods of the greatest teaching Order the Church has ever seen. By the time Carroll returned, the long span of the history of contemplative life in this country had begun with the founding of the first Carmelite Convent at Port Tobacco in the summer of 1790, and before he yielded the burden of the archiepiscopate to his successor in 1815, religious Orders of women, devoted to the spiritual life and to teaching, were to be established as the beginning of that history of labor and sacrifice the profound significance of which to the progress of the Faith here can never be fully estimated. Before his death, other religious Orders of women—Dominicans, Visitandines, Daughters of Charity, Sisters of Charity of Nazareth, and Sisters of Loretto at the Foot of the Cross—were to be established in his vast ecclesiastical province, while the oldest community, that of the Ursulines of New Orleans, was then approaching its centennial. He lived also to see the restoration of the Society of Jesus (August 7, 1814), and the founding of other religious Congregations devoted to missionary and educational work. The important factor in this beginning of religious life is the sense of stability these communities gave to the young Church. Their very presence in the populous centers of Catholic activity had a steadying effect upon turbulent or disorderly elements in the ranks of the clergy and laity.

On all sides Bishop Carroll sensed the vigorous youth of a Church, freed at last from penal restrictions and from vague canonical jurisdiction, which it was his duty and honor to lead. And a leader he proved himself to be, especially in the matter of reëstablishing Church discipline. In fact so solidly did he create order in the Church that the Statutes of the Synod of 1791 were considered by the prelates of the Provincial Council of 1829 as the *magna charta* of all ecclesiastical legislation of the future, and they ordered that these decrees be reprinted as part of their own enactments in 1829. "When we look back," they wrote, "upon all the circumstances of the time and conditions which existed at the period that the Venerable John Carroll, of happy memory, Bishop of Baltimore, held the Diocesan Synod of 1791, we greatly admire the zeal, prudence and learning with which so many laws for the benefit of the Church were passed."

One of the keenest of all observers of Catholic progress in this country during the first half-century of our hierarchical life, Bishop Bruté of Vincennes, wrote about the Synod of 1791: "We must read over the Synod of 1791, for the form and its authority will be a good standard. In every line you see the Bishop. In all you see how extensively he had studied; and the spirit of faith, charity and zeal in that first assembly has served as a happy model for its successor." [1]

The synodal legislation of 1791 is in reality the corner stone of the edifice erected by our prelates during the century which

[1] Cited by Shea, *op. cit.*, III, 398.

followed down to 1884. Carroll's statutes not only inspired all subsequent conciliar decrees but were the norm of practically all the legislative enactments of the seven Baltimore Councils from 1829 to 1849. Only in one respect was there a striking difference, the problem of trusteeism. Bishop Carroll had coped successfully with the trustee evil in Boston, New York, and Philadelphia and was later to curb its rise in Baltimore. There is little doubt that he did not foresee the extent to which the unruly spirit of priests and laity would disturb the peace of the Church in the United States. The silence in the 1791 statutes on the trustee question is significant. Equally so is the silence in the Agreement of 1810 when, with his first suffragans about him, every aspect of Catholic life was thoroughly analyzed. Sixty years later, Archbishop Hughes of New York was to pen a striking page on Carroll's attitude toward trusteeism:

The venerable Archbishop Carroll, who himself took part in the revolution by which American independence was won, wished to assimilate, as far as possible, the outward administration of Catholic Church property in a way that would harmonize with the democratic principles on which the new government was founded. With this view he authorized and instituted the system of lay trustees in Catholic congregations. Regarded *a priori*, no system could appear to be less objectionable, or more likely both to secure advantages to those congregations, and at the same time to recommend the Catholic religion to the liberal consideration of the Protestant sentiment of the country. It would, he thought, relieve the priest from the necessity and painfulness of having to appeal from the altar on questions connected with money, touching either the means of his own support, repairs of the church, or other measures essential to the welfare of his congregation. It would at the same time secure the property, by the protection of law, for the perpetual uses to which it had been set apart and consecrated. It would be a bond of union between the priest and the people. It would be a shield to protect the minister of the altar from the very suspicion of being a money-seeker, and at the same time a means to provide for his decent maintenance. All these were no doubt the considerations which moved the venerable and patriotic Archbishop to adopt and recommend the system of lay trustees. On paper and in theory that system was entirely unobjectionable. It was well calculated to gain the confidence of a mind so generous and so liberal as that of the first Archbishop of Baltimore. But in practice it became the bitter chalice of his old age. It led to violent strifes in Charleston and in Norfolk. It led to riots and bloodshed in Baltimore and Philadelphia. Archbishop Carroll, when there were but two churches in the city of Baltimore, was doomed to witness the congregation of one of them assembling at the house of divine worship on Sunday with loaded muskets in their hands. He was doomed even during his own administration to see an excommunicated priest inaugurated by lay trustees in another church in Philadelphia; and to undergo a legal prosecution at the hands of lay trustees, in the civil court, for a simple act of episcopal jurisdiction. It is impossible to tell what would have been the consequence of that prosecution had it not been for the high character which the good prelate had sustained, and for the high estimation in which he was held by the whole community of Philadelphia, Protestant as well as Catholic. After his death, similar results of lay-trusteeship followed in the church of St. Mary in Philadelphia. Whoever will turn to the press of that city in the years 1821, 1822, 1823, and 1825, will see melancholy evidence of its workings in social strifes, religious enmities, schism, lawsuits, fearful riots, and bloodshed. The evils which manifested themselves in these churches on a grand scale, were witnessed in a minor degree in almost every congregation throughout the country, under the government of lay-trustees.[2]

The purpose Carroll had in mind when he issued (October 27, 1791) the letter of convocation for the Synod were: (1) the mode of preserving episcopal succession in the See of Baltimore; (2) the question of a coadjutor or a division of the diocese; (3) uniformity of Church discipline throughout the United States; (4) strengthening the bonds of unity with the Holy See; (5) regulations on the administration of the sacraments; (6) clerical discipline; and (7) safeguarding his priests and people from the religious indifference and worldliness so prevalent in the country after the Revolution.

Among the twenty-two priests present, when the Synod opened on November 7, 1791, ten were representatives of the older clergy who had labored under his direction as prefect-

[2] *Works*, II, 550-551.

apostolic, and twelve were newcomers, among them the three pioneers of the Sulpician community—Fathers Tessier, Nagot, and Garnier. There were seven absentees from the Maryland missions. Philadelphia and New York were not represented. Father John Thayer arrived on November 10, from Boston. No priest from the Kentucky missions was present, nor were there any from the vast Northwest Territory or from the Southland.

The ceremonies of the Synod began with a procession of the clergy from Bishop Carroll's house to St. Peter's pro-Cathedral near by, and Bishop Carroll formally opened the sessions with a discourse on the meaning of the Synod. Fathers Leonard Neale and William Elling were named promoters and Father Francis Beeston was appointed secretary to the assembly.

The sessions lasted four days and the legislation enacted concerned the administration of the sacraments, the observance of holy days of obligation and of Sunday Mass, regulations for clerical life, and the support of the missions. In the fifth session (November 10) the Blessed Virgin Mary was chosen as patroness of the diocese, and the Sunday within the octave of the Assumption was made the principal diocesan feast day.

Among the twenty-four statutes passed by the Synod, some are of major importance as revealing the problems facing these first conciliar legislators of the American Church. The priests had found many Catholics who were not certain of having been baptized; others had been baptized privately; others still had been baptized by non-Catholic ministers. To relieve them of their anxiety, the Church law on rebaptizing *sub conditione* was made clear; but priests were warned to make a thorough investigation in each case. To avoid similar difficulties in the future pastors were to begin baptismal registers. In the case of adult converts who had been validly baptized, it was not necessary to supply the ceremonies. The Sacrament of Confirmation, except when danger of death was present, was not to be conferred on children until they had reached the use of reason and were properly instructed, especially in the doctrine of the Sacrament of Penance. Linked with the necessity of keeping the churches, the altars and the vestments in a state of cleanliness, was stressed the duty of supporting the priests. In every parish two or three men of standing and virtue were to be chosen either by the pastor or the congregation to take up the collection at all the Masses. No further privilege, however, such as the spending of the parochial funds, was given to these *curatores*. Parochial funds were to be divided in accordance with the ancient custom of the Church into three parts: one for the support of the priests; one for the relief of the poor; and another for the upkeep of the church itself. Stipends should be received in such a way that all appearances of avarice or simony be excluded. The cassock was to be worn by the priests in the celebration of Mass, and the surplice also in the exercise of other public functions of the ministry. Children about to make their first Holy Communion were to be advised to make a general confession beforehand. Pastors were warned not to delay first Holy Communion too long, but care was to be taken lest the children be permitted to approach the sacred table too early. A far-reaching decree was the one inflicting suspension *a divinis* on any priest exercising faculties for confession without the approbation of the bishop, and the faithful were to be instructed that confessions to unauthorized priests were invalid. The pain of suspension was also decreed against any priest who should change his residence from one congregation to another without permission. The Sacrament of Extreme Unction was to be conferred on all, even to little children who had not reached the use of reason, who were in danger of death.

The longest decree is that on the Sacrament of Marriage. Strangers were not to be united in the bonds of matrimony until the three proclamations of the banns had been made and not without sufficient testimony from the pastor of the place where they formerly lived that they were free to marry. No one should be permitted to marry who was ignorant of the fundamental doctrines of the Church. The principal truths which had to be known and understood before the ceremony were then given by means of a quotation from the Council of Lima (probably that of 1567). This was especially cited because of the difficulties many pastors had found among the colored portion of their flocks. The truths which were to be known were—that God is the Creator of all things, the rewarder of good and evil; the three Persons in God; the Incarnation, Death and Resurrection of the Savior; necessity of belief in Jesus Christ for salvation; sorrow for sins committed; the duty of obedience to the laws of God and the Church; and the love of God and of one's neighbor. Mixed marriages were to be discouraged as much as possible. The Fathers of the Synod realized how difficult it would be to avoid marriages with non-Catholics, especially in those places where few Catholics resided; but the pastors were urged to exercise every holy influence to prevent these unions.

The following rules were then laid down for the regulation of these marriages: (1) Catholics should be warned of the grave consequences that frequently followed upon such unions and they should be exhorted to show Christian fortitude in restraining themselves from entering the marital state with those not of their own faith; (2) if the pastors saw that their admonitions were not heeded, every care should be taken to surround the Catholic party with safeguards for the preservation of his or her faith; (3) the non-Catholic party should be required to promise before God and several witnesses that there would be no opposition to the education of the children in the Catholic faith; (4) pastors should proceed cautiously in their attempt to dissuade the Catholic party from such a marriage lest the same take place before a non-Catholic minister; (5) where such a risk is present, the pastor was permitted to proceed with the marriage providing no impediment was present; (6) no mixed marriage, however, was to be blessed with the blessing as prescribed in the Mass *pro sponso et sponsa.*

Regulations for Mass on Sundays were prescribed. The Litany of the Blessed Virgin was to be recited before Mass, since the

Mother of God was the principal patroness of the diocese; where it was possible to have a *Missa cantata,* the *Asperges* was to be sung, and the Mass with a choir trained to sing the proper parts was to be celebrated with all the dignity of the ceremonial. At the end of the Gospel, the prayer for the civil authorities of our country was to be read,[3] the Gospel in the vernacular was to follow, the banns to be published, notices made of feasts and fasts, and then a short sermon was to be given of an exhortatory nature in order that all present should strive for higher Christian perfection. At the afternoon services, commonly called Vespers, the prescribed psalms and prayers were to be sung. This was followed by the Benediction of the Most Blessed Sacrament with the proper hymns and prayers. Hymns in English were permitted at this service. These rules had in view a church where more than one priest was stationed. If, however, there were but one priest, after Mass the whole congregation was to recite with him the *Pater Noster, Ave Maria, Apostles Creed,* and the *Acts of Faith, Hope* and *Charity.* Then the children and those needing instruction were to remain, and the Catechism was to be taught to them by the priest in charge of the mission. The next decree reads as follows:

At the beginning of our episcopate we have been impelled by an ardent desire to make the Blessed Virgin Mary the principal patroness of our diocese, so that by Her intercession, faith and love of God and sanctity of life in the people committed to our care may flourish and increase more and more. We were consecrated first Bishop of Baltimore on the feast of the Assumption and we are led to honor Her as our patron and we exhort our venerable colleagues to venerate Her with a great devotion and often and zealously commend this devotion to their flock, so that in Her powerful patronage they may rely on Her protection from all harm. We decree also that the Sunday within the octave of the feast of the Assumption, or that feast itself if it falls on a Sunday, shall be the principal feast of the diocese on which the people should be excited to receive piously and religiously the Sacraments of Pen-

---

[3] This prayer, composed by Dr. Carroll, will be found in Guilday, *Carroll,* II, 432, and in the *Eulogy, etc.,* xv-xvii.

ance and Holy Eucharist. In order to foster the piety of the faithful we shall direct our humble prayers to the Apostolic See to obtain abundant spiritual favors, concerning which, if they are granted, we shall speak hereafter.

The difficulty merchants and workingmen found in attending Mass on holydays of obligation was recognized and pastors were directed to deal with each case as wisely as possible, in case Mass could not be celebrated at a time convenient to all. Two decrees regulated clerical dress and domestic affairs in the presbyteries and the vicars-general of the diocese were requested to use the highest caution in this regard. A further decree legislated for the support of the clergy. The colonial Catholics of Maryland had a long and honorable record for generosity to the Church, but with congregations rising in the cities and towns there was danger that Church support, unless properly regulated, would fall off. Hence the divine precept of such support was recalled, and the faithful were to be admonished from time to time that those who did not do their duty were not worthy to receive absolution and that they would have to answer for the "crass ignorance and vice of those poor people who because of the woeful parsimony of the rich, remain altogether ignorant of Christian instruction." Along with the statutes was sent to each priest an instruction regarding the amount of stipends etc., and this was to be read to the congregation.

The decrees of the Lateran Council on the Paschal precept of confession and communion were to be enforced and pastors were directed to warn their flocks from time to time that they ran the danger of loss of Christian burial unless this duty was fulfilled annually.

We have here no doubt one of the chief abuses which Bishop Carroll had found in his visitation as prefect-apostolic. Congregations were not compact social groups at the time. Catholics were scattered. Priests were few, and it was almost impossible to minister to all. Neglect was present; and although the Lateran decree was to be rigorously obeyed, pastors were to exercise extreme caution before refusing Catholics the right of Christian burial. If the neglect was not accompanied by contumacy or contempt for the Church, if it were not a notorious neglect of years, and if the dead person's moral character was such that he or she had not lost the respect of the community, the pastor should not act imprudently, but should ask the advice of the vicar-general of his district or of the bishop. If this was impracticable, then he should proceed charitably and mercifully to judge the case before him, and to act upon the principle that the discipline of the Church was not for the punishment of the dead but for the salutary effect it should have on the living.

These twenty-four decrees were passed on November 10, and signed by Bishop Carroll and the priests present. Before closing the Synod, Carroll addressed them on the matter of proposing to the Holy See either a division of the Diocese of Baltimore or the election of a coadjutor. The Synod ended with a sermon by Father John Ashton on the priesthood, and then the *Te Deum* was sung and the sessions came to a close.[4]

A few days later, Bishop Carroll issued a Circular on Christian Marriage, ordering that in the future all Catholics entering into the marriage state before any but their lawful pastors would not be admitted "to reconciliation and the Sacraments, till they shall agree to make public acknowledgment of their disobedience before the assembled congregation, and beg pardon for the scandal they have given."

The following year (May 28, 1792) Dr. Carroll issued the first *Pastoral Letter* to the American Church.[5] The document was genuinely admired by all, regardless of creed, at the time. The topics discussed in the *Pastoral* are: the advantages of Catholic education; Georgetown College; necessity of vocations to the priesthood; the founding of St. Mary's Seminary, Baltimore, by the Sulpician Fathers; the maintenance of the clergy; support of

[4] Contrary to the general opinion the decrees of 1791 were sent to the Holy See for approbation (Guilday, *Carroll*, II, 443-444).

[5] Printed in the *National Pastorals etc.* (ed. Guilday), 1-15.

the Church; attendance at Mass on Sundays and holy days of obligation; prayers for the dead; devotion to the Mother of God; and the patronal feast of the diocese, the Assumption of the Blessed Virgin Mary.

What is strikingly characteristic of this legislation of 1791 and of the episcopal mind which framed it is its supreme conservatism and mildness of statement. A new Church was being brought into the broad stream of juridic authority at Baltimore during those November days of 1791. Practically every aspect of Church law had to be considered in these our earliest enactments, and it would not be surprising, considering the times and the condition of the Church here, if laws of a more stringent and peremptory kind had been passed. But Bishop Carroll displayed in these decrees that consummate prudence and far-sightedness which few pioneers possessed. Future Councils under his successors in the See of Baltimore would gradually build upon the legislation of 1791 and ere long the simple direct appeal of Catholic loyalty to God and to the discipline of the Church that lies at the heart of Carroll's enactments would be forgotten in the stress of meeting the many complex problems which accompanied our growth in the United States; but shrewd prelates all through these years would realize that the Councils of Baltimore were simply and quietly building the House of God upon the foundations John Carroll laid so wisely.

CHAPTER VII

THE MEETING OF THE HIERARCHY (1810)

FOR thirty-eight years (1791-1829) the Church in the United States was to be guided by the conciliar legislation of Bishop Carroll's Synod. During the years which followed to his death in 1815, one of the important measures in Carroll's eyes for the stabilization of Church discipline was the division of the episcopal burden.

His first act in creating Church discipline was to ask for a division of the diocese with a second See at New York or Philadelphia, the Susquehanna River to be the boundary line. Failing to obtain this, he then asked for a coadjutor who would share the burden and would be ready to take his place in case of death. Dr. Carroll's choice was Father Laurence Graessl of Philadelphia, then thirty-nine years old. Bishop-elect Graessl died in October, 1793, before the official documents were received from Rome. On the advice of the older clergy, the name of Father Leonard Neale, then stationed at Philadelphia, was sent to Propaganda (1794), but owing to the disturbed political conditions in Europe the bulls for his consecration did not reach Baltimore until the summer of 1800. Bishop Neale was consecrated on December 7, 1800, and returned to Georgetown College to resume the presidency of that institution. During the fifteen years of his coadjutorship, Bishop Neale seems to have taken little part in the administration of the diocese. Carroll then decided to request the Holy See to divide the Diocese of Baltimore; on April 8, 1808, by the briefs, *Ex debito pastoralis officio* and *Pontificii muneris,* Baltimore was made a metropolitan See and Sees were created at Boston, New York, Philadelphia and Bardstown. Cheverus was appointed to Boston, Concanen to New York, Egan to Philadelphia, and Flaget to Bardstown. The bulls necessary for the consecration of the three American prelates (Concanen had been consecrated at Rome on April 24, 1808) reached Archbishop Carroll in August, 1810, and immediate plans for this important ceremony were decided upon.[1] Bishop Egan was consecrated at St. Peter's, the pro-Cathedral of Baltimore, on October 28, 1810; on November 1, in the same church, Bishop Cheverus was consecrated; and three days later, in St. Patrick's Church, Baltimore, Bishop Flaget was consecrated. The fortnight spent with the venerable metropolitan enabled the prelates to make a thorough survey of Church conditions here, to reach an objective estimate of the value of the 1791 statutes, and to come to a common agreement on certain extensions of the prevailing laws which they considered necessary as a preliminary to what was to have been the First Provincial Council of 1812. Archbishop Carroll's three suffragans were men of exceptional character and experience. All three had resided long enough in their respective dioceses to be familiar with those problems which were of local origin or development.

When the five prelates began their deliberations after the consecration of October-November, 1810, they probably did not realize that the status of Church progress and discipline would require a whole fortnight's discussion in order to reach a decision upon a uniform system of diocesan control.

The decisions reached at this first Meeting of the American hierarchy prove how wisely Carroll and his priests had legislated nineteen years before. First in order of importance, the five prelates considered the necessity of holding a Provincial Council. They felt, however, that it would be best to study their own diocesan problems anew from the vantage of the episcopal

[1] For a documentary explanation of the appointment of Bishop Concanen, cf. Hughes, R., *The Right Rev. Richard Luke Concanen, O.P., etc.* (Fribourg, Switzerland, 1926), 29-113. Bishop Concanen died at Naples, June 19, 1810.

dignity which had been conferred on them, and that within two years (1812) they would be better informed on all those topics which were bound to arise in a Provincial Council.

The Meeting of 1810 is a singular one in this respect, that, without any of the formalities surrounding a synodal or conciliar assembly, the five prelates passed a series of "resolutions or ordinances" which were made obligatory on all the congregations of the Province of Baltimore. In one sense, however, these ordinances were a more precise wording of the decrees of 1791. Pastors were again warned not to permit strange and unknown priests to exercise any functions "before they exhibited authentic proofs of their having obtained the Bishop's permission," and this warning was given also to those lay people who were in charge of the churches, chalices and sacred vestments. Baptism was to be administered no longer in private houses except in cases of necessity. The people were gradually to be brought to the realization that Catholics should be married in church, but it was thought best not to issue an ordinance to that effect at the time. The fourth resolution reads:

The pastors of the Faithful are earnestly directed to discourage more and more from the pulpit, and in their public and private conferences an attachment to entertainments and diversions of dangerous tendency to morality, such as to frequent theatres, and cherish a fondness of dancing assemblies. They likewise must often warn their congregations against the reading of books dangerous to Faith & morals and especially a promiscuous reading of all kinds of novels. The faithful themselves should always remember the severity with which the Church, guided by the Holy Ghost, constantly prohibited writings calculated to diminish the respect due to our Holy Religion.

All Catholics known to be Freemasons were debarred from the Sacraments, "unless these persons seriously promise to abstain forever from going to their lodges and professing themselves to belong to their Society, and Pastors of Congregations shall frequently recommend to all under their care never to join with or become members of said fraternity."

Further deliberations during the fortnight resulted in a second series of regulations. The first of these was the decision to hold a Provincial Council in November, 1812. While recognizing the value of diocesan synods, they deemed it wiser to represent to the Holy See the inconvenience of these assemblies at the time, and to ask that the time of convoking these synods be left to the discretion of the respective bishops. If, however, there was neglect in the matter, the archbishop was empowered to "take lawful measures for the convocation of such Synod." Moreover, the Church law requiring annual visitations of the diocese was considered impracticable at the time and "would prove an insupportable burden to the Bishops." Each Ordinary was to be free to arrange for these official visits at his own convenience. Part of the diocese, however, should be visited each year. Although the next resolution cannot be linked with the selection in 1808, of Bishop Concanen for New York by the Holy See itself, its significance can scarcely be ignored:

In case the Holy See will graciously permit the nomination to vacant Bishopricks to be made in the United States, it is humbly and respectfully suggested to the Supreme Pastor of the Church to allow the nomination for the vacant Diocese to proceed solely from the Archbishop and Bishops of this ecclesiastical Province.

An echo of the quarrel between the seculars and regulars in England can be heard in the following resolution, urging upon the superiors of religious Orders and Congregations not to change their subjects who have been entrusted with the care of souls without the consent of the Ordinary. Confidence in the coöperation of these superiors is generously expressed, and there is even a favorable word on the question of diocesan priests who wish to leave the secular priesthood to become members of these religious communities. In no way will the bishops interfere with the recall of regulars whose presence is required elsewhere for the welfare of all such Orders or Congregations. This particular ordinance is exceptionally well phrased and has a historical place in the long quarrel which ended in England many years after our bishops had settled the question for the United States. Priests living on the confines of another diocese were to be permitted, under certain conditions, to exercise priestly functions in both dioceses, and again the law regarding strange priests is emphatically expressed. The Douay Bible was to be used in all books of devotion and in reading the Gospel during Mass. The following ordinance should be given in full:

It is being made known to the Archbishops and Bishops that there exists a difference of opinion and practice among some of the clergy of the United States concerning the use of the vernacular language in any part of the public service, and in the administration of the Sacraments, it is hereby enjoined on all Priests not only to celebrate the whole Mass in the Latin language, but likewise when they administer Baptism, the Holy Eucharist, Penance and Extreme Unction, to express the necessary and essential form of those Sacraments in the same tongue according to the Roman ritual, but it does not appear contrary to the injunctions of the Church to say in the vernacular language the prayers previous and subsequent to those Sacred forms, provided however, that no translation of those prayers shall be made use of except one authorized by the concurrent approbation of the Bishops of this ecclesiastical Province, which translation will be printed as soon as it can be prepared under their inspection. In the meantime the translation of the late venerable Bishop Challoner may be made use of.

Registers were to be kept for baptisms, marriages and burials in each church or congregation. Again the ruling regarding baptism in private houses is laid down, and where it is impossible to have sponsors the child was to be baptized with the usual ceremonies "but only receives what is called private baptism." The stipend-offering for Masses was fixed at fifty cents. A further word is added about the celebration of marriages in the church, and priests were cautioned against permitting lay people to take perpetual vows of chastity whilst living in the world.

A uniform ritual for the Benediction of the Most Blessed Sacrament was to be composed and copies sent to the clergy at an early date.

This second and more detailed series of resolutions is signed by the five prelates and is dated November 19, 1810.[2] When the next two years had passed, the War of 1812 had begun, and there was some reluctance on the part of Bishop Cheverus to make the long and arduous journey to Baltimore for the proposed Provincial Council. The vacancy in the Sees of New York and New Orleans, he considered as a hindrance to any attempt to bring about a more uniform system of Church discipline. Bishop Egan was not in the best of health at the time, and Archbishop Carroll was beginning to show the signs of decline. The death of Bishop Egan on July 22, 1814, and the appointment by the Holy See of Bishop Connolly to New York on November 6, 1814, no doubt had their influence in persuading Archbishop Carroll not to call the Provincial Council. His death on December 3, 1815, passed the problem on to his successors. Fourteen years later, under the fourth Archbishop of Baltimore, Dr. Whitfield, the First Provincial Council of 1829 was to be held at Baltimore.

[2] The two sets of regulations are printed in Guilday, *Carroll*, II, 589-596.

PART III

THE SEVEN PROVINCIAL COUNCILS OF BALTIMORE

(1829–1849)

CHAPTER VIII

THE FIRST PROVINCIAL COUNCIL OF BALTIMORE (1829)

TWICE under Archbishop James Whitfield (1829, 1833) and five times during the régime of his successor, Archbishop Samuel Eccleston (1837, 1840, 1843, 1846, and 1849), the bishops of the Province of Baltimore met in solemn provincial assemblies to deliberate upon, and to legislate for, the uniformity of Church discipline in the United States. Owing to the fact that Oregon City in 1846 and St. Louis in 1847 had been erected into archiepiscopal Sees, Archbishop Eccleston had considered the advisability of calling a plenary council in 1848; but the great distance prevented Archbishop Blanchet of Oregon from coming to Baltimore. Uncertainty over the extent of his metropolitan jurisdiction determined Archbishop Peter Richard Kenrick of St. Louis to take part in the 1849 Council, not indeed as a suffragan of Baltimore but as one of the presiding prelates. For this reason the Seventh Council of 1849 is styled a Provincial Council and its legislation was acknowledged as prevailing over the whole of the United States, Oregon and St. Louis included.

The method followed in treating these seven Provincial Councils is kept as uniform as the subject-matter will permit. First, as far as possible a brief survey of the state of the Church in this country at the opening of each Council is given; this is followed by a list of the more important problems each assembly had to solve; then the convocation, deliberations and decisions of each Council are given. To this is added a concise statement of the decrees passed by the Council and the epistolary cor-

81

respondence between the Fathers of the Council with the Holy See and others is summarized. While the narrative is kept as strictly as possible to the work of the Council itself, the whole forms a synopsis of Church progress in its more salient aspects.

As has been stated, when the Meeting of the Hierarchy ended on November 19, 1810, Archbishop Carroll, his coadjutor, Bishop Leonard Neale, and the suffragans of Boston (Cheverus), Philadelphia (Egan) and Bardstown (Flaget) decided to hold the first Provincial Council in 1812. The convocation for this assembly was indeed sent out by Dr. Carroll in June, 1812, but later it was decided to postpone the Council, and during the delay Bishop Egan and Archbishop Carroll died. Archbishop Neale (1815-1817) was in declining health and the postponement was continued. Archbishop Ambrose Maréchal who succeeded Neale in 1817 and who presided over the American Church for the next eleven years was not favorably inclined toward a provincial assembly in spite of the constant urging of some of his suffragans, especially Bishop England of Charleston, S. C.[1] There is much to be said in favor of the archbishop's reluctance to call his suffragans together. The condition of the Church in the larger centers, such as New York, Philadelphia, Norfolk, Richmond and Charleston was not favorable to this general assembly; and Dr. Maréchal believed it more prudent to wait until the local situation had righted itself under the guidance of his suffragans before bringing together an official meeting of the prelates. The two views prevalent at the time—that of the archbishop and that of Dr. England and some of his

[1] The complex situation of Church affairs during these years (1817-1828) and the reason for Dr. Maréchal's opposition to a Council are given in the *Life and Times of John England*, II, chap. xxi. (*Antecedents to the First Provincial Council*) 68-110. Dr. Brownson's tribute to Bishop England in this respect will be found, *ibid.*, 502-503. "The Church in this country," he writes, "owes to Bishop England the celebration of Provincial Councils which have given form and consistency to the hierarchy and order to her internal economy. . . . It is right that the praise of originating and promoting these most important assemblies should be given to the eminent Bishop of Charleston." *Brownson's Quarterly Review*, L, 158.

colleagues in the hierarchy—represented two different modes of
action in the face of the confusion created by unruly priests and
laity and by the action of Rome in the direct appointment of
prelates (of which Dr. England was one) to Sees in this country. Dr. England's correspondence with the archbishop during
these years (1821-1828) brings into relief these two views; and
his constant appeal for a national assembly to create a uniform
Church discipline, while meeting at every turn a negative answer from the archbishop, has this paramount value, that we
are enabled to realize vividly the many pressing problems which
eventually Dr. Maréchal's successor faced when the First Provincial Council was convened during the first year of Archbishop
Whitfield's régime. In one of Dr. England's letters (April 26,
1827) there is a fair and just statement of the conflict of
opinion on the question:

I am under the impression that you neither wish for, nor intend
to summon, a Synod. I am bound, as well from the general principles of charity, and also from my firm belief of your good inten-
tions, and my respect for your zeal and virtues, to feel convinced,
as I do sincerely, that you do in your conscience judge it would
be improper to call one. Thus without examining, what it would
be folly to guess at, what might be the reason for your determination, I believe that determination to have been made, and as you
believe, correctly. My judgment leads me altogether to an opposite
result. I not only think it would be useful, but I believe it absolutely necessary, and that the evils which unfortunately do exist will
scarcely if at all, and only after increase of extent and duration, be
healed before one is called. And my not more frequently and earnestly pressing the subject upon your consideration is not the result
of any doubt, but of absolute despair of your coming into my view
of the subject. I therefore content myself with doing as much as
acquits my own conscience without uselessly annoying you.

Later (June 25, 1827), he wrote to the archbishop:

That is my humble opinion. The deranged and unsettled state
of the American Church can be reduced to order and peace and
permanent system only by Provincial Synods of the American
Hierarchy. That much as I would value even the temporary quiet

and highly as I would esteem and reverence and faithfully as I would obey a Papal legate, I solemnly and earnestly deprecate and am averse to this extraordinary mode of doing what I think can be better done by the proper and ordinary mode of a Provincial Synod. Because the usual mode of a Synod has not been tried. Because the usual mode of a Synod is more congenial to the practice of the Church. Because the usual mode of a Synod is more congenial to the old canons of the Church. Because the usual mode of a Synod has been prescribed by the last general council. Because the usual mode of a Synod has been found most beneficial in those places in which it has been followed. Because the usual mode of a Synod has been preferred by most holy Prelates whose example is most precious and useful in the Church. Because the usual mode of a Synod is more in accordance with the spirit of our National institutions, and because it is the mode which will best please the flock and insure their support to its resolutions. Whereas placing the power in the hands of an individual appears to me an encroachment upon the rights of Diocesan Bishops, and an attempt to reduce them to the level of Vicars-Apostolic. It destroys what Cardinal Bellarmine calls the republican part of Church government, and properly states to be one of its characteristics, and is calculated in this country to create a great moral obstacle to the continuance and progress of our Faith. I could add many more reasons, which make the conviction in my mind strong, and not easily to be shaken, but for my present purpose this is enough. That purpose being respectfully to declare that so far as I am concerned, though I suppose that concern will be estimated, perhaps, as it deserves, as not very great, I cannot contemplate the future prospects of the American church without most painful apprehension; that I humbly conceive proper measures have not been taken to prevent the evils which I dread, and that having no other power but that of declaring my impression, I am anxious to relieve myself from all responsibility for the consequence by making this plain but painful declaration to you.[2]

Whatever hopes there were of inducing the archbishop to call a Provincial Council at the time were abandoned owing to

[2] In a letter to Bishop Bruté (June 4, 1828) Bishop England expresses the opinion that perhaps after all it would be better not to unite the suffragans, since it was evident to many at the time that the South and North would eventually separate, and "that in such an event there should not exist too strong a bond to unite Churches which ought to sever. In plain practice, at present, every American Diocese is a Popedom, and Archbishop is a useless name."

the precarious state of Dr. Maréchal's health. He died on January 29, 1828, and was succeeded by James Whitfield who was consecrated fourth Archbishop of Baltimore on May 25 of that year. Although sharing Maréchal's attitude toward a national assembly of the hierarchy, Dr. Whitfield eventually (December 18, 1828) wrote to his suffragans convoking the Council for October 1, 1829, and asked them for suggestions on the questions to be discussed in the meeting. Dr. England's reply (December 26) reveals some of the vexed questions which had arisen since the Synod of 1791. Among these were: the best method of educating candidates for the priesthood; the best method of counteracting the pernicious influences of the anti-Catholic groups in the country, of regulating the instruction of Catholic youth, and of encouraging and supporting religious communities, especially of women devoted to educational work; the best method of publishing and distributing Catholic books on doctrinal questions; and "the laying down of general principles of discipline upon which we might enact our respective Diocesan Statutes with as much of an approach to uniformity as possible." [3]

Uniformity of discipline was the principal need of the Church in the United States during the score of years which followed the Meeting of 1810. It was not easy of attainment, for misrule had spread under incompetent leadership in New York and Philadelphia and New Orleans. The Church here during this period of its infancy was sadly hampered by the presence of priests who knew not how to obey and of laity who were interpreting their share in Catholic life by non-Catholic church systems. On the other hand, uniformity, when it did come, and it came quickly after the promulgation of the legislation of 1829, was considerably accelerated by the fact that the Church here consisted of one ecclesiastical province coterminus with the nation. Canals and roadways were in operation and interstate commerce was already highly developed. The country was

[3] The letter is printed in Guilday, *England*, I, 117-118.

one and united in 1829; more so than it had ever been since the close of the Revolutionary War. States were multiplying, as were also dioceses within the Baltimore Province. There were at the time (1829), not counting Richmond which had been vacant since Bishop Kelly's abandonment, nine suffragan Sees—Boston, New York, Philadelphia, Bardstown, Charleston, Cincinnati, St. Louis, New Orleans, and Mobile—and the jurisdiction of their bishops covered the twenty-eight States and Territories then constituting the Union. Their hierarchy at the time consisted of the archbishop, Dr. Whitfield, then 59 years old; Flaget who was 66; England, 43; Fenwick, 61; Rosati, 40; Fenwick (S.J.), 47; Dubois, 65; David, 69; Portier, 34; Conwell, 71; and De Neckere, 29, who, though it was not known when the Council opened, had been appointed to New Orleans on August 2, 1829.

Of these eleven bishops, three were absent from the Council. Bishop Dubois had been summoned to Rome on September 30, 1829; Bishop Portier left for Europe in April, 1829; and Bishop David was prevented from attending owing to illness. Bishop Conwell of Philadelphia had been called to Rome in 1828 and relieved of all jurisdiction over his diocese, but returned while the Council was in session (October 7, 1829), though not permitted to exercise a deliberative vote by the Fathers of the Council. His place was occupied by Father William Matthews of Washington, D. C., who had been appointed Administrator Apostolic of the Diocese of Philadelphia. The *Synodales* present, therefore, were: Whitfield, Flaget, England, Fenwick (O.P.), Rosati, Fenwick (S.J.), and Matthews, and in this order do we find the decrees signed.

It would be of considerable assistance in estimating the decretal legislation passed in 1829 if we possessed accurate statistics of the Church here at that time. None, however, exist. The *Laity's Directory* of 1822 has a section devoted to the "Present State of Religion in the Respective Dioceses"; [4] but we

[4] Pp. 81-121.

have no certain source between this date and the first volume of the little *Catholic Directory* of 1833. Shea has given what he estimates to be a fair census for 1829, based upon the Council's letter to the pope (October 24, 1829) and places the Catholic population as five hundred thousand in a population of twelve million.[5] The exact number of priests and churches in 1829 is unknown, but the problems before the Fathers of the Council were identical in all parts of the country.

Apart from the anxieties cognate to the normal growth of the Church, such as Catholic education, the supply of the clergy, the work of the religious communities of men and women, Catholic devotional life and the spiritual discipline of the laity, especially in the administration of the sacraments, the chief difficulty before the assembly of 1829 was that of securing a legal and satisfactory method of safeguarding Church property. This problem we know under the general, though somewhat loose, term *trusteeism*. There was nothing inherently vicious in the trustee system, and it might have prevailed, owing to legal methods in use for the incorporation of Church property, had it not been for the injection of certain elements of discord which created an impossible situation, so far as Catholic discipline is concerned, namely, the encroachment of lay influences upon the spiritual jurisdiction of the priests and bishop and the rise of the obnoxious right of patronage to which rebellious trustees laid claim. Out of this came the disorders of the first half-century of Church discipline in the United States; disorders which created dissensions, tumults, scandals, schisms and eventually heresy:

From St. Peter's Church in New York City to Holy Trinity Church in Philadelphia, then down the Atlantic seaboard to Baltimore, Norfolk, Charleston and Savannah, and then westward to New Orleans, the standard of rebellion had been raised by groups of laymen who were fighting for a principle which would have

[5] *Op. cit.*, III, 191. Bishop Rosati gives this same estimate in a letter in the *Annales*, IV, 599. Bishop England (*U. S. Cath. Misc.*, IX, 293) places the number as more than 600,000.

ended, as Carroll once told them, "the unity and Catholicity of the Church." [6]

The serpentine trail of trusteeism winds its vicious way along the highroad of canonical legislation from 1791 to 1884. None of the *Pastoral Letters* during that time is silent on the question; and while to-day the problem is practically non-existent, it was a principal cause of confusion in the external relations between the hierarchy and the Catholic body during that hundred years. Another problem of an internal nature which had an equally disturbing effect upon the peace of the Church and which can hardly be said to have been settled satisfactorily by any of the Seven Provincial Councils was the mode of filling vacant Sees in the American Church.

During the ten months which followed the letter of convocation to the Council, Archbishop Whitfield carried on, with the assistance of the professors of St. Mary's Seminary, active preparations for the assembly. The procedure to be observed had already been outlined by Pope Benedict XIV in his *De Synodo Dioecesana* (1756), and it was decided that all questions to come before the Council should be analyzed and studied by three committees: *De Fide et Disciplina, De Sacramentis,* and *De Moribus Clericorum.* On the eve of the Council (September 30, 1829) the seven prelates who were to direct the proceedings met at the archbishop's house and general rules were agreed upon for their guidance:

1. Nothing would be sanctioned by the Council which could not be easily carried into execution.
2. No decree would be binding upon the faithful until the Holy See had given its approval.
3. Nothing would be brought before the consideration of the Fathers of the Council for decision apart from the questions which were settled upon in advance, unless by a two-thirds' vote permission were obtained.

[6] Guilday, *England*, I, 355; *id.*, "Trusteeism," *Hist. Records and Studies,* XVIII (1928), 7-73; Dignan, "Peter Antony Malou (1753-1827)," *Records,* Amer. Cath. Hist. Society (December, 1931-March, 1932).

4. The sessions would begin at ten in the morning; the private conferences at four in the afternoon. Neither were to exceed three hours' duration.

The officials appointed were: *Promoter*, Bishop Fenwick (Boston); *Secretary*, Rev. Edward Damphoux, S.S.; *Assistant Secretary*, Rev. Francis P. Kenrick; *Master of Ceremonies*, Rev. John J. Chanche; and *Chanters*, Fathers Lhomme and Radanne. Certain prominent ecclesiastics were invited: Father Francis Dzierozynski, Superior of the Jesuits in the United States; Father Joseph Carrière, the Visitator of the Sulpicians, then on an official tour of inspection in this country; Father John Tessier, Dean of the Faculty of Sacred Sciences in St. Mary's Seminary and Vicar-General of the Archdiocese of Baltimore; and Father Louis Deluol, Rector of St. Mary's Seminary. Fathers Tessier, Deluol and John Baptist Damphoux (then President of St. Mary's University) acted as *theologians* for Archbishop Whitfield. There were present also the *theologians* chosen by the bishops: Fathers F. P. Kenrick (Flaget), Simon G. Bruté (England), Louis de Barth (Fenwick, O.P.), Augustus Jeanjean (Rosati), Anthony Blanc (Fenwick, S.J.), and Michael Wheeler (Matthews). On October 5, Father John Power, Vicar-General of New York, was admitted as the representative of Bishop Dubois. In all the conciliar body consisted of twenty-two persons. To these should be added three prominent lawyers who were invited to attend the ninth public session (October 13)—Roger B. Taney, then Attorney-General of Maryland and later Chief Justice Marshall's successor in the Supreme Court of the United States, John Scott and William J. Read, who were asked to assist the prelates in the legal aspects of Church property incorporation.

During the fifteen days of the Council (October 3 to October 18, 1829), there were held thirteen private and thirteen public congregations and the customary three solemn Sessions. Thirty-eight decrees were enacted by the Council. Some were merely the reiteration with necessary changes of the Statutes of 1791 and 1810, and the others were directed to the newer set of problems which had arisen in Church discipline since Carroll's death (1815-1829).[7]

The first, second and third decrees emphasized the jurisdiction of the bishops over all priests laboring in their respective dioceses and legislated against the removal of members of the religious Orders in pastoral capacity without the consent of the Ordinary. This part of the decree was an echo of an old problem which, as has been seen, had arisen in England several centuries before; and, although several enactments on the same question will be made in subsequent Councils, it is to the credit of the American Church that its internal discipline was never seriously threatened on this score as was the Church in England until nearly the end of the century. These initial decrees likewise regulated another disorder which apparently was existent at the time: the migration of priests without permission from one diocese to another. Priests were obliged to accept the mission entrusted to them by the bishop and to remain in the diocese to which they were attached, nor were priests who came to any of the dioceses to be accepted unless their official papers were in proper order. A clause was added by Propaganda to the first decree safeguarding the privileges which had been granted to certain religious Orders by the Holy See. The Fathers excluded from the first of these declarations one beneficed parish in New Orleans, control of which was then in litigation between Bishop Rosati and the trustees.[8] A fourth decree ended the system of co-pastors which existed in several places and gave us the uniform system we now have of pastor and assistants. The fifth decree is the earliest canonical legislation against the evils of trusteeism. In the future, wherever possible, no new churches

---

[7] The short history of the Baltimore legislation (*Baltimore Catholic Mirror*, XXXV, October 25, 1884) praises these decrees in eloquent terms: "How well they were framed and how singularly fortunate they were in meeting the anitcipated needs of the times!"

[8] Rothensteiner, *History of the Archdiocese of St. Louis* (St. Louis, 1928), I, 433.

were to be erected unless the deeds were made out in the bishop's name. The constitutional system already established by Dr. England for the Diocese of Charleston was excluded from this legislation, and Propaganda later added a clause safeguarding the rights of the regular clergy in this respect. Henceforth the alleged right of patronage claimed by certain groups of trustees was declared illegal in Church discipline. Further legislation was necessary in subsequent Councils, but in retrospect it may be admitted that from 1829 onwards, the influence of the trustee system began to wane. Later, the Fathers of the Council were obliged to insist with Propaganda on the non-existence of the *jus patronatus* in this country, as declared in their sixth decree, which also removed the control of Church funds from the trustees. The interpretation of this decree in the *Pastoral Letter to the Laity*, issued at the close of the Council, left no further room for tergiversation in the matter:

We further declare to you, that no right of presentation or patronage to any one of our churches or missions, has ever existed or does now exist canonically, in these United States, and, moreover, even if it were desirable to create such right, which we are far from believing, it would be altogether impossible canonically to do so, from the manner in which the church-property in these states is vested; and that even did we desire to create such right, it would not be in our power, after what we have learned from eminent lawyers in various states, to point out any mode in which it could be canonically created; the nature of our state constitutions and the dispositions of our state legislatures regarding church-property being so perfectly at variance with the principles upon which such property must be secured, before such right could be created. It is our duty, as it is our disposition, so to exercise that power which resides in us, of making or changing the appointments of your pastors, as to meet not only your wants but your wishes, so far as our conscientious convictions and the just desires and expectations of meritorious priests will permit, and we trust that in the discharge of this most important and most delicate duty, we shall always meet with your support; as our only object can be your spiritual welfare, for the attainment of which we are, at the risk of our eternal salvation, to lay aside all prejudice and partiality respecting those whom we appoint.

Bishops were exhorted in the seventh and eighth decrees to withdraw canonical faculties from any priest who should in the future abet or instigate lay interference in the spiritual concerns of the Church, and to place any church retaining an unapproved clergyman under interdict.[9] Propaganda softened the original wording with the clause: "When all other means apparently fail." The ninth decree, ordering the uniform use of the Douay version of the Bible, contained the words: "Since it has the approval of the Holy See." Propaganda deleted this clause, because the Holy See had never given its approbation to any version in the vernacular. This did not, however, prevent the Fathers from approving the Douay version for the United States and since that time it has been commonly used. The need of a uniform Ritual was pressing owing to the varied training of the clergy and a tenth decree legislated for the common use of the Roman Ritual. In the eighth private congregation (October 13) the task of compiling and editing a *Ceremonial* in English was entrusted to Bishops England and Rosati, and a decree (thirty-one) to this effect, without mentioning the names of these two prelates, was passed. The tenth to the twentieth decrees legislated for the proper administration of the Sacrament of Baptism, the keeping of accurate registers for baptism, confirmation, marriages, and burials, the selection of sponsors for baptism and confirmation, the baptism of non-Catholic children, the form to be used in baptizing adults, the use of Latin in administering the sacraments, and the churching of women. Propaganda made but few changes in the wording of these decrees. In the baptism of non-Catholic children in danger of death, the Sacred Congregation added that they not only might be but should be baptized. The Council had ordered the churching of women to take place in the church, but Propaganda added: "Wherever Mass was said," since the Ritual does not prescribe the church as

[9] A later writer describes the situation as that of "practical unaccountability of priest to bishop and in turn of layman to priest" (*Balt. Cath. Mirror*, XXXV, October 25, 1884).

the necessary place for the ceremony. The Sacred Congregation also more or less advised against churching women who had not made their Easter duty or who had not been previously to confession. Propaganda passed without comment the second part of the twentieth decree permitting the use of an English translation after the administration of the sacraments and in funeral obsequies, wherever such use should be considered expedient before mixed congregations.

To the twenty-first decree which stated that the Sacrament of Confirmation was not to be administered to children who had not reached the use of reason, Propaganda added: "except in danger of death." The twenty-second decree laid down the rule that none should be confirmed without presenting a card from the pastor or confessor, and Propaganda deleted this lest it savor of a violation of the seal of confession. The cards were to contain simply the name or names taken in confirmation and were to be given to all who were admitted to the Sacrament. The twenty-third decree brought to an end the missionary privilege of celebrating Mass wherever the priest found it convenient. Hereafter only churches and stations approved by the bishop, except in very special cases, and only then for a few occasions, were to be used. The purpose behind this regulation was to urge congregations to build and support chapels and churches.

The twenty-fourth decree dealt with the proper care of the church and altar, and the twenty-fifth strongly urged the bishops to see to the erection of confessionals in the churches. This decree originally forbade all confessions to be heard privately, but Propaganda limited it to women and girls, permitting however the use of a *crates* so placed as to be *in loco patenti*. The twenty-sixth decree reiterated the legislation of 1791 on the proper preparation for the Sacrament of Marriage and, while not strictly enjoining confession and communion beforehand, urged each bishop to issue an enactment to that effect. It is significant that the severe disapproval of mixed marriages as found in the Statutes of 1791 and 1810 is not repeated by the Fathers of 1829. Decrees twenty-seven, twenty-eight, twenty-nine, thirty and thirty-two legislated for the spiritual life of the clergy. The dress of the priest was to be in keeping with his calling; the cassock, surplice and biretta were to be worn in all sacred functions according to the rules of the Ritual; priests were to avoid worldly amusements, such as games of chance. The original decree forbade all card-playing, but Propaganda considered this too rigorous, commenting on the fact that St. Charles Borromeo had not mentioned card-playing in his first diocesan Synod. Preaching was strictly enjoined on the pastors, and catechism classes were to be instituted in all the churches and stations. Daily meditation, the annual retreat, spiritual reading, the prayers preparatory to Mass and thanksgiving afterwards, and other pious exercises were urged upon the clergy. The thirty-third decree forbade the promiscuous use of unapproved catechisms and prayer-books and notice was given that a catechism, based on that by St. Robert Bellarmine, adapted to the needs of the American Catholics, would be prepared and issued with the approbation of the Holy See. It is interesting to note that Propaganda inserted the clause on Bellarmine's catechism.[10]

The thirty-fourth decree contains the first general legislation on Catholic parochial schools. The decision arrived at, writes Burns, was clear and imperative.[11] Many boys and girls especially of poor parents were in grave danger of the loss of their faith and of the corruption of their morals, owing to the lack of Catholic schools; the Fathers therefore decreed:

We judge it absolutely necessary that schools be established in which the young may be taught the principles of faith and morality, while being instructed in letters.

Moreover, in the next (thirty-fifth) decree they legislated for what was then a crying need—textbooks which would not con-

[10] This beginning of the much-discussed question of a uniform Catechism for the United States is treated in Guilday, England, I, 313-314.
[11] Principles, Origin and Establishment of the Catholic School System in the United States (New York, 1912), 299.

tain, as the majority in use did contain at the time, erroneous and deliberately false statements regarding Catholic doctrine and worship and Catholic history. The decree referred only to textbooks being used by teachers in Catholic schools, but it reveals also the unfortunate plight of the Church both at that time and even down to our own day in the effort of our leaders to purify this stream of inaccurate knowledge on Catholicism which flowed uninterruptedly throughout the common school system. To stop the spread of this anti-Catholic training, the Fathers decided upon the foundation of a Catholic Tract Society for the purpose of disseminating books and pamphlets on Catholic doctrine and on the history of the Church. It was decided also in the fifth private congregation (October 9) to incorporate this society under the laws of Maryland and to support it by mutual financial assistance among the prelates. The thirty-seventh decree dealt with the required official approbation by the Holy See of all the decrees of the Council and the bishops were urged, as soon as this was known, to hold synods for the purpose of applying this uniform legislation to their dioceses. A final decree called for a second Provincial Council within three years "unless for a grave reason the archbishop should postpone the same."

In signing the decrees, Archbishop Whitfield used the term: *definiens subscripsi,* and the suffragans, the words: *consentiens subscripsi.* The Sacred Congregation seems to have taken alarm at this difference of authority and ordered that in the printed copy all should use the term: *definiens subscripsi.* Propaganda also changed the initial words of the decrees from *with the counsel and consent of the suffragans* to *together with the bishops of the Province of the United States.*

The Council came to a close with the prescribed ceremonies at a third Solemn Session on October 18, which fell that year on Sunday. Archbishop Whitfield celebrated Solemn Pontifical Mass, and Dr. England "preached a charity sermon which, though containing some excellent passages, was considered greatly inferior to some of his other discourses, and very unequal in itself." [12] The Bishop of Charleston who may be said to represent the conciliar party in the hierarchy, was not entirely satisfied with the results of this first meeting of the bishops in twenty years; but his fears were groundless, for the legislation of 1829 has formed the basis of all subsequent canonical enactments. What Dr. England desiderated was a closer and more frequent union between the prelates for mutual support in those problems which were common to all the dioceses. This, the seven Provincial Councils did bring about gradually.

In point of time, the first two official documents emanating from the Council were the two *Pastoral Letters,* one to the laity and the other to the clergy, dated October 17, 1829, and written by Dr. England.

Both the *Pastorals* are in the nature of a commentary on the thirty-six decrees enacted by the Council, and the one to the clergy is a remarkably well-written summary of clerical life, piety and zeal.[13] It has a unique place in the history of the Church here since it is the only document of its kind ever issued by the hierarchy. The decrees were sent to the Holy See with a letter dated October 24, 1829, congratulating Pius VIII upon his accession to the throne of Peter, and pledging the loyalty of the American Church, clergy and laity, to the Vicar of Christ. It is in this letter that the well-known passage occurs:

Not two centuries have elapsed since, in a remote and obscure corner of Maryland, a little band of Catholics guided by a few missionaries, exiles from their native land, flying from the cruel persecution inflicted on them for adhering to the faith of their forefathers, laid the foundations of this American Church. It is scarcely forty years since this body of the faithful in the United States of America was found sufficient to demand in the opinion of the Sovereign Pontiff the erection of the first episcopal see at Baltimore. Not twenty years have rolled by since a decree of the Holy

[12] *United States Catholic Miscellany,* IX (October 31, 1829), 142.
[13] These *Pastorals* as well as all the others issued by the Councils will be found in *National Pastorals of the American Hierarchy (1791-1919),* ed. Guilday (Wash., D. C., 1923).

Pontiff, Pius VII, exalted the Church of Baltimore with the dignity and rights of a Metropolitan, and like a joyful mother of children she has beheld in recently erected suffragan dioceses, quickened by a heaven-bestowed fruitfulness, an offspring in new churches, which it has borne to Christ. Nevertheless, we see so many blessings bestowed by God on these rising churches, such increase given to this vineyard, that those who planted, and those who watered, and those who harvested and tread the overflowing winepress, are compelled to confess and admire wholly "the finger of God." The number of the faithful increases daily, churches not unworthy of Divine worship are everywhere erected, the word of God is preached everywhere and not without fruit; the hatred and prejudice spread against the Church and the faithful vanish; holy religion, once despised and held in contempt, receives honor from her very enemies; the priests of Christ are venerated even by those without; the truth and divinity of our faith is proclaimed and vindicated from the calumny of heresy and unbelief not only in churches and from pulpits, but from the press in widely scattered periodicals and books. Six ecclesiastical seminaries, the hope of our churches, have already been established, and are governed in holy discipline by pious and learned priests; nine colleges under ecclesiastical control, the glory of the Catholic name, have been erected in different States to train boys and young men in piety, arts, and higher branches of science; three of these have been chartered as universities by the legislatures; thirty-three monasteries and houses of religious women of different orders and congregations, Ursulines, Visitandines, Carmelites, Sacred Heart, Sisters of Charity, Loretto, etc., are everywhere established in our dioceses, whence emanate not only the observance of the evangelical counsels, and the exercise of all other virtues, but "the good odor of Christ" in the pious training of innumerable girls; houses of religious of the Order of Preachers and the Society of Jesus, of secular priests of the Congregation of the Mission, and of St. Sulpice, from which as centres priests are sent out to missions; many schools where the poor of both sexes are taught gratuitously; hospitals where these examples of Christian charity were formerly unknown, are now daily given by religious women to the great benefit of souls and of religion. These, Most Holy Father, are the signal benefits which God has bestowed upon us within a few years.

A second letter written the same day to Pius VIII asks for the privilege of using the simpler form in baptizing adults, for that of blessing baptismal water by the short form wherever it was found necessary, owing to the great distance separating many of the priests from a church, according to a formula granted to the missionaries of Peru by Paul III, and for the prolongation of the Paschal season from the first Sunday of Lent to Trinity Sunday. These three privileges were granted through Propaganda in an audience with Pius VIII on September 26, 1830; the first, however, of using the simpler form of baptism was conceded for twenty years only. The decrees of the Council were confirmed, with certain changes which have already been noticed, in a general congregation of Propaganda on June 28, 1830, and the letter of approval sent to Archbishop Whitfield on October 16 that year. There is apparently no record of a reply from Pius VIII (who died on December 1, 1830) to the letter of the hierarchy.

The *acclamationes* sung by the archdeacon and the responses chanted by all priests at the closing Session of the Council reflect even at this distance the joy all felt in the work of the Council. The first of these responses was as follows:

We praise thee, O Lord, who wonderfully enlightenest from the eternal mountains; who hast in thy wonderful benignty brought this Provincial Council to its wished-for results; to thee be praise, to thee power and empire for ever and ever!

The *Te Deum* and the prescribed prayers followed, and that evening after Vespers the *Pastoral Letter to the Laity* was read by Dr. England, and Solemn Benediction of the Most Blessed Sacrament was given by Archbishop Whitfield.

Thus was laid the corner stone of ecclesiastical discipline in this country. As the most imposing ceremony held up to that time, the Council of 1829 marks an historic moment in the Church here. It gave to Catholicism in the United States a dignity in the eyes of all which enhanced the position of the Church and strengthened our priests and people for the then unsuspected demands which would be made upon their courage and loyalty during the next score of years. The Council of 1829 did more; it brought the American Church into closer union with the supreme administration of the Sacred Congregation de Propaganda Fide and stimulated that filial devotion to the Holy See which has ever been the greatest source of joy to bishops, priests and laity of the Church in the United States.

CHAPTER IX

THE SECOND PROVINCIAL COUNCIL OF BALTIMORE
(1833)

NOT all that was discussed in the private congregations and in the meetings of committees during the Council of 1829 found its way into the formal decrees enacted by that assembly. Rules, for example, were decided upon for dealing with clerics whose lives were not in keeping with the lofty spiritual ideals of the priesthood. A long discussion occurred on the advisability of founding a Catholic publishing house in Baltimore, and the encyclical letter of Pius VIII regarding the dissemination of Catholic books was read; the question of erecting a national or central Seminary for the Province of Baltimore was treated at length. The problem of the support of the churches, to be so arranged as to avoid the necessity of trustees in the future, was also discussed. The office of St. Gregory (May 25) was to be said in future throughout the whole Province. An attempt was made to settle upon a uniform course in sacred theology for candidates for the priesthood; confession preparatory to the Sacrament of Marriage, mixed marriages and the publication of the banns were treated but no decision of a decretal nature was reached. Bishop Flaget was requested to write to the Society of the Propagation of the Faith (Paris-Lyons) a letter of thanks for its support of our missions. The Statutes of the Synod of 1791 were ordered to be printed as a preface to the decrees of 1829. In the only historical account of the Council of 1829 we possess—that sent each day by Dr. England to the *United States Catholic Miscellany* of Charleston, it is evident that many minor problems arose but were in the judgment of the prelates postponed to future assemblies. Some of these were to be considered in the Second Provincial Council of 1833. To understand the enactments of 1833, something should be added here on the progress of the Church in the interim.

There was a particularly significant meaning to the visit made by Archbishop Whitfield and the attending prelates to Dougho-regan Manor on October 20, 1829, to pay their respects to the last of the Signers of the Declaration of Independence, Charles Carroll of Carrollton. As the foremost Catholic layman in the United States and as the most venerable of all its citizens after the deaths of Jefferson and Adams, on July 4, 1826, Charles Carroll stood at that time for all that the Church asked of her faithful—obedience to the voice of the Vicar of Christ in spirit-ual matters and unswerving loyalty to sane American ideals. The non-Catholic mind was then smarting under the passage of the Bill of Catholic Emancipation in England (April 13, 1829), and the Catholic Church here was on the threshold of the long and bitter fight its enemies were to wage, from the creation of the American Protestant Association in New York City in 1830 to the outbreak of the Civil War, against equality of political rights and privileges for Catholic American citizens. The burn-ing of churches by mobs of anti-Catholics from 1831 onward, the vicious attacks made upon Roger Brooke Taney, the scurril-ity which crowded the pages of hundreds of Protestant religious magazines, not to speak of the daily press, and the constant mis-representation of Catholic tenets, worship, and of the historical past of the Church—all created an atmosphere for the assembly of 1833 quite different from that of the First Provincial Council four years previous. Internal disorders also were not completely curbed by the stern decrees of 1829, and the potency of evil in trusteeism had not been lessened when the Council of 1833 opened its sessions. The juridic situation in the Church in New York and Philadelphia remained in its former unfortunate state and was to last in fact until Dr. Dubois and Dr. Conwell were called to their reward.

During the interim, in pursuance of the thirty-seventh decree of 1829, three diocesan synods were convened.

The first was that of Charleston, held on November 21, 1831, and was carried out in strict conformity to the rules laid down by Benedict XIV. The canons of 1829 were read, together with the letter of approval from Propaganda, and each decree was explained to the priests present. A lengthy debate took place on the decrees regarding baptism, but no change was made. Decrees twenty-five, twenty-six and twenty-seven elicited some opposition, especially the last, on the use of the cassock and surplice and clerical dress, as did also the question of erecting parochial schools. Before the Synod closed, Bishop England secured the consent of his priests for the creation of a clerical fund "for the support of the infirm, decayed or destitute priests of the diocese." [1]

The second, the Diocesan Synod of New Orleans, was convoked by Bishop Leo de Neckere, who had been consecrated in 1830 at the age of twenty-nine as a successor to Bishop Du Bourg, and who thus became the first Bishop of New Orleans. The Synod was opened on February 26, 1832, with twenty-one priests in attendance, according to the form prescribed in the Roman Ritual. The decrees of the First Provincial Council of 1829 were read and promulgated. Serious attention was given to the formation of a society for the dissemination of Catholic literature, and some few local amendments to the Baltimore decrees were added. [2]

The third of these assemblies was the first Diocesan Synod of Philadelphia, held in St. Mary's Church, on May 13-15, 1832, with thirty priests present under Bishop Francis P. Kenrick, then coadjutor to Dr. Conwell. The decrees of 1829 were formally promulgated for the diocese, and stress was placed upon the canon forbidding the erection of any church in the future without episcopal approbation, and without being deeded to the

---

[1] *United States Catholic Miscellany*, XI (Nov. 27, 1831), 174.
[2] *U. S. Cath. Misc.*, XI (April 21, 1832), 342; Shea, *op. cit.*, III, 669.

bishop. Nineteen decrees in all were enacted, all in harmony with the Council of 1829. Local legislation consisted in the prohibition to ask any remuneration for the administration of the sacraments, although voluntary offerings were permitted. Especially were all offerings to be refused from penitents. The Blessed Sacrament was not to be kept in the presbyteries nor should the priest carry It on his person except for sick calls. Days were selected for the Benediction of the Blessed Sacrament, and midnight Masses on Christmas were forbidden.[8] The question of a diocesan seminary was introduced and met with warm support from all the clergy present. That same year saw the beginning of the St. Charles Borromeo Seminary in Philadelphia.[4]

That there was opposition on the part of Archbishop Whitfield to the convocation of the Second Provincial Council became apparent after the publication of the decrees of 1829 early in 1831. In this attitude he found a determined opponent in Bishop England of Charleston. The latter's correspondence with the Holy See in 1831-1833 constantly repeats for the benefit of Pope Gregory XVI and the Sacred Congregation the theme that the surest means of promoting the progress of the Church in the United States was through Provincial Councils. When it was evident that the archbishop meant to postpone the Council in the autumn of 1832, Dr. England boldly wrote to him (June 10, 1832): "I feel myself canonically bound by the prorogation to attend on the first of October, unless I am canonically released; your summons is not necessary; for it is an act of the council confirmed by the Pope and pointing out only one mode of avoiding the meeting." Propaganda had written to Dr. Whitfield, owing to Bishop England's insistence, that a Provincial

---

[8] *Statuta provincialia et dioecesana* (Philadelphia, 1897), 1-8. For a non-Catholic attack on the synod, *cf. U. S. Cath. Misc.,* XI (June 2, 1832), 390, 398.

[4] McDonald, *The Seminary Movement in the United States (1784-1833),* (Wash., D. C., 1927). Before the opening of the Second Provincial Council, besides St. Mary's Seminary in Baltimore and Mount St. Mary's at Emmitsburg, the Dioceses of Bardstown, St. Louis, Charleston, Cincinnati and Philadelphia had begun seminary training.

Council should be called in the autumn of 1832, if for no other reason than that of defining the geographical limits of the American Sees. The death of Bishop Fenwick (O.P.) of Cincinnati on September 26, 1832, again focused the attention of the prelates on one of the unfinished parts of the conciliar legislation of 1829, namely, the mode of nomination to vacant Sees. Dr. England arrived in Rome on Christmas Day, 1833, and lost no opportunity of persuading the Holy See of the necessity of the Council. The American dioceses, he told Propaganda, were "a parcel of disunited congregations, having no common consultation, no unity of action, no rallying point, growing daily more jealous, and more divided, and having no practical union." [5] In agreement with Dr. England were Bishops Rosati and Francis P. Kenrick, and all three were determined to create the system of these triennial assemblies which lasted until 1849. Propaganda eventually wrote to the archbishop (May 4, 1833) practically insisting upon the convocation of the Council, and the archbishop, though expressing his disapproval, proceeded at once to summon his suffragans for the following autumn. Dr. England's action in Rome and a series of articles on the necessity of a triennial Council in the *Catholic Herald* (Philadelphia), signed by "Philo-Canon," annoyed the archbishop, as Dr. England found to his humiliation in the sessions of the Council itself. The archbishop believed that the decrees of 1829 had not been fully applied through diocesan synods and that further legislation would be premature, if not unwise. Other factors which entered into his attitude have no bearing on the canonical legislation itself and may be passed over in silence.

The opening Session of the Council was held on Sunday, October 20, 1833. The archbishop celebrated Solemn Pontifical Mass, at which Dr. England preached on the nature of Church government, the utility of councils, and the benefits likely to arise from their celebration in this country. The prelates present were: Bishops David, England, Rosati, Fenwick (S.J.), Dubois,

[5] England to Rosati, Rome, January 14, 1833: Guilday, *England,* II, 249.

Portier, Francis P. Kenrick, Rese, and Purcell. Bishop Flaget was unable to be present, owing to the infirmities of old age. The officials of the Council were: *Promoters,* Bishop Fenwick (S.J.) and Father Deluol, Vicar-General of the Archdiocese of Baltimore; *Secretaries,* Fathers Damphoux (then Pastor of the Cathedral) and John Hoskyne; *Master of Ceremonies,* Father Chanche; and *Chanters,* Fathers Radanne and Fredet. The consulting *theologians* were: Father William McSherry, Provincial of the Jesuits; Father Nicholas D. Young, Provincial of the Dominicans; Fathers Tessier, Jeanjean, Eccleston, De Barth, Andrew Byrne, Odin, Chanche, John Power, Peter Mauvernay, John Hughes, William Matthews and Simon Bruté. The Council was composed of ten prelates and twenty priests. Two congregations, the one private in the archbishop's house in the morning, the other public in the Cathedral in the late afternoon, were held daily for a week. The second Solemn Session, the Mass of Requiem for the deceased prelates (Fenwick, O.P., and De Neckere) was celebrated on October 24, at which Fenwick's successor who had been consecrated ten days before, Bishop John B. Purcell, preached the customary panegyric.

The official *Acta et Decreta* give no record of these private and public congregations. All we have in print are the decrees, eleven in number, with an appendix of documents concerning the same.

The first three decrees contain a geographical delineation of the dioceses. In opposition to Dr. England's party in the Council, it was decided to ask the Holy See to suppress the See of Richmond and to restore Virginia to the jurisdiction of Baltimore. The old, and by that time abandoned, political division of East and West Jersey was preserved, Philadelphia having jurisdiction over West Jersey and New York over East Jersey, and the counties are named within each section. Boston had jurisdiction over all New England. Detroit which had been erected in 1833, and to which Frederic Rese had been appointed as Bishop, possessed jurisdiction over Michigan and the Northwest Territory. The original Diocese of St. Louis (now divided into forty dioceses)[6] consisted of the State of Missouri, Arkansas Territory, and western Illinois. Eastern Illinois and Indiana were to constitute the new Diocese of Vincennes which the Fathers asked for in the first decree. The old Diocese of Bardstown was confined to Kentucky and Tennessee, and Cincinnati to the State of Ohio. The Diocese of New Orleans comprised the States of Louisiana and Mississippi; and Mobile, the States of Alabama and Florida. Apart from the Diocese of St. Louis, these limits were logical and presaged the further delineations which were to be decided upon by the Holy See within a few years.

The fourth decree, the most important passed by the Second Provincial Council, concerns the mode of nominating to vacant Sees in the United States. The fifth and sixth decrees, to Dr. England's disappointment, placed the Indian missions of the Far West and the Liberian Mission in Africa under the care of the Jesuits. Bishops Rosati and Fenwick (S.J.) were appointed a committee to prepare an edition of the Roman Ritual adapted to the wants of the missionaries in the country, to which was to be appended an English version of the more important parts. The bishops were admonished that the decree of the Council of Trent on the erection of diocesan seminaries should be faithfully obeyed. The question of a central seminary, as advocated by Bishop England, was discussed, but the project was not accepted owing to the fact that his plan involved the creation of a national seminary in Ireland to supply all the dioceses.[7] The ninth decree was an attempt to bring about uniformity in the use of textbooks in Catholic schools and colleges, and the presidents of the three principal Catholic educational institutions, Georgetown University, St. Mary's University, and Mount St. Mary's, Emmitsburg, were appointed a committee to supervise the preparation of suitable textbooks.[8] For the better control of

[6] A map will be found in Rothensteiner, *op. cit.,* I, 415.
[7] McDonald, *op. cit.,* 62-63.   [8] Burns, *op. cit.,* 250.

the exercise of sacerdotal faculties, the Council abolished the privilege which the bishops had enjoyed since 1810 of empowering priests to officiate in neighboring dioceses. The final (eleventh) decree convoked the Third Provincial Council for the third Sunday after Easter (April 16), 1837.

All the suggestions of the Council were favorably acted upon by Propaganda with the exception of the suppression of the See of Richmond. In its meeting on May 18, 1834, the Sacred Congregation drafted an instruction regarding nominations to vacant Sees, and word to this effect was sent to the American hierarchy on June 26, 1834. The fatherly and sympathetic letter of Gregory XVI to the Fathers of the Council (dated April 23, 1834) gave consolation to our prelates, and the Apostolic brief of June 17, 1834, ratified all that had been accomplished by the Council as well as the Instructions sent by Propaganda.

Among these Instructions, the important one is that fixing for the time being the mode of filling vacant Sees in the United States. Up to this time (1833) several methods had been used in the selection of our bishops. The first was the privilege granted by the Holy See in 1788, for that one time only, of direct nomination which placed Father John Carroll over the nascent American Church. The second was the privilege given to Dr. Carroll of naming his coadjutors (Graessl and Leonard Neale). The third was direct appointment by the Holy See as in the case of Bishops Concanen, Connolly, England, and Kelly. A fourth method was the choice by the Archbishop of Baltimore and his suffragans of Bishop David as coadjutor to Dr. Flaget. The fifth was the selection of Bishops Purcell, Fenwick (O.P.), Fenwick (S.J.) and others by the suffragans who were interested, without recourse to the metropolitan.[9] Some unified system was necessary, wrote the Fathers of the Council of 1833 in their fourth decree, to secure to the Church bishops eminent for

[9] McCarthy, "Historical Development of Episcopal Nominations in the Catholic Church of the United States (1784-1884)" in *Records,* American Catholic Historical Society, XXXVIII (Dec., 1927), 335-336.

doctrine, piety and zeal; and the method they proposed, while involved, had all the requisite restraints upon the *laissez-aller* system in vogue previously. The decree runs as follows:

When a See becomes vacant all the Bishops of the Ecclesiastical Province vote upon whom they think worthy of being appointed to the vacant See. Since this voting can be done more accurately and easily at a Provincial Council, if a Provincial Council is to be held within three months of the death of the Bishop, the Bishops of the Province should not vote upon the names of the candidates, but should wait till they meet in Council before they write the names to the Sacred Congregation. Assembled in Council in such a case, after a discussion, they shall determine what priests merit appointment to the vacant See or to a coadjutorship according as the case may be. When, however, the See becomes vacant at a time when no Provincial Council is to be held, another plan should be followed. So lest a See might be too long without an incumbent, it is exceedingly necessary and fitting that each Bishop keep sealed and directed to his Vicar General to be opened at his death, a duplicate list of the three priests whom he deems best fitted to succeed him. The Vicar General should take care to send one of these lists to the Archbishop and the other to the neighboring Bishop or to the Senior of the neighboring Bishops. On reception of the list the neighboring Bishop will write to the Archbishop inclosing his opinion with regard to the candidates. When this has been done or within a reasonable period if the neighboring Bishop does not write, the Archbishop will communicate to all the Bishops of the Province, the neighboring Bishop included, the names of the proposed candidates together with his personal opinion in the matter. He should add other names to this list proposed by the deceased Bishop if the list does not seem to him to be the best selection. After receiving the letter of the Archbishop, each suffragan will write directly to Propaganda expressing his choice and giving his opinion concerning the three or six candidates as the case will be if the Archbishop has added to the list. In the case of a vacancy of the Metropolitan See, the letter of the deceased Archbishop designating the names of the three priests should be sent by the Vicar General to both the neighboring and the senior suffragan Bishop. In this case the senior suffragan will do all those things which are determined in the case of a suffragan's election to be performed by the Archbishop. If among the letters of the

deceased Bishop or Archbishop there is not found the one designating three names to succeed him, the Vicar General must immediately inform the neighboring Bishop or the senior of two neighboring Bishops, so that the neighboring Bishop may designate the
names of three priests to be sent by letter to the Archbishop. The
Archbishop having received the letters will write to all the Bishops
and will follow out the prescriptions already indicated when the
letters of the deceased Bishop or Metropolitan are found. If the
neighboring Bishop should neglect entirely to write to the Archbishop the latter will send three names to all his suffragans, the
neighboring Bishop included. If it is a question of the election of
an Archbishop, the senior suffragan will do all those things to be
done by the Archbishop in the election of a candidate to a suffragan See. When it is a question of the election of a coadjutor,
except where the Holy See might determine a different method of
action, the Bishop who desires the coadjutor will send a list of
three names to the Archbishop and suffragan Bishops and a petition requisitioning the coadjutor to the Sacred Congregation. The
Archbishop and the suffragan Bishops will communicate to the Congregation their views on the matter. All these prescriptions are
to be followed carefully; the Congregation insists upon it. It wishes
to emphasize the fact, that the names thus sent are not really nominations, elections or requests, but properly and solely recommendations, imposing no obligation on the Congregation to select any of
the candidates mentioned.

Complicated as the method proved to be, it was the one used
with some slight changes until the First Plenary Council of
1852, and it had a certain kind of practicalness so long as the
Church in the United States comprised one ecclesiastical province. After the creation of the metropolitan Sees of Oregon
(1846) and St. Louis (1847), so much confusion arose that a
change had to be made, as will be seen in the story of subsequent Councils. Dr. England brought to the attention of Cardinal Weld, while in Rome in May, 1834, the more serious aspects of the problem, stating that "the nomination to American
Sees is a much more important affair than in any other part
of the Church," and that the selection of any but American citizens for the episcopate would undoubtedly convince "the Ameri-

can people of the alleged incompatibility of Catholicism with the American Republic." [10]

The *Pastoral Letter* of the Council, dated October 27, 1833, and written by Dr. England, is in some respects a more valuable historical document than the *decreta* of the Council. Deploring the lack of churches and priests to meet the increasing number of the faithful, the Fathers appealed to the priests to redouble their efforts to satisfy the spiritual demands of their flocks and urged Catholics in outlying districts, where no priest could be had, to meet regularly on Sundays for prayers and catechetical training. Frequent reception of the Sacraments of Penance and Holy Communion was advocated, and parents were strongly urged to foster vocations to the priesthood among their sons. Immigration was on the increase and the Fathers were fearful of the loss of faith in the ranks of the newcomers, if sufficient priests were not at hand to cope with the spiritual work involved in their care. Closely allied to this was the need of a Catholic education for the rising generation of the Church, and even more so the necessity of preparing the minds of adult Catholics to meet courageously the opposition to the Church. Shea says that no one seemed to comprehend the fact that the current of anti-Catholic feeling "was gaining ground steadily and becoming a menace to the peace and harmony of the country." This is not altogether exact, for the Fathers signalize the situation in the *Pastoral Letter* in the following paragraph:

We notice, with regret, a spirit exhibited by some of the conductors of the press, engaged in the interests of those brethren separated from our communion, which has, within a few years become more unkind and unjust in our regard. Not only do they assail us and our institutions in a style of vituperation and offence, misrepresent our tenets, vilify our practices, repeat the hundred times refuted calumnies of days of angry and bitter contention in other lands, but they have even denounced you and us as enemies to the liberties of the republic, and have openly proclaimed the fancied necessity of not only obstructing our progress, but of using their

[10] Guilday, *England,* II, 268.

best efforts to extirpate our religion: and for this purpose they have collected large sums of money. It is neither our principle nor our practice to render evil for evil, nor railing for railing: and we exhort you rather to the contrary, to render blessing, for unto this are you called, that you, by inheritance, may obtain a blessing. Recollect the assurance of the Saviour—"Blessed are you, when men shall revile you, and persecute you, and say all manner of evil against you falsely for my sake; rejoice and be exceeding glad: because your reward is very great in heaven: for so they persecuted the prophets that were before you." We are too well known to our fellow-citizens to render it now necessary that we should exhibit the utter want of any ground upon which such charges could rest. We, therefore, advise you to heed them not: but to continue, whilst you serve your God with fidelity, to discharge, honestly, faithfully, and with affectionate attachment, your duties to the government under which you live, so that we may, in common with our fellow citizens, sustain that edifice of rational liberty in which we find such excellent protection.

Little of a progressive nature can be attributed to the Second Provincial Council, except the fact that the principle was sustained of a triennial meeting of the hierarchy. The three years' interim before the convocation of the Council of 1837 was one of the alarming periods in American religious history and its portents will be reflected in the deliberations of the Fathers, especially in their *Pastoral Letter* that year to the faithful.

CHAPTER X

THE THIRD PROVINCIAL COUNCIL OF BALTIMORE (1837)

WITHIN twelve months after the last Solemn Session of the Council of 1833, Archbishop Whitfield passed away (October 19, 1834) in his sixty-fourth year, and was succeeded by Dr. Eccleston who had been consecrated coadjutor-Archbishop of Baltimore a month earlier (September 14). He was then thirty-three years old and the next five Provincial Councils were to be held under his presidency. The hierarchy in 1837 consisted of Dr. Eccleston and thirteen prelates—Bishops England, Rosati, Fenwick (S.J.), Dubois, Francis P. Kenrick, Purcell, Rese, Chabrat, then coadjutor to Flaget, Flaget himself, Bruté, Clancy, coadjutor to Dr. England, David, who had resigned, Portier and Blanc. Nine of these attended the Third Provincial Council. Bishop Dubois of New York declined to take part in the proceedings and was represented by Father Felix Varela in the Council. Bishop Rese of Detroit resigned during the Council itself. Bishop Flaget was in Europe at the time. Bishops David and Portier were unable to be present.

The outstanding fact in the three years' interim was the swift and amazing alignment of the anti-Catholic forces in the Republic. The "Shame of Massachusetts," as the burning of the Ursuline Convent of Charlestown, Massachusetts, on the night of August 11, 1834, was known; the attack made by Samuel F. B. Morse of telegraph fame on the Leopoldine Association of Vienna in his *Imminent Dangers to the Free Institutions of the United States through Foreign Immigration and the Present*

112

State of the Naturalization Laws,[1] published in 1835; the beginning of a vicious and immoral anti-Catholic literature—*Six Months in a Convent* by Rebecca Reed (1835); *Plea for the West,* by Lyman Beecher who was partly responsible for the Charlestown outrage; the *Downfall of Babylon* by the ex-priest, Samuel Smith, then editor of the *Protestant,* the organ of the American Protestant Association which had been founded by a group of ministers in New York City in 1830; the *Awful Disclosures of Maria Monk* (1836), and a number of salacious novels which were avidly read and liberally distributed by peddlers and hawkers especially in the Middle West—all these made it apparent to the most sanguine of our Catholic leaders that a dangerous moment had come in the tolerant spirit of the decade.[2] The antipathy bred of the freedom granted to Catholics in the British realm through the Act of Emancipation (1829) was bearing luxuriant fruit in Canada and the United States, and Orange lodges were being established in all the principal centers of population as a "preventative against Popery." There are, it must be admitted, certain social, industrial and political factors in this recrudescence of anti-Catholic feeling; but the most salient factor of all is the fear engendered in Protestant circles by the extraordinary increase of Catholics at this time. We have seen in the *Pastoral Letter* of 1833 the alarm in the hearts of our bishops that the Church would not be able to cope with the ever-growing number of the faithful. Between 1830 and 1840, the Catholic population more than doubled, as did also, by the spiritual laws that dominate within the Fold, the means—priests, teaching and nursing sisters, schools and colleges, and welfare organizations.

It was with the consciousness that their flocks looked to them with anguished eyes that the prelates met at the archbishop's

[1] *Cf.* Connors, F. J., "Samuel Finley Breese Morse and the Anti-Catholic Political Movements in the United States," *Illinois Cath. Hist. Review,* X (October, 1927), 3-42.

[2] *Cf.* Godecker, *Simon Bruté of Rémur: first Bishop of Vincennes* (St. Meinrad, Ind., 1931), 300-301; Guilday, *England,* II, cc. xxxi-xxxii.

house on Sunday, April 16, 1837, to open this third national Catholic assembly. Solemn Pontifical Mass was celebrated by Archbishop Eccleston, and Dr. Kenrick preached the opening sermon on the spirit of wisdom in the Church. All those present remarked the harmony which prevailed and all felt that beneficial results would arise from the meeting.[3] The customary profession of faith was then made by those bishops who were in attendance for the first time (Chabrat, Clancy, Bruté and Blanc) and the conciliar officials were elected. Bishop Fenwick and Father Deluol, Vicar-General of the Archdiocese, were named *Promoters;* as *Secretaries,* Fathers Damphoux and Charles I. White were selected. The *Masters of Ceremonies* were Father Lhomme and Hugh Griffin, while Fathers Radanne and Fredet were again selected as *Chanters.* Those invited formally to take part in the deliberations were: Father William McSherry, Provincial of the Jesuits of the Maryland Province; Father P. J. Verhaegen, Superior of the Missouri Jesuits; Father Thomas Mulledy, S.J., President of Georgetown University; Rev. John J. Chanche, President of St. Mary's University; and Rev. Thomas Butler, President of Mount St. Mary's College. The consulting *theologians* were: Father Louis de Barth (Kenrick); Father Peter Richard Kenrick (Bruté); Father John Hughes (Clancy); Father Peter Schreiber (Eccleston); Father S. T. Badin (Purcell); Father Regis Loisel (Rosati); Father Ignatius Reynolds (Chabrat); and Father Augustin Verot (Blanc). Bishop England did not choose a *theologian.*

In all, five private and five public congregations were held between April 17 and 22, and on April 20, the second Solemn Session, the Mass of Requiem for the deceased prelates (Archbishop Du Bourg of Besançon, Cardinal de Cheverus of Bordeaux, and Archbishop Whitfield) was sung by Bishop Fenwick of Boston, and Dr. England preached on the doctrine of Purgatory, concluding his discourse with a well-merited tribute to the three prelates who had passed away since the Council of 1833.

[3] *U. S. Cath. Misc.,* XVI (April 29, 1833), 335.

Special rules were made for the public congregations so that everyone taking part in the discussions should have the opportunity of giving his opinion. It was decided to petition the Holy See for a second 'diocese in Pennsylvania, at Pittsburgh. At the second private congregation Bishop Rese offered his resignation to the assembled prelates and the same was accepted. In the final private congregation it was decided to ask the Holy See for Sees at Nashville with jurisdiction in the State of Tennessee, at Dubuque, with jurisdiction in the State of Wisconsin, and at Natchez, with jurisdiction in the State of Mississippi.

Eleven decrees were enacted in this Third Provincial Council. The first decree warned the bishops to use great care in ordaining for the priesthood *titulo missionis* only those candidates who showed unmistakable signs of aptitude for missionary work and who should first take the oath of devoting themselves to the missions. The Sacred Congregation inserted in the original wording of this decree the phrase *ex Apostolico indulto,* lest the sense be that the bishops had the inherent right to ordain *ad titulum missionis.* The second decree emphasizes the duty of the faithful to support their pastors. In many parts of the country, the decree says, old and infirm priests were being neglected by the people in this regard, and it was decided that a Clerical Fund be started in each diocese, from the benefits of which, however, all unworthy priests and those living in disobedience to authority should be excluded. The third decree announced that the *Ceremonial* published in accordance with the thirty-first decree of the First Provincial Council was to be followed in all the churches of the country. Propaganda ordered, however, that the *Ceremonial* be sent first to Rome for approbation. The third decree, a further enactment in the matter of safeguarding Church property, ordered that all ecclesiastical property be secured by the best means the local civil law afforded. The original wording of this decree contained a phrase which Propaganda considered a reflection on the honesty of the bishops and the same was deleted. The fifth decree legislated for uniformity in following the Roman Ritual. The sixth decree prohibited priests from bringing contentious ecclesiastical cases before civil tribunals, and Propaganda inserted the word "strictly" in order to leave no room for doubt in the cases in question. The seventh decree put a stop to a growing abuse which had given cause for scandal —collections made by priests in neighboring parishes or dioceses without the written permission of the Ordinary. All ecclesiastics guilty in this regard were to be suspended without delay. Abuses which had become apparent in the Church music of the day were deplored in the eighth decree, and pastors were warned that in the Holy Sacrifice of the Mass the music was to serve divine worship, and not to overshadow it. Hymns in the vernacular were not to be permitted during Mass or Solemn Vespers. The ninth decree made known that the Fathers of the Council had decided to ask the Holy See to abrogate the obligation of hearing Mass on the Mondays after Easter and Pentecost, and the tenth decree requested the same privilege for the fast on Wednesdays and Fridays in Advent. The final decree was a convocation of the Fourth Provincial Council for the fourth Sunday after Easter (May 17) in 1840.

At the last Solemn Session, Bishop Rosati sang Solemn Pontifical Mass and Dr. England preached in a lucid and forcible manner on the constitution of the Church and the nature of the powers which Christ had committed to its dispensation.[4] The *acclamationes* and *Te Deum* were then sung and the decrees signed by the prelates. The letter to Pope Gregory XVI, dated April 22, 1837, contained expressions of filial loyalty on the part of the American hierarchy for the Holy See and of gratitude to Almighty God for the evidences of Catholic progress throughout the world. The situation in this country was then described and the Holy Father was besought not to interpret the state of mind in the United States toward the Church by the violence which had recently occurred. The hatred so openly manifested was indeed causing a more widespread knowledge of the Faith

[4] *U. S. Cath. Misc.*, XVI (May 6, 1837), 343.

and was creating in Catholic ranks a deeper zeal and a more profound love for the Vicar of Christ who was then so bitterly assailed. The immigration problem is then mentioned and the Holy Father was asked to erect as soon as possible the three new Sees requested in order to help cope with the large number of Catholics then taking part in the frontier movement toward the West. The number of priests was woefully inadequate but great hopes were placed upon the religious Orders already established in the United States, and the pope was asked to support the hierarchy whenever it was found necessary to nominate any member of these Orders to the episcopate. Propaganda's Instruction on the decrees (September 2, 1837) approved the enactments of the Council, with the changes already mentioned, and in its letter of that date announced the fact that Gregory XVI had created the new Sees requested by the Council.

The following priests were selected for the same: for Natchez, Father Thomas Heyden; for Dubuque, Father Mathias Loras; and for Nashville, Father Richard Miles, O.P. Father John Hughes of Philadelphia was chosen coadjutor to Bishop Dubois of New York. The resignation of Bishop Rese was not accepted since the Holy See decided to await his arrival in Rome. The dispensations asked were granted by the Holy See. The request, however, to abrogate the fast on the Fridays of Advent was not granted; but if the bishops found that there was an occasion of sin in continuing the same, then the Holy See would reconsider its decision and grant the required dispensation. An Apostolic Rescript of January 17, 1841, proclaiming the *Manual of the Ceremonies used in the Catholic Church,* compiled by Bishop Rosati, the official ceremonial for the United States, belongs to the epistolary documents of this Council.[5] One of the most imposing of all Church ceremonies up to this time occurred at the close of the Council, when on April 26, 1837, Archbishop Eccleston and eight of his suffragans participated in the consecration of St. John's Church, in Frederick, Maryland.

[5] *Concilia habita etc.,* 152-154.

The *Pastoral Letter,* issued on April 22, 1837, is the most re-markable document of its kind in the history of the American Church. Its courageous defense of the Faith, its striking de-nunciation of the persecution in which Catholics were then plunged by the wholesale intolerance of some of their Protestant fellow citizens, and its dominant demand for equal rights and for fair play make the *Letter* almost unique. It speaks frankly of the shame of the Massachusetts legislature in not giving jus-tice to the defenseless Ursulines of Charlestown. It pillories those members of the Protestant ministry who were causing the spread of obscene literature in the country and warned them that the social reaction would do irreparable damage to the morality of the rising generation. Anti-Catholicism, the prelates boldly said, meant anti-Christianity. Catholics were encouraged to reflect upon the spirit of forbearance and courage shown by their ancestors in the Faith in the ages of pagan persecution and to realize that "this very misrepresentation of our tenets, of our principles and of our practices exhibits the best proof that the doctrine which we believe and teach cannot be successfully as-sailed by fair argument nor our principles rendered odious by honest exposition."

The climax to this remarkable letter is in the reply made re-garding Catholic allegiance. Calmly and serenely those who were authors of the charge of a divided allegiance were told:

We owe no religious allegiance to any State in this Union, nor to its general government. No one of them claims any supremacy or dominion over us in our spiritual or ecclesiastical concerns: nor does it claim any such right or power over any of our fellow-citizens, of whatsoever religion they may be: and if such a claim was made, neither would our fellow-citizens, nor would we submit thereto. They and we, by our constitutional principles, are free to give this ecclesiastical supremacy to whom we please, or to refuse it to every one, if we so think proper: but, they and we owe civil and political allegiance to the several States in which we reside, and also, to our general government. When, therefore, using our undoubted right, we acknowledge the spiritual and ecclesiastical supremacy of the chief bishop of our universal church, the Pope or bishop of

Rome, we do not thereby forfeit our claim to the civil and political protection of the commonwealth; for, we do not detract from the allegiance to which the temporal governments are plainly entitled, and which we cheerfully give; nor do we acknowledge any civil or political supremacy, or power over us in any foreign potentate or power, though that potentate might be the chief pastor of our church.

The *Pastoral* contains also what is practically the last word on the evils of trusteeism, and also the first word in these Charges of our hierarchy on the Catholic Press.

The three years which intervened between the Councils of 1837 and 1840 were not marked with any cessation of the anti-Catholic movement which had been organized in 1830. The stirring appeal of the prelates through their *Pastoral Letter,* which was widely printed in the public press and commented on favorably by the better class of journals, had no appreciable effect in stilling the more militant members of the Protestant Churches, and it was realized that it would be only a question of time before violent outbreaks would occur in many parts of the country. The Council of 1837 deserves respect for the courageous manner in which it met the coming issue; but at the same time it must be confessed that, without having planned any concerted action to make the doctrines of the Church better known, the Fathers of the Council left the Catholic body, as Dr. England so often said, in "detached squads," and therefore all the more vulnerable to their enemies. The peak of the anti-Catholic agitation was to be reached in the presidential campaign of 1840.

CHAPTER XI

THE FOURTH PROVINCIAL COUNCIL OF BALTIMORE (1840)

THE Province of Baltimore in 1840 contained the archiepiscopal See of Baltimore (including the vacant Diocese of Richmond) with the suffragan Dioceses of Boston (1808), New York (1808), Philadelphia (1808), Bardstown (1808), Charleston (1820), Cincinnati (1821), St. Louis (1826), New Orleans (1826), Mobile (1829), Detroit (1833), Vincennes (1834), Dubuque (1837), Nashville (1837), and Natchez (1837). In the Republic of Texas, the Prefecture-Apostolic of Texas had been established in 1839, and the Diocese of the Two Californias, then Mexican territory, had been erected on April 27, 1840, as a suffragan to Mexico City, with San Diego as the episcopal city. All the sixteen American suffragan Sees, with the exception of Natchez, were filled, while New York had been given a coadjutor in John Hughes who was consecrated on January 7, 1838. The *Metropolitan Catholic Directory* for 1840 gives the following statistics for 1840: Churches and chapels, 454; stations, 358; clergymen in the ministry, 399; clergymen otherwise employed, 100; ecclesiastical institutions, 16; clerical students, 141; colleges for young men, 18; female religious institutions, 28; female academies, 47; and charitable institutions, 76. The number of Catholics is not stated in the *Directory,* but it has been estimated by Shea as about one million.[1]

So far we have been able to record but three diocesan synods outside of Baltimore from 1829 to 1837. Between 1837 and

[1] Shaughnessy, *Has the Immigrant Kept the Faith?* (New York, 1925), 125.

1840, there was, so far as the sources show, only one such synod, that of St. Louis convoked by Bishop Rosati on April 21, 1839, with twenty-two diocesan priests and seventeen members of religious Orders in attendance. The principal work done was the promulgation of the decrees of the Baltimore Provincial Councils, special attention being given to the decrees of the Council of 1829; and certain local enactments which have lasted almost to the present were issued at that time.[2]

There was some opposition to the convocation of the Fourth Provincial Council of 1840, on the part of the prelates whose Sees were far removed from Baltimore, and the sentiment was abroad that the time had come to create other metropolitan Sees in order to save the bishops from the fatigue of traveling such great distances. "The present arrangement," one critic wrote, "requires four weeks' constant travelling for one week of hasty deliberation. . . . New metropolitan Sees might be erected in the distances. National councils might be celebrated every ten years, and provincial and diocesan synods held at the shorter intervals required by the canons."[3] The Middle West was growing in self-consciousness, ecclesiastically as well as politically. Dr. Eccleston obeyed the decree of 1837 and sent out the usual letter of convocation late in January, 1840, summoning his suffragans to Baltimore. In Dr. England's reply (February 21), there is a plea that a Catholic census should be taken up officially by the bishops, and the chief note struck in his outline of the method to be used was that the native and foreign elements in the Church here be carefully tabulated.

On May 16, a preliminary meeting took place in Dr. Eccleston's house with the archbishop and Bishops Flaget, Rosati, Kenrick, Purcell, Blanc, and de la Hailandière present. Also present by the special privilege conferred upon him of a deliberative vote in the Council was the Primate of Lorraine, Count de Forbin-Janson, Bishop of Nancy and Toul. The only impor-

[2] Rothensteiner, *History of the Archdiocese of St. Louis*, I, 739-740.
[3] *U. S. Cath. Misc.*, XIX, 292.

tant decision reached was that the prelates would not be limited to one *theologian*. The solemn opening of the Council was on Sunday, May 17. The archbishop celebrated Solemn Pontifical Mass, and Dr. England preached. The opportunity was somewhat unique; it was the golden jubilee of the establishment of the American episcopate and the Bishop of Charleston rose nobly to the occasion. Bishops Rosati and Fenwick were appointed *Promoters,* and Fathers Damphoux and Charles I. White, *Secretaries.* The same priests who had been *Masters of Ceremonies* and *Chanters* in the Council of 1837 (Fathers Lhomme, Radanne, and Fredet) were reappointed, with Father James B. Donelan as *assistant-Master of Ceremonies.*

Five private and five public congregations were held. At the first private congregation (May 18), Bishop Fenwick proposed that in the future only those priests who were citizens of the United States should be proposed for the episcopate here, and the motion was carried. The erection of a See at Pittsburgh was again recommended for immediate action by the Holy See. Bishops Kenrick, Blanc and Loras argued for the election of the *Promoters* in the Council, but no action was taken. At the first public congregation that afternoon in the cathedral, there were present: Fathers Charles P. Montgomery, O.P., Provincial of the Dominicans, Father Joseph Prost, C.SS.R., Superior of the Redemptorists; Fathers Deluol, S.S., Chanche, S.S., and Kenney, as *theologians* to the Archbishop of Baltimore; and the following *theologians* to the different bishops: Peter Chazelle, S.J. (Flaget); John Power and John Barry (England); Joseph Lutz (Rosati); Vincent Badin (de Forbin-Janson); Henry Coskery (Fenwick); Michael O'Connor (Kenrick); John McElroy, S.J. (Purcell); John Bouillier, C.M. (Blanc); Gilbert Raymond (Loras); Benedict Bayer (Miles), and Peter Lefebre (Hailandière).

That morning, Dr. England preached to a crowded audience in the cathedral on the unchanged and unchangeable doctrine of the Church. At the next morning's private congregation, Bishop

England presented a petition from some naval officers who were Catholics asking for a special prayer-book for their use. Action on the petition of the Catholics of Springfield, Illinois, for the erection of a diocese in that part of the State was postponed as inexpedient at the time. The petition sent by Bishop Flaget to the Holy See to remove his episcopal city from Bardstown to Louisville was acted upon favorably. At the same meeting the Fathers listened to the interesting report on the Indian missions, read by Father Verhaegen, S.J., the Provincial of the Society of Jesus in Missouri.[4] The project of erecting a See in Wisconsin and of restoring the See of Richmond was discussed. Dr. Kenrick pleaded also for the erection of the See of Pittsburgh. In the third private congregation (May 20) the first five decrees of the Council were passed. Father Moriarty, Superior of the Augustinians, came to the public congregation that afternoon and endeavored to arouse the interest of the prelates in the burning question of the National Education Act then under discussion by the hierarchy of Ireland. No action was taken on this plea. The second Solemn Session, the Mass of Requiem for the deceased prelates was said on Thursday (May 21) by Bishop de la Hailandière, the successor of Bishop Bruté who had passed away on June 20, 1839, the only prelate to die in the interim. The sermon was preached by Bishop Purcell. At the end of the ceremony the Apostolic Letter of Gregory XVI of December 3, 1839, on the Slave Trade was read.[5] The fourth private congregation (May 22) was devoted to several questions, one being the request to the Holy See for the abrogation of the fast on the vigil of the feast of Saints Peter and Paul and the extension of the dispensation granted in 1834 *ad decennium* of the abstinence on Saturday in perpetuity. A second problem upon which no decretal action was taken was the formal request of some of the Western bishops for a division of the Province of Baltimore. There was considerable discussion

[4] The Report will be found in extenso in the *U. S. Cath. Misc.,* XIX, 367.
[5] A translation is in the *U. S. Cath. Misc.,* XIX, 281.

over the problem of asserting the Church's stand on secret societies, and it was decided to refuse the sacraments to Catholics who belonged to these forbidden groups. Labor unions which savored of this same secrecy were deprecated, especially because their meetings led to excessive drinking. Temperance societies were also brought up for favorable discussion, and it was decided that confraternities to give mutual encouragement to frequent the sacraments should be encouraged. The Fathers decided to ask for a number of new offices of Saints and that the feast of St. Patrick be given *duplex* rank in the United States. The Council agreed to send letters of sympathy to the Archbishops of Cologne and of Gnesen-Posen who were then in duress by the action of the Prussian government on account of their stand regarding mixed marriages. Several important matters were disposed of during the fifth and last private congregation. A final decree *de vita et honestate clericorum* was passed at this meeting, and it was decided to hold the Fifth Provincial Council on the fourth Sunday after Easter (May 14), 1840. The third Solemn Session with which the Council closed was held on Sunday, May 24, 1840, and Dr. England preached on the marks of the true Church.

The Fourth Provincial Council was the largest held up to that time. In the first (1829), the archbishop had as his co-legislators five bishops and one diocesan administrator. In the Council of 1840, eleven years later, there were twelve bishops, four only of whom had been present in 1829—Flaget, England, Rosati and Fenwick (S.J.).

The eleven decrees reflect the mind of the hierarchy as a conclusion to the week's discussions. The first decree renewed the former legislation regarding the ceremonies for mixed marriages. No sacred vestments were to be worn by priest or bishop on these occasions, and priests were warned to remind the faithful of all the grave evils which resulted so often from these unions. Every care should be taken beforehand to safeguard the faith of the Catholic party, and of the children of both sexes.

In every case security must be given for the baptism and Catholic education of the children of these marriages and solemn promises before God were to be exacted to that effect from the non-Catholic party. Priests were permitted to wear the cassock and bishops the ordinary house-dress for the ceremony. The second decree reënacted the ruling of the Council of 1829, that there should be one pastor to each congregation and that the assistants were not to invade the pastor's rights without his permission. The third decree regulated the vexed question of stole-fees and the bishops were asked to lay down rules for the equitable division of these in the first diocesan synod held after the Council. The fourth decree admonished the faithful to keep Sunday holy and to avoid places where intoxicating drinks were sold, especially on that day consecrated to the Lord. The fifth decree recommended the establishment of temperance societies in all the parishes. The taking of a pledge to refrain entirely from the use of liquor was praised. All Ireland was alive at the time to the crusade of the celebrated Father Theobald Mathew, who was to come to the United States in 1849 and to whom is due in a large measure the Catholic temperance movement which began here at that time. The sixth decree called attention again to the grave risks the public or common school held for the Faith of Catholic boys and girls who were obliged to listen to the Protestant Bible, sing Protestant hymns, and hear sermons against the Church. The clergy and Catholic parents were advised to assert their civic rights in this grave question for it could not be denied at the time that the common schools were being used as annexes to the Protestant churches. Nothing is said about the establishment of Catholic parish schools and, no doubt, had Bishop Hughes who was in Europe during the Council been present, the result of his relations with the public school authorities in New York City would have influenced our prelates to develop the legislation of 1829 on this question. But the bishops considered it prudent only to direct the pastors to prevent Catholic pupils in these schools from being forced to join in Protestant religious services. The seventh decree concerned the rule of the Church against Catholics joining secret societies and warned the faithful that the sacraments would be denied to those who disobeyed this injunction. No specific societies were mentioned in the decree but it was understood that the Freemasons and Oddfellows were particularly under the ban of the Church.

Evidently, the Fathers of the Council were not satisfied with the situation of Church property incorporation, for a decree was passed insisting upon the necessity of properly securing all movable and immovable property and stating that if this security could be obtained in no other way, then the property was to be handed down by means of last wills and testaments, drawn up according to the provisions of civil law. Propaganda's reaction to this decree was an Instruction (December 15, 1840) of such an involved nature that it was modified in the Council of 1843. Priests were no longer to hold ecclesiastical property in their own names. In the ninth decree the bishops were requested to see that registers of ordinations and of the acceptance of priests into their dioceses be scrupulously kept, and the various offices held by the clergy were to be noted therein. The tenth decree, a summary of the Tridentine legislation on clerical life, is of an exhortatory nature, appealing to the priests to be zealous in the work of the Vineyard and blameless in their private and public lives.

The documents appended to the decrees in the *Concilia habita etc.* are numerous and highly interesting as revealing the minds of the bishops and their interest in the broader aspects of Catholic progress in the world. The letter to Pope Gregory XVI (May 24, 1840) stands out in these conciliar sources for the dignity and beauty of its language and sentiments. "In our days," the Fathers write, "the Church is greatly agitated, and many things fill the paternal heart of your Holiness with anguish; not among the lightest of which may be regarded the evils which flow from the persecution which in many parts of

Europe, religion endures at the hands of the ambitious and the wicked." The condition of the Church in France and Spain and the enmity shown to the Holy See in Italy and in Rome are deplored. The sad situation of the Catholics in Poland, the martyrdoms in China and the persecution of the faithful in the Hawaiian Islands are mentioned with sympathy; but the Holy Father should not lose heart. "Where are they to be found," the American bishops wrote, "who, relying upon the sword, oppressed the Church! From the rubbish of Nero's tomb, the traveler beholds the mausoleum of the Vatican! Look at the cliffs of St. Helena, whilst amidst the applause of the Christian world, Rome, exulting in triumph, receives to her bosom Pius returning from his exile!" They tell the pope that they have drafted a letter of consolation to the Archbishops of Cologne and of Gnesen-Posen to "congratulate them for having been found worthy of suffering reproach in the name of Jesus." All over the vast land of America priests and people were rejoicing in the gallant stand of these two prelates, and the letters to both are masterpieces of Christian fearlessness. "Courage," they wrote, "courage, Confessors, Martyrs, Champions of Christ! Be of good cheer! He who has hitherto contended for you and with you, He will bestow upon you the crown!"

A further letter to the Leopoldine Society of Vienna (May 22, 1840) offers to that association the sincere thanks of the American Church for the support it had so generously given to our progress. Through the alms of Vienna, the life of the Church here had been quickened in every aspect and the harvest sown by the Society was being reaped in the erection of churches, seminaries, colleges, monasteries, orphanages, hospitals and schools, in the increase of religious Orders of men and women, and in the ever-widening field of the preaching of the Gospel. Pope Gregory's answer (December 19, 1840) is a touching reply to the loyal utterance of our bishops, and Propaganda's letter (December 19, 1840) tenders high congratulation to the American prelates for their zeal and devotion.

The Sacred Congregation announced that the See of Richmond had been restored to the Church here and that Father Richard Whelan had been chosen by the Holy Father as its bishop. Father Chanche was selected to fill the See of Natchez and Father John Odin was selected as coadjutor to Bishop Rese of Detroit. The solemnity of the feast of Saints Peter and Paul was changed to the Sunday within the octave of June 29, unless the feast itself fell on that day, and the Holy See had dispensed from the fast formerly kept on the vigil of the feast. The dispensation from abstinence on Saturday, unless it was a fast day, was made perpetual, and new offices were added to the calendar for the Church here. The long and involved method for the safeguarding of ecclesiastical property, as described in Propaganda's decree of December 15, 1840, need not be analyzed since it was found too cumbersome to be put to practical use, although it formed the basis for the subsequent legislation of 1843.

Again, as in former Councils, the *Pastoral Letter* to the clergy and laity is a mirror in which the manifold aspects of Catholic thought and action can be clearly seen. In spite of the growing intolerance toward the Church, the bishops witnessed progress on all sides. They recalled to the minds of the faithful that the "Shame of Massachusetts" still stained the escutcheon of that noble State, "the cradle of our liberties, the first field of honor of our federation." The libels against the clergy issued by the enemies of the Church had decreased, but it was still true that "the pulpit and the press are industriously used for our defamation," though apparently not with the same violence "nor upon the same system of preconceived action for our destruction." Parents were solemnly warned of the dangers their children encountered in non-Catholic educational institutions. "Long and melancholy experience" had proven the truth of this attitude, as well as that shown by the prelates of former Councils, on the question of the textbooks in use in those schools and colleges. "We can scarcely point out a book in general use in the ordinary schools, or even in higher seminaries, wherein covert and insidious efforts are not made to misrepresent our principles, to distort our tenets, to vilify our practices and to bring contempt upon our Church and its members." Mixed marriages are treated in a way that left no room for doubt on the Church's stand, and our bishops speak of the "very many instances of bitter repentance, unavailing as respects the progeny," which had come under their observation: "From the earliest period of the Christian dispensation, we find the code of discipline opposed to those marriages of members of the Church with persons estranged from her communion." The bitter political situation of 1840 called for a strong paragraph on the sacred obligation of the ballot. Bribery and venality were to be avoided as worthy only of renegades to the country. The danger of riches, of intemperance, and of the seductions of the world are described; and the spirit of generosity toward Church support encouraged by pointing to the benefactions of the Societies of Lyons and Vienna.

So noteworthy was the legislation of the Council and so influential for good were the deliberations of the prelates that leaders in the hierarchy, such as Dr. England, might well be pardoned for the sentiment that more time should be given to these triennial assemblies. "Surely," the Bishop of Charleston wrote, "one week in three years is by no means sufficient to transact the business of this large ecclesiastical province, even with the acknowledged assiduity and industry of the bishops. Many things are passed over lightly, and several that ought to be examined are laid aside." But the next decade was to see the beginning of other provinces in the United States with the consequent distribution of the burden of legislating for the Church in the United States.

CHAPTER XII

THE FIFTH PROVINCIAL COUNCIL OF
BALTIMORE (1843)

FOUR members of the American hierarchy passed away during the interim between the Councils of 1840 and 1843. Bishop John B. David of Bardstown (who had resigned in 1833) died on July 12, 1841; Bishop John England, the "Father of our Provincial Councils," [1] died on April 11, 1842; Bishop Henry Conwell of Philadelphia closed his pathetic career on April 22, 1842; and Bishop John Dubois, whose episcopate was equally crowded with tragic misfortune, died on December 20, 1842. The new prelates of the interim were: Bishop Peter Richard Kenrick, coadjutor to Bishop Rosati of St. Louis, who was consecrated on November 30, 1841; Bishop Richard Vincent Whelan, who was to reconstruct Church life in the long vacant See of Richmond and who was consecrated on March 21, 1841; Bishop Lefebre who was consecrated as coadjutor to Bishop Rese of Detroit on November 30, 1841; Bishop John Mary Odin, C.M., who was consecrated as Vicar-Apostolic of the Republic of Texas on March 6, 1842; and Bishop John J. Chanche who had been consecrated for Natchez on March 14, 1841. The Diocese of Charleston had not been filled when the Council of 1843 convened at Baltimore.[2]

The Church in the United States constituted still in 1843 one ecclesiastical province with Baltimore as the metropolitan See. There were fifteen suffragan Sees and the Vicariate-Apostolic of

---

[1] *Brownson's Quarterly Review*, I, 158.
[2] *Cf.* "A Statistical Survey of the Church in the United States in 1841," in *Records,* American Catholic Historical Society, XXXVIII (1927), 193-206.

Texas which Republic would soon (1845) be admitted into the Union. The *Metropolitan Catholic Almanac* for 1843 gives the number of priests in the country as 579—Baltimore, 69; Detroit, 19; Cincinnati, 47; Vincennes, 34; Dubuque, 11; St. Louis, 77; New Orleans, 52; Natchez, 4; Mobile, 18; Charleston, 19; Richmond, 7; Louisville, 50; Nashville, 7; Boston, 34; New York, 71; and Philadelphia, 60.[3]

Three diocesan synods were held in 1842. The second Diocesan Synod of Philadelphia was convoked by Bishop Kenrick for May 22 to 26, 1842, and was held in the Church of St. John the Evangelist, with fifty-five priests present. The decrees of the Provincial Councils of Baltimore were promulgated in the diocese. The new Ritual was made obligatory. Abuses which had crept into Church music were to be corrected *quantocius*. Pastors were obliged to the law of residence, and parochial limits to be strictly observed in the administration of the sacraments, the only exceptions being for German and French priests who were permitted to attend their own flocks. Rules were laid down for a just division of *stipendia* between pastors and assistants; confessionals were to be erected in all the churches, and special regulations for the confessions of women and girls were passed, with exceptions for the deaf and those who were ill. Visiting priests were obliged to present a *Celebret,* although pastors were allowed a certain amount of liberty so that the laws of hospitality be not broken. The quarterly conferences of the clergy were to be attended by all who were not excused, and parochial registers were to be kept under the pain of suspension. Catholics only were to be admitted as sponsors for baptism and confirmation. Marriage before any but the pastor or his delegate was to be treated as clandestine and punished by excommunica-

[3] Pp. 137-143, where the names of the priests will be found in the order above. Apparently, no statistics were available for the Vicariate of Texas. *Cf.* Fitzmorris, *Four Decades of Catholicism in Texas (1820-1860)*, (Washington, D. C., 1926). In the body of the little *Almanac* five priests are listed for the Diocese of Richmond (108-109). The figures given for Boston and Mobile are those of the year 1842 (p. 150).

tion, incurred *ipso facto* and reserved to the Ordinary. Further rules for safeguarding the sanctity of the matrimonial contract were passed. Since no Catechism had been formally adopted by the Baltimore Councils, Dr. Kenrick adopted Butler's Catechism in English and the German Catechism of Canisius, known as the Augsburg Catechism, issued in 1836.[4]

The first Diocesan Synod of Boston was held at the close of the clergy retreat (August 12-17, 1842) and was attended by thirty priests under the presidency of Bishop Fenwick. The decrees of the Baltimore Councils were promulgated and the Ritual which had been published in 1841 was made obligatory in the diocese. Strict adherence was to be given to the canonical law that in the future no new church should be erected unless the deeds were made in the name of the Ordinary. Any abetting of the trustee system was equivalent to suspension *a divinis.* Pastors were enjoined to live within their parishes and the Tridentine law of residence enforced. Midnight Mass on Christmas Day was forbidden owing to the danger of disorders from anti-Catholic malcontents. The collection of money at the doors of the churches was strictly forbidden and the rules laid down in the Council of 1840 *de vita et honestate clericorum* were to be sedulously followed by the clergy.

Owing to the unsettled condition of affairs in the Diocese of New York during the episcopates of Bishops Connolly and Dubois, no diocesan synod could be held. With the succession of John Hughes to the See, it was deemed expedient to convoke the first of these assemblies, and on July 28, 1842, Dr. Hughes issued a circular letter to the clergy requesting their presence at a spiritual retreat (August 21-29), at the close of which the diocesan synod was to be held on the three following days.[5] Each priest was required to bring a copy of the decrees of the Council of Trent and a copy of the decrees of the Provincial Councils of Baltimore (which had been printed in 1841). The

[4] *Statuta Provincilia et Dioecesana* (Phila., 1897), 9-16.
[5] *Works,* I, 313-314.

synod was held in St. John's College, Fordham. A number of statutes for the better administration of church affairs was submitted by Bishop Hughes. Shea has summed up these regulations as follows:

These statutes required a baptismal font in every church with a fixed pastor, and the administration of the sacrament there and not in private houses, except in danger of death. The Roman Ritual was to be followed in all cases. The custom of the diocese in not preparing the young for confirmation till after their first communion was retained. Rules were adopted for the reverent administration of the Holy Eucharist to the sick and its proper reservation in the tabernacle. Suitable confessionals were to be set up in all churches within three months. Priests were not to officiate at marriages unless four days' previous notice was given, in order to prevent rash and sometimes forbidden unions, and the marriage was to be celebrated in the parochial district to which the parties or one of them belonged. The faithful were to be warned from time to time against contracting marriage before a civil magistrate, or any but a Catholic clergyman. The marriages of Germans were to take place before a priest having charge of a German congregation. No priest was to officiate at a marriage where the parties had been or were to be married by a Protestant clergyman. Catholics were to be warned against mixed marriages, and no such marriage was to be performed without a dispensation, and a pledge of the non-Catholic party that the Catholic one should enjoy full liberty of conscience to practice her religion, and that the children should be brought up Catholics. The celebration of Mass with proper and becoming vestments and the altar neatly kept was prescribed: and all churches were required to have a proper cope, veil, monstrance, and censer for the office of the Benediction of the Blessed Sacrament. No priest was to be absent from his church on Sunday without permission. Funeral services were not to be held in houses, or in English, and funeral orations were discountenanced. Steps were to be taken to prevent the burial in consecrated ground of those who had by their lives and the neglect of the sacraments cut themselves off from the body of the church. In the important matter of church property it was enacted that trustees should not expend, without leave of the pastor of the church, money contributed by the faithful for the maintenance of religion and the clergy. Neither pastor nor trustees were to make any extraordinary outlay exceeding one hundred dollars without the permission of the Bishop. Priests were required, under pain of suspension, to report infringements of this rule. They were to prepare an inventory of all ecclesiastical property, and to present to the Bishop at his visitation a statement of the financial condition of the church, and for this purpose were to have free access to the minutes and account books of the trustees. No priest was to hold the title of church, parochial residence, or cemetery in his own name, but to have it vested in the Bishop of the diocese. All persons engaged in taking part in the public services of the Church and in teaching were to be appointed by the priest in charge of the parochial district. No meetings were to be held in the church or basement without his leave. The letting of pews by auction was discountenanced. Provision was made for a cathedraticum or regular annual contribution from each church for the maintenance of the Bishop. The faithful were to be warned against secret societies or the taking of oaths to support factions, and the sacraments were to be denied to those who persisted in adhering to such organizations, which had wrought great evils among the laboring classes, leading to perjury and the sacrifice of human life.

On September 8, 1842, Bishop Hughes issued a *Pastoral Letter* to the faithful on the evils of trusteeism.[6] The *Pastoral* treats of the administration of the sacraments, the application of the general laws of the Church to local conditions, the enactment of rigid laws for the Sacrament of Matrimony, secret societies, and the tenure and administration of ecclesiastical property. New York was the last stage of the fight made by belligerent laymen for the control of Church property and Dr. Hughes explained that, owing to the State laws on the question, he had "hitherto declined executing the statutes of the decrees of the Baltimore Councils on the subject." The time had come, however, for a just and adequate reconstruction of the situation and the statutes issued by the Synod made it impossible for the older system to continue. The attacks in the daily press on this part of the *Pastoral Letter* and Dr. Hughes' reply are the beginning of the bitter fight which was to continue for the next few years and to end in victory for the Church authorities. Dr. Hughes did not condemn the trustees indiscriminately. "I must say," he

[6] *Works*, I, 314-327.

writes (November, 1842), "that in all my intercourse with the trustees of New York, and I may add of the diocese generally, I have found them, with very few exceptions, as respectful to me in my official character, as zealous for the good of their religion, as any other members of the Church." It was the power of the trustee system to interfere in the spiritual administration of the Church which he had determined to end.[7]

Pastoral Letters, such as that issued by Bishop Kenrick of St. Louis (December 3, 1842)[8] reënforcing the decrees of 1840, took the place of formal synodal legislation. The chief burden of this pastoral was the necessity of erecting a seminary in the city of St. Louis.[9]

If one may judge the conditions prevailing in Catholic life here when the Fifth Provincial Council opened its meetings on May 13, 1843, by the topics discussed in the *Pastoral Letter to the Laity,* it is apparent that nothing of an exceptional nature in the matter of national ecclesiastical jurisdiction demanded the attention of the prelates. These years (1840-1843) are the first part of a decade of tremendous progress in the American Church. In their letter to Pope Gregory XVI, the prelates wrote that in all parts of these vast regions (*in vastissimis vero regionibus*) the number of priests, churches, religious institutions, schools and of the faithful were daily on the increase (*quotidie crescit*). As a sign of progress, they say, in one diocese alone forty-three churches had been erected since the Council of 1840.

The preliminary meeting of the Council took place on May 13 in the archbishop's house, with the following prelates present: Archbishop Eccleston, Bishops Fenwick, Portier, Purcell, Chabrat, Blanc, Hughes, Miles, De la Hailandière, Chanche, Whelan, Lefebre, Peter Richard Kenrick, and John Odin. On Sunday, May 14, the first Solemn Session of the Council was held. Solemn Pontifical Mass was celebrated by Bishop Portier in the cathedral in the presence of the prelates. Bishops Francis

---

[7] *Works,* I, 334.   [8] *U. S. Cath. Misc.,* XXII, 212.
[9] Rothensteiner, *op. cit.,* I, 836-840.

Patrick Kenrick and Loras, and Father Richard S. Baker arrived in the meantime and were present. Bishop Fenwick of Boston preached the sermon.[10] The officials chosen were: *Promoters,* Bishops Portier and Chanche; *Secretaries.* Fathers Damphoux and Charles I. White; *Masters of Ceremonies:* Fathers Lhomme, Thomas Foley, and Jenkins; and *Chanters:* Father Blenkinsop and Rev. Mr. Parsons.

At the first private congregation (May 15) the question of selecting priests for new and vacant Sees was discussed, and that same afternoon, the first public congregation was held in the cathedral. Besides the prelates, the following priests were invited to be present: Louis Deluol, Superior of St. Mary's Seminary; John Timon, Superior of the Vincentians; Peter Joseph Verhaegen, S.J., Provincial of the Missouri Province; and Patrick Moriarty, the head of the Augustinians in this country. Twenty other priests—*theologians* to the bishops—were present, among them the future prelates: Henni, Verot, and Lynch, and such outstanding ecclesiastics as Mazzuchelli, Penco, C.M., and James Ryder, S.J. At the second private congregation (May 16) it was decided to ask the Holy See to erect new dioceses at Pittsburgh, Chicago, Milwaukee and Little Rock. The following day (May 17), the creation of a vicariate-apostolic for Oregon was agreed upon.[11]

The second Solemn Session was held on May 18, with Pontifical Mass, celebrated by Bishop Blanc of New Orleans, and Bishop Hughes of New York preached. It was the first time

---

[10] "Thus opened the fifth Provincial Council of the American Church, whose hierarchy, assembled from every segment of the great republic, stands unsurpassed by any other portion of their brethren throughout the world, for virtue, learning, apostolic zeal and devotion to the See of Peter, the mother and mistress of all" (*U. S. Cath. Misc.,* XXII (May 27, 1843), 375).

[11] By the year 1843 all Russian, French and Spanish claims to the Oregon territory were practically relinquished, leaving the United States and Great Britain as the sole claimants. The question of ownership was a mooted one in 1843, and the famous cry of "54° 40' or fight" was heard in some political quarters. The United States government began organizing the territory in 1843, although it was only in 1848 that Oregon was created a territory within the nation.

that this illustrious prelate was heard in a Provincial Council. The bishops whom he eulogized were among the pioneers in the establishment of the Church here, and Dr. Hughes, though cool and self-possessed in the pulpit, won the sympathy of his audience, clergy and laity, by the emotion which he could hardly suppress.[12]

The afternoon of the same day saw the prelates gathered in the archbishop's house for the fourth private congregation when the customary letter to the Holy Father was written. At the fifth private congregation (May 19), the See of Hartford for Connecticut and Rhode Island was decided upon, and in the last (eighth) private congregation, the archbishop left the chair while Bishop Portier offered the usual resolution of thanks to the archbishop for his kindness and hospitality during the Council. Up to this time Dr. Eccleston had presided over the Provincial Councils of 1837, 1840, and 1843, and had won the good will of all the prelates and priests by the freedom and courtesy shown during the deliberations and for the impartial and dignified manner "in which he discharged his duty even under those occasional circumstances that he might himself be inclined to designate as exceedingly delicate." [13]

The third and last Solemn Session was held Sunday, May 21, with Solemn Pontifical Mass celebrated by Bishop Chanche, the sermon being delivered by Bishop Purcell. During these eight private congregations, the eleven decrees of the Council were voted by the prelates, and these were then promulgated in the public congregations and Sessions which followed. The *acclamationes* and the *Te Deum* brought the Council to a close, and it was not without emotion that an acclamation in behalf of the faithful at large was sung. It was exquisitely worded, calling upon Almighty God to fill the hearts of all with peace, to banish enmities, contentions, wraths, quarrelings and dissensions, that the charity of brotherhood might abide in them and keep them one in love as in faith, obedient to their prelates in order

[12] *U. S. Cath. Misc.,* XXII, 375.   [13] *Ibid.*

that here on earth they might all enjoy a foretaste of the peace which shall be eternal in God's glory.

Eleven decrees were passed by the Council of 1843. In the first of these, it was stipulated that the regulations passed by the Fourth Provincial Council of 1840 in regard to ecclesiastical property held in the name of the bishops had proven to be more rigorous than practical. With the consent of the Holy See, the Council of 1843 modified these to suit the laws of the respective States. Each bishop was required within three months after his consecration to make a will securing the ecclesiastical property in his charge by the laws of his State and to deposit a copy of the will with the archbishop. The archbishop was required to do the same and to deposit a copy with the senior suffragan.[14] The second decree has relation to an abuse about which little can be found in the extant sources, namely, that the laity were no longer permitted to use a dedicated or consecrated church for a public meeting. The third decree declared any Catholic to be *ipso facto* excommunicated who should attempt remarriage after being divorced by the law of the State. The fourth decree restricted the marriage law of the *Tametsi* to the city of Detroit. The *Tametsi* [15] nullified any marriage not contracted before the parish priest or the Ordinary and before two witnesses. It bound, however, only in those places where it was formally promulgated. Consequently, it was held to be applicable in all those dioceses which were once a part of the Diocese of Quebec, in the old Spanish province of Louisiana, and in California. The Fathers of the Council decreed that the *Tametsi* was not to bind except in those dioceses where it was known to have been so promulgated, and they intended to ask the Holy See for a dispensation for the city of Detroit.

The Tridentine decree regarding the residence of pastors

---

[14] Desmond, *The Church and the Law* (Chicago, 1898); Baart, *The Tenure of Catholic Church Property in the United States* (Marshall, 1900). See also bibliography in Bartlett, *The Tenure of Parochial Property in the United States of America* (Wash., D. C., 1926).

[15] Council of Trent, Sess. xxiv, c. 1.

was to be enforced, lest the faithful miss Mass on Sundays and holydays, and in order that the sick might not be neglected. This decree urges that statutes to this effect be promulgated in local diocesan synods. The bishops were warned in the sixth decree to admonish pastors not to incur any rash debts by building or repairing churches, and ordered that a yearly report of the parish finances be sent to the Ordinary and that no Church property should be alienated (sold, mortgaged or leased), without the bishop's consent. Priests were requested not to mix their personal financial matters with those of the parish, lest scandals arise. All financial matters pertaining to Church funds were to be kept in a book for that purpose, and this should be open for the inspection of the bishop at the time of visitation. The eighth decree prescribed the Roman Ritual as compiled by Bishop Rosati for the entire Church in the United States. Permission was given to print an appendix containing prayers in the vernacular, but priests were admonished to use only the Latin forms in all services. The ninth decree made the erection of confessionals in the churches obligatory, as had been decreed in the First Provincial Council of Baltimore. The sacristy was excluded as a confessional, unless it was a room accessible to the public. The publishing houses of Baltimore and Cincinnati which were then printing Catholic books under the direction of some of the clergy were given the approval of the Council. The eleventh and last decree legislated for the prompt and assiduous attention of the sick and their frequent reception of the Sacraments of Penance and the Holy Eucharist. Priests were admonished in their sermons on Sundays and holy days not to teach vain or intricate things, but what was necessary for the eternal salvation of their flocks and not to dwell upon those things which might arouse admiration for eloquence, but upon what was edifying and promoted the increase of piety.

The decrees are signed by Archbishop Eccleston and fifteen suffragan bishops, together with Father Richard S. Baker, Administrator of Charleston.

The letter of the Council to Pope Gregory XVI is couched in the same lofty eloquence as those of previous assemblies. With their eyes, hearts, and minds turned to the successor of St. Peter and to the See of Rome, as to the sun of eternal light, they praise the splendid progress the Church of God has made under his supreme guidance. At the great Rock of Peter the world was taking refuge, they wrote, in order that it might escape the floods of idolatry, superstition, heresy, and vice which were sweeping over the world. To the Vicar of Christ, hands are stretching from Asia and Africa, seeking the bread of light. The progress of the Faith in the United States gave encouragement to all the hierarchy. As a sign of that progress they mention the great increase in parochical life and social welfare since the Council of 1840. They gave high praise to the work of the Jesuits in the Indian missions of the Rocky Mountains and to the work being done among the Negroes of Liberia. The attacks upon the Church were not decreasing, and anti-Catholic books and pamphlets were being distributed in all parts of the country, especially among the ignorant and unlettered, while the cry of Catholic disloyalty to American principles was gaining in volume. There is little doubt that our prelates, while silent on the subject in their *Pastoral Letter* to the faithful, were conscious of the intense anti-Catholic movement which was to break out into violence the following year.

The decrees of the Council were approved by letter from Cardinal Franzoni, Prefect of the Sacred Congregation of Propaganda Fide, on September 30, 1843, and the following appointments made to the new Sees, the erection of which was approved by the Holy See: Pittsburgh, Michael O'Connor; Little Rock, Andrew Byrne; Chicago, William Quarter; Hartford, William Tyler; and Milwaukee, John Henni.

Ignatius Reynolds was appointed to the vacant See of Charleston. John McCloskey, the future (first) American Cardinal, was appointed coadjutor to Bishop Hughes of New York, and John B. Fitzpatrick, coadjutor to Bishop Fenwick of Boston.

The Vicariate-Apostolic of Oregon was likewise erected by the Holy See, and Francis Norbert Blanchet named as first Vicar-Apostolic. Pope Gregory XVI responded to the conciliar letter on December 2, 1843, congratulating the Fathers of the Council upon the great progress of the Church here, without, however, making any reference to the anti-Catholic spirit abroad in the United States at the time.

The *Pastoral Letter* of 1843 is the shortest written during the seven Provincial Councils. It appeals to all to make public profession of the Faith, whenever the divine honor or the edification of one's neighbor was in question, and it takes cognizance of the fact that in industrial centers Catholics were being ostracized and in some cases could only obtain employment through apostasy. The instruction of the young in the truths of religion is brought forcibly to the attention of parents, and the methods used in the common schools to poison the minds of Catholic boys and girls is categorized as "plainly opposed to the free genius of our civil institutions." Parents were admonished to "avail themselves of their natural rights, guaranteed by the laws," and to see "that no interference with the faith of their children be used in the public schools, and no attempt made to induce conformity in anything contrary to the laws of the Catholic Church." All secret societies bound by oath were to be shunned under penalty of being refused the Sacraments. Catholics were encouraged to strengthen the social bonds which should unite them to their non-Catholic neighbors, and to practice strict integrity in the daily concerns of life, in the fulfillment of all engagements, in their peaceful demeanor, in obedience to the laws of the nation, in their respect for civic authorities, and in their unaffected exercise of charity, as a barrier to the widespread animosity toward their Church. The "enormous evils" of intemperance at the time bring forth a sturdy paragraph on the value of total abstinence, although the prelates remind the faithful that temperance in the use of wine or other liquors is a virtue. "It would not be advisable," they write, "to impose or to assume generally the obligation of total abstinence, since, considering human frailty, it might become a snare of souls, and change a lawful act into sin, and add to the sting of conscience the terror of despair." The pledge did not impose any new moral obligation, since all were held to the virtue of temperance. Likewise the "enormous scandal" of divorce was exposed, for the bishops "were determined to employ the severest authority of the Church" against any of the faithful "guilty of so heinous a crime and to cut them off from her communion." After a paragraph on the Rocky Mountain Missions and the Mission in Liberia, the *Pastoral* closes by expressing gratitude to God for "the admirable change which His grace has wrought in the minds of many in England" through what is now known as the Oxford Movement, "the effects whereof are seen even in this country." The conversion of Orestes Brownson the following year (October, 1844) focused the attention of the entire country upon the movement which was to bring so many intellectual leaders into the Church within the next decade.

CHAPTER XIII

THE SIXTH PROVINCIAL COUNCIL OF
BALTIMORE (1846)

DURING the interim between the Councils of 1843 and 1846 religious freedom reached its lowest ebb in this country. Never before or since, even during the cruelest days of the colonial penal laws against Catholicism, had there been such scenes of violence and animosity against the Church of Rome. All our traditions of civil and religious equality were overthrown, apparently beyond all hope of saving them for the future; for these years witnessed the climax of the first period (1829-1844) of antagonism to freedom of conscience in the land. The story of the outbreak does not enter into the history of canonical legislation in the United States; in fact, one looks in vain in the *Acta et Decreta* of the Council of 1846, or in its *Pastoral Letter to the Clergy and Laity,* for any expression of sorrow or resentment over the outrages committed by the Native-Americans in that truly terrible year of 1844.

Although the violence of the Native-Americans was worst in Philadelphia, every civic center with a large Catholic population suffered from the movement. Baltimore was not spared. The brother of Rev. John Breckenridge (1797-1841) who had been so ably refuted by John Hughes in Philadelphia in 1833-1835—Rev. Robert J. Breckenridge (1800-1871), and who succeeded him in the pastorate of the Second Presbyterian Church in Baltimore (1832-1845), was one of the bitterest opponents the Catholic faith has ever had in the United States. As editor of the *Baltimore Literary and Religious Magazine,* Robert published a series of articles, later printed in book form under the title *Papism in the XIX Century in the United States* (1841). The chapter on the Third Provincial Council of 1837 is a vicious personal attack upon the prelates, particularly on Bishop England. Another chapter contains an unspeakable page on Archbishop Eccleston. The book is typical of the kind of literature spread broadcast at the time. The licentious work of a Spanish apostate priest, Anthony Gavin—*A History of Popery,* to which was appended a scurrilous *History of the Papacy in the United States,* appeared the year of the Council of 1846, calling upon "every true lover of freedom and religion" to resist the further extension of the Church in this country: "Shall Americans sleep, while the 'Man of Sin' is thus active in his work; thus extending his dominion? Or shall they, in the spirit of holy love, cluster around the banner which the spirit of the living God has lifted up against him? *Let American Christians answer!"*

Of the crimes committed against defenseless Catholics in Philadelphia and elsewhere, of the rioting, the acts of arson, the outrages and murders, little need be said here. Honest citizens of all faiths were shamed by the Native-American Terror. But the fact itself needs to be recalled, if only to bring out into bolder relief the great Christian charity and civic nobility of the Fathers of the Council of 1846; for, in none of the published documents of the assembly is there any mention of these outrages and only a general reference is made to Catholic loyalty in the *Pastoral Letter* of that year.

The progress of the Church showed no slackening between 1843 and 1846. As a result of the deliberations of the Council of 1843, five dioceses (Chicago, Milwaukee, Pittsburgh, Hartford, and Little Rock), making in all twenty-one suffragan Sees, together with the Vicariate of Oregon, were created. There were, at the opening of the Council, twenty-six bishops, six hundred and seventy-five churches, seven hundred and nine priests,[1] twenty-two seminaries, fifteen colleges, and over one

---

[1] The secular clergy numbered 508; the religious Orders in the country were: Augustinians, 8; Dominicans, 12; Jesuits, 103; Vincentians, 30; Re-

million Catholics.[2] There were at this time fourteen Catholic weekly and monthly publications; among the latter were the *United States Catholic Magazine* (Baltimore), the *Catholic Expositor* (New York) and the *Catholic Cabinet* (St. Louis); while *Brownson's Quarterly Review* (Boston) had then reached its second volume since the conversion of that eminent philosopher.

Among the problems which occupied the attention of the prelates at the time were: the creation of new dioceses; the organization of the Church in the former Republic of Texas, which was annexed to the United States in 1845; the spiritual care of Catholics in the army; and higher education for Catholic youth.

Three diocesan synods were convened during the interim. The second Diocesan Synod of New Orleans was called by Bishop Blanc on April 21, 1840, and thirty-seven priests attended. The decrees of the five Councils of Baltimore were formally received and made obligatory in the diocese and by this act it was understood that the Archbishop of Baltimore was metropolitan over New Orleans. The use of the Roman missal, ritual, ceremonial and breviary was enjoined on all the clergy. Regulations for the reception of priests into the diocese were made and it was decreed that no ecclesiastical benefice was to be permitted in the future. Priests were again warned not to have any part in the lingering trustee troubles, and in the future no new church edifice would be allowed unless the deeds were made in the name of the bishop. Strict financial accounts were to be kept by the pastors, and the trustees were to be excluded

---

demptorists, 25; Eudists, 4; Fathers of the Most Precious Blood, 8; Holy Cross, 3. There were 32 Brothers of St. Joseph, 4 Viatorian Brothers; and the following nuns: Dominicans, 30; Carmelites, 36; Ursulines, 44; Religious of the Sacred Heart, 141; Sisters of Charity of Emmitsburg, 368; Sisters of Charity of Dubuque, 19; Visitandines, 162; Sisters of Mercy, 29; Sisters of Loretto, 156; Sisters of the Good Shepherd, 8; Sisters of Notre Dame—Cincinnati and Oregon, 14; Sisters of Providence, 46; Sisters of St. Joseph, 13; and Sisters of the Most Precious Blood, 4, making a total of 1140 nuns where a score of years before there were less than a hundred. *Cf. Catholic Cabinet*, II (1845), 633-634.

[2] *Metropolitan Catholic Almanac* (1845), 185.

from all temporal administration of church property. The law regarding clandestine marriages prevailed and all such unions were declared invalid. Pastors were not to exercise jurisdiction outside the limits of their own parishes, and all who died as members of forbidden secret societies were to be denied Christian burial.[3] This same year (1844) saw the final overthrow of the trustee system in New Orleans; and, as Bishop Blanc expressed it in a *Pastoral* on May 16, 1844, the beginning of a new and better order was visible in the diocese.

The first Diocesan Synod of Vincennes was called by Bishop de la Hailandière on May 12, 1844, with twenty-four priests in attendance. The regulations of the Councils of Baltimore were made obligatory in the diocese, and among the local enactments was a remarkable decree urging the priests to preserve all the documentary material which came into their possession for the future history of the Church in Indiana. The statutes passed for the maintenance of ecclesiastical discipline were noted at the time as being uncommonly wise and prudent.[4]

The first Diocesan Synod of Pittsburgh was convened by Bishop O'Connor on June 16, 1844, with twenty priests present. The statutes were largely repetitions of the conciliar legislation of Baltimore. Bishop O'Connor expressed the desire to have the feast of the Immaculate Conception specially honored in the diocese. A committee of priests was named to make collections for a diocesan seminary, and the diocese was given the regular official family of chancellor, secretary, and clergy examiners. Permanent rectorships were also established. Strict rules were issued for the preservation of church records, and it was urged upon the clergy to begin at once a system of Catholic parochial schools.[5]

---

[3] *Synodus Dioecesana Neo-Aurelianensis Secunda habita mense Aprilis anno 1844* (New Orleans, 1844). *Cf. U. S. Cath. Magazine*, III (1844), 541-542; Shea, *op. cit.*, IV, 269-270.

[4] *U. S. Cath. Magazine*, III (1844), 405.

[5] *Statuta Dioecesis Pittsburgensis lata in Synodo dioecesana habita 1844* (Pittsburgh, 1854).

Beyond these three synods there is apparently no record of any similar assembly in the other suffragan dioceses.

The Sixth Provincial Council of Baltimore opened its sessions in the archbishop's house on May 9, 1846. On March 31, 1846, Archbishop Eccleston issued a circular letter asking for special prayers for the coming Council and urging the faithful to receive Holy Communion frequently in order that "the favor of Heaven may be more effectively invoked on the proceedings of the approaching Provincial Council." [6] There were present: Archbishop Eccleston and twenty-three bishops, representing almost all the suffragan dioceses. One beloved link with the past who went back to the days of Carroll and Neale—Benedict Joseph Flaget—had reached the advanced age of eighty-three and was unable to make the long and arduous journey from Louisville. Bishop Fenwick of Boston was then in his last illness; he died on August 11, 1846. Bishop Rosati had passed away while on a visit to Rome on September 25, 1843, and Bishop Diego y Moreno of California died before the Council opened (April 30, 1846). Bishop Francis N. Blanchet of Oregon was unable to come owing to the great distance and the lack of traveling facilities.[7] Bishop Barron was then in Liberia. The first Solemn Session of the Council took place on Sunday, May 10, in the cathedral. Solemn Pontifical Mass was celebrated by Archbishop Eccleston, and Bishop Purcell preached "a very eloquent, argumentative and impressive sermon, in which the venerable Prelate showed the divine character of our Holy Church and vindicated it." [8] An eyewitness has described the opening scenes of the Council. A vast concourse of people filled the cathedral and the adjacent streets looking on "with breathless interest while this largest assembly of prelates and clergymen ever convened in the Union," was gathered together from

[6] *U. S. Cath. Magazine,* V, 281.
[7] Bishop F. N. Blanchet was consecrated titular Bishop of Drasa at Montreal on July 25, 1845, after traveling around Cape Horn to London, thence to Boston, and from there to Montreal, a journey of 22,000 miles.
[8] *U. S. Cath. Misc.,* XXV, 365.

all parts of the United States to legislate for the American Church.[9] One innovation was made—every evening in the cathedral one of the prelates preached to the throngs that were in attendance. Among these were: the future Archbishop of Baltimore, Martin John Spalding; Bishops John Hughes, Michael O'Connor, Francis P. Kenrick, and John McCloskey, the future Cardinal.

The new prelates who took the customary conciliar oath were: Bishops O'Connor (Pittsburgh), Byrne (Little Rock), Quarter (Chicago), McCloskey (New York), Tyler (Hartford), Reynolds (Charleston), Henni (Milwaukee), and Fitzpatrick (Boston). The *Promoters* were Bishops Portier and Chanche, who had served in this capacity in the Council of 1843; Fathers Damphoux and Lhomme were selected as *Secretaries,* and Father Lhomme acted also as *Master of Ceremonies.* The *Chanters* were Father Parsons and Rev. Mr. Henniss.

At the first private congregation the following prelates were appointed to prepare the formal letters of the Council: Bishop Peter Richard Kenrick (to the Holy Father, Gregory XVI); Bishop Francis Patrick Kenrick (the *Pastoral Letter to the Clergy and Laity*); Bishop Portier (to the Society for the Propagation of the Faith, Lyons); and Bishop Henni (to the Leopoldine Society of Vienna). The first public congregation (May 11) saw in attendance the heads of the religious Orders in the country and the *theologians* appointed by the different bishops; in all thirty-one priests, among whom were many who had grown old in the service of the Church. The third private congregation is of historic interest, for the prelates then promulgated the first decree of the Council, naming the Blessed Virgin Mary Immaculate as Patroness of the Church in the United States and petitioning the Sovereign Pontiff to transfer her feast to the Sunday within its octave.[10]

[9] *U. S. Cath. Magazine,* V (1846), 341.
[10] Macleod, X. D., *Devotion to the Blessed Virgin Mary in North America* (New York, 1866), 28-29; McKenna, Bernard A., *The Dogma of the Immaculate Conception* (Washington, D. C., 1909), 517.

The second Solemn Session, the Mass of Requiem for the deceased prelates was celebrated by Bishop Chanche, and the panegyric given by Bishop Peter Richard Kenrick of St. Louis. One prelate, his own predecessor, Bishop Rosati, had passed away during the interim between the Councils of 1843 and 1846. There was no doubt in the minds of the prelates that in Rosati's death the American Church had lost one of the most remarkable bishops in Christendom.

In the fourth private congregation the Fathers decided to ask the Holy See for the privilege of inserting in the Office and Mass of December 8 the word *Immaculate* and in the Litany the invocation: *Queen, conceived without original sin, pray for us.* In the fifth and last private congregation, the Fathers expressed their appreciation of "the great kindness and warm hospitality" extended to them by the archbishop and the Catholics of Baltimore. The final Solemn Session took place on Sunday, May 17, in the cathedral. Archbishop Eccleston celebrated Pontifical Mass and Bishop Reynolds of Charleston preached on the unity of the Church. "He well represented," it was said at the time, "his great predecessor the illustrious England." [11] The ceremonies ended with the *acclamationes* and the *Te Deum* and the solemn procession back to the archiepiscopal residence.

Four decrees only were enacted by the Council of 1846. The first, already mentioned, was the choice of the feast of the Immaculate Conception as the patronal feast of the Church in the United States. The second, echoes the old problem which had disturbed the harmony of missionary life in England for many years: secular priests leaving their dioceses to join religious Orders without the permission of the Ordinary. The Fathers of the Council asked that the Holy See issue a declaration on the subject for all who had been ordained *titulo missionis,* to the effect that written permission from the Ordinary was necessary. The Fathers were strongly of the opinion that the banns should be announced before the celebration of marriage, according to

[11] *U. S. Cath. Misc.,* XXV, 373.

the mind of the Councils of the Lateran and of Trent, and the reply of the Sacred Congregation was not only favorable, but extended the practice to mixed marriages also. In the fourth decree, pastors were strictly forbidden to administer the Sacraments of Matrimony and Baptism to the faithful of other dioceses in all cases where they could easily receive these sacraments from their own pastors. The last decree announced the coming Seventh Provincial Council for the fourth Monday after Easter (May 9) in 1849. The decrees are signed by Archbishop Eccleston and twenty-two bishops.

Judging from the decrees alone, it would appear that the Council of 1846 was hardly necessary. The published *Acta* are the most meager of any in the *Concilia habita etc.*, and the contemporary notices we have for the sessions are of little value for the history of canonical legislation. The ceremonies, however, were so imposing and splendid in their observance of the Ritual, and the interest aroused by the evening sermons of the prelates so intense, that little else except descriptions of these have come down to us. There is one immortal honor that must always be united with the memories of the Council—the action taken in regard to the patronal feast of the Immaculate Conception, eight years before the solemn definition of the dogma itself by Pius IX (1854).

The official documents on the Council are not many. Cardinal Franzoni, Prefect of the Sacred Congregation de Propaganda Fide, wrote on September 15, 1846, praising the Council for its decree on the Immaculate Queen of Heaven and enclosing a rescript from Pius IX (Gregory XVI had passed away on June 9, 1846) which granted the privileges the Fathers had requested. In his letter, Cardinal Franzoni wrote:

It is not surprising that after the erection of new dioceses, the enactment of decrees, and other proceedings of former councils, religion should have obtained such an increase in the United States, the solicitude of the clergy should have shone forth so conspicuously, and religious institutions, both male and female, should have become so flourishing. To derive still more abundant fruit from the labors which you so indefatigably sustain, in conjunction with the beloved members of the secular and regular clergy, the fathers of the Council very wisely determined to invoke, in a special manner, the most powerful aid and protection of the holy Mother of God, and our holy Father Pius IX most willingly confirmed the wishes of the Council that has selected the *Blessed Virgin, conceived without sin,* as the patroness of the Church in the United States of America.

Pius IX wrote on June 13, 1847, explaining to the archbishop that the cause of the delay was the death of Gregory XVI. The new pope rejoiced over the great increase of the faithful in the United States and gave his consent to the creation of the new Sees asked for by the Council—Albany, Buffalo, and Cleveland.[12] Bishop McCloskey was appointed to Albany; Father Timon, C.M., to Buffalo; and Father Amadeus Rappe, to Cleveland.[13]

The American bishops were informed by Propaganda in its official instruction of July 3, 1847, that in the future in the selection of bishops for vacant Sees, care should be shown to nominate for sections of the country where German Catholics predominated priests who were of that race or who were familiar with the language and customs of the people. This part of the letter runs as follows:

Among the qualifications of a bishop, is certainly to be reckoned a knowledge of the language in use among those over whom he presides. Wherefore, as large numbers of Germans annually emigrate to the United States where they permanently settle, you will carefully provide that bishops, to be appointed for these dioceses whose population is German, be well acquainted with their language. Those dioceses should also be provided with priests who speak the German language.

[12] In his letter to the hierarchy, Pius IX "manifests his love and admiration for the young Church of the West, destined in his prophetic opinion, to make up for the melancholy losses in Europe" (*Balt. Cath. Mirror,* XXXV, November 8, 1884).

[13] Bishop John Hughes of New York had urged upon the Council the creation of a See at Plattsburg, but this was not acted upon.

Moreover, the bishops were to provide priests who were able to preach and hear confessions in that language. There is also in the official documents printed with the *Acta et Decreta* of the Council a new form of oath to be taken by the bishops-elect before their consecration. Certain clauses to which Carroll and some of the prelates since his day had objected because they were liable to be misunderstood by those outside the Church were eliminated.[14] An interesting pen sketch of the Sixth Provincial Council appeared in the August, 1846, issue of the *United States Catholic Magazine*.[15]

A final ceremony has its place in the history of the Council of 1846. At its last private congregation the prelates unanimously voted to present to Archbishop Eccleston who had up to that year presided over four of the Provincial Councils, "a cross and the vases and ornaments belonging to the archiepiscopal *chapelle* as tokens of their veneration and attachment." This was done the following October by Bishop Francis P. Kenrick, the chairman of the committee appointed for that purpose. "The courtesy, dignity and kindness which have marked your intercourse with your colleagues," Kenrick wrote to the archbishop (October 23, 1846), "the wisdom and moderation with which you have presided over these deliberations, and the unbounded hospitality which you have exercised towards them, demanded some expression of their admiration and gratitude. On me has devolved the pleasing duty of presenting these sacred ornaments in the name of all."[16]

The *Pastoral Letter to the Clergy and Laity,* while short and concise, reflects the spirit of optimism which prevailed in the Council, in spite of the three fearful years of anti-Catholic violence which preceded the convocation of that assembly. The return of "so many distinguished individuals in England to the Catholic communion, from which that illustrious nation was

[14] *U. S. Cath. Magazine,* VI, 503.
[15] Reproduced in Shea, *op. cit.,* IV, 28.
[16] *U. S. Cath. Magazine,* VI, 688-689.

torn by the strong arm of the civil power, has filled us with joy," the Fathers wrote, and they predicted truly that the example of these conversions would have considerable influence upon many intellectually trained men and women in the United States who were seeking the truth. Many, it was true, who were struggling forward toward truth and unity, would be "drawn back by the interests of this world" and would "love the glory of men rather than the glory of God." The faithful were asked, therefore, to redouble their prayers and spiritual exercises in order that Almighty God would shower His graces upon all who were sincerely in search of the true faith. Again, the love and veneration of the Church in the United States were pledged to the Holy See. The zeal and generosity of the Society of Paris-Lyons was held up as a model to American Catholics. A final paragraph contains the announcement of the Council's action in placing the Church here under the august patronage of the Immaculate Queen of Heaven.

The war with Mexico was beginning while the Council was in session, and when the next provincial assembly met in 1849, jurisdiction in the United States had been immensely increased by the addition of the Republic of Texas and the old Spanish Southwest. During the Council, the government had requested through Buchanan, then Secretary of State, for Catholic chaplains to accompany the American army, and Fathers McElroy and Rey of the Society of Jesus were chosen. It was stated at the time that there were eleven hundred Catholics in the first army sent to the border. Father Rey was killed after the capture of Monterey under General Scott, who, it was reported, wept when informed of his untimely fate.

CHAPTER XIV

THE SEVENTH PROVINCIAL COUNCIL OF BALTIMORE (1849)

THE letter of convocation for the Seventh Provincial Council of Baltimore—the last Provincial Council to legislate nationally for the Church in the United States—was sent out to the members of the American hierarchy on September 23, 1848.

The changes which had occurred in the diocesan structure of the Church since the close of the last Council (May 17, 1846) were important in themselves and were the beginning of a hierarchical development which has continued until our own times. On July 24, 1846, by the Brief *Universi dominici*, Pius IX erected the vast Archdiocese of Oregon City, and in accordance with the wishes of Archbishop Blanchet, created within the province the suffragan Sees of Nesqually, Walla Walla, Fort Hall, Colville, Vancouver, Princess Charlotte Island and New Caledonia.[1] Three of these dioceses (Vancouver, Princess Charlotte and New Caledonia) were in Canadian territory. No more ambitious ecclesiastical foundation was ever conceived than this; and while it failed, it shows the profound faith Archbishop Blanchet had in the future of this great section of the United States and Canada. On February 28, 1848, he held the first Provincial Council of Oregon, which was attended by his brother, Bishop Blanchet of Walla Walla, and by Bishop Modeste Demers of Vancouver—the only two suffragans appointed up to that time.

The creation of the Oregon Province in what the Bishop of St. Louis always regarded as part of his own diocese was later

[1] De Martinis, *Jus Pontificium etc.*, VI, 6.

readjusted by the Holy See. On July 20, 1847, St. Louis became a Metropolitan See, by the Brief *Apostolici muneris,* but the choice of its suffragan Sees was left to the next Provincial Council of Balimore.[2]

The American Church now consisted of three Provinces: Baltimore, St. Louis and Oregon. Strictly speaking, the Seventh Provincial Council should have been the First Plenary Council; but the great distance prevented the Archbishop of Oregon and his suffragans from attending the Council. The pallium for Archbishop Kenrick did not reach the United States until August, 1848, and was conferred on Peter Richard by his brother, Bishop Kenrick, at Philadelphia, on September 3, 1848. However, the problem of the geographical extent of his metropolitan jurisdiction was not entirely settled, and Kenrick, though at the head of a province, sat in the Seventh Provincial Council as one of the presiding prelates of Baltimore.[3] The additional Sees of Albany, Buffalo, Cleveland, and Galveston between 1846 and 1849 brought the number of American dioceses up to twenty-nine.

When the Council met on May 5, 1849, several familiar faces were absent. Bishop Fenwick of Boston had passed away on August 11, 1846, and was succeeded by Bishop John Bernard Fitzpatrick, who had been consecrated as his coadjutor in 1844. Bishop de la Hailandière resigned the See of Vincennes on July 16, 1847, in a pathetic farewell letter to his flock,[4] and was succeeded by Rt. Rev. John Stephen Bazin, who was consecrated on October 24, 1847, and who died six months later on April 23, 1848. Bishop Maurice de St. Palais, who succeeded him, was consecrated on January 14, 1849.

In the treaty of peace between the United States and Mexico

---

[2] *Ibid.,* 40.

[3] It appears that the question of metropolitan dignity for St. Louis had been privately discussed in the Sixth Provincial Council of Baltimore (1846) and that at the suggestion of Bishop Francis P. Kenrick the question of the suffragan Sees was deferred (*Cf. Kenrick-Frenaye Letters,* 263, note. Philadelphia, 1920).

[4] *U. S. Cath. Magazine,* VI, 557.

at Guadalupe Hidalgo on February 2, 1848, New Mexico and Upper California were ceded to the United States and the spiritual jurisdiction over the Catholics in this territory passed to the American hierarchy. It was estimated at the time that New Mexico had about forty thousand Catholics and that there were about forty churches.[5]

A preparatory meeting took place at the archbishop's house on May 5, 1849. The *Promoters* chosen were again Bishops Portier and Chanche. The *Secretaries* were Fathers Lhomme and Damphoux. The *Masters of Ceremonies* were Fathers Lhomme and Rev. Mr. Francis E. Boyle. Father Gillet, C.SS.R., and Parsons were chosen as *Chanters*.

A larger number of *theologians* chosen by the respective prelates appeared at this Council; and there were also present as consultors the superiors of the Sulpicians, Vincentians, Benedictines, Dominicans, Augustinians, Jesuits, and Redemptorists. Among the *theologians* were the future bishops and archbishops —Thaddeus Amat, Thomas Foley, James Wood, John Loughlin, Augustin Verot, James O'Connor, William Elder, John J. Conroy, Michael Heiss, and Bernard O'Reilly, and such nationally known priests as Charles I. White, John McCaffrey, William Starrs, Charles Constantine Pise, and James Ryder, S.J.

The first Solemn Session was held the following day, Sunday, May 6, in the cathedral. Solemn Pontifical Mass was offered by Archbishop Eccleston, and the sermon was preached by Archbishop Kenrick of St. Louis. After the Mass, the conciliar oath was taken by the new bishops present for the first time— Rappe (Cleveland), Timon (Buffalo), Martin J. Spalding (Louisville), Maurice de St. Palais (Vincennes) and Vandevelde (Chicago).

At the first private congregation on May 7, the Fathers of the Council decided to solicit the Holy See for three new provinces or metropolitan Sees: *New Orleans,* with suffragan Sees at Mobile, Natchez, Little Rock, and Galveston; *New York,*

[5] *Metropolitan Catholic Almanac* (1849), 252-254.

with suffragan Sees at Boston, Hartford, Albany, and Buffalo; and *Cincinnati,* with suffragan Sees at Louisville, Detroit, Vincennes, and Cleveland. To the metropolitan jurisdiction of St. Louis, the Bishoprics of Dubuque, Nashville, Chicago and Milwaukee were assigned.

Added to these petitions was another which deserves special attention as reflecting the mind of the prelates on the organization of the Church in the United States. A resolution was unanimously passed asking the Holy See to confer upon the Archbishop of Baltimore the honor of the primacy, with its respective rights and privileges, over all the Sees in the United States. It was with the hope that Pius IX would confer this dignity upon the Baltimore metropolitan that they fixed upon the year 1850 for the First Plenary Council of the American Church. In its letter of approbation of the decrees of the Council of 1849, the Sacred Congregation de Propaganda Fide deferred action upon this request, without, however, stating its reason for the same.

It was also decided at this meeting to solicit the Holy See for permission to hold a Plenary or National Council at Baltimore in 1850. This request was embodied in the final decrees of the Council, but the Holy See postponed the assembly until 1852.

At the first public congregation (May 7), after hearing from the *theologians* present, the Fathers decided to petition the pope to make a doctrinal declaration on the Immaculate Conception of the Blessed Virgin Mary.

In the second private congregation (May 8), attended also by Bishop Andrew Byrne of Little Rock who arrived that day, the decision was reached to request the Holy See to erect a See at Savannah with jurisdiction over the Catholics in the States of Georgia and Florida, as suffragan to Baltimore. Bishop Hughes of New York requested that a coadjutor be appointed to Bishop Tyler of Hartford on account of his failing health.

The customary letters were decided upon at the third private congregation (May 9): the one to the Holy Father was entrusted to Bishop Michael O'Connor of Pittsburgh; the *Pastoral Letter* to Bishop F. P. Kenrick of Philadelphia; the letter to the Society for the Propagation of the Faith (Lyons) to Bishop Portier; and the one to the Vienna Leopoldine Association to Bishop Henni of Milwaukee.

The second Solemn Session, during a Council, as has already been pointed out, witnesses the celebration of a Solemn Mass of Requiem for all the bishops and priests of the province who had passed away since the last Council. Bishop Portier celebrated this Solemn Mass on May 10, and Bishop Purcell preached.

At the next private congregation (May 11), it was decided that in all the churches of the United States a collection be taken up on the Sunday within the octave of the feast of Sts. Peter and Paul, namely on July 1, for the Holy Father.[6] At this congregation it was decided to ask the Holy See for the erection of new Sees at Wheeling (in western Virginia), at St. Paul (to embrace the Territory of Minnesota), and a Vicariate-Apostolic for New Mexico.

At the sixth private congregation (May 12), in addition to the Sees decided upon the day before, the Fathers determined that the Diocese of Wheeling should be in the Province of Baltimore, and that the Diocese of St. Paul be included in the Province of St. Louis. They requested also that a vicariate should be erected in the "Indian Territory," the limits to be between the Rocky Mountains on the west, the States of Arkansas and Missouri on the east, and the Territory of Minnesota on the north.

Then, as was customary, in this final private congregation, the archbishop withdrew, and Archbishop Peter Richard Kenrick took the chair while a motion was made to thank Dr. Eccleston

[6] Owing to the political disorders created in Rome by the "Young Italy" party, Pius IX was obliged to leave Rome on November 24, 1848. He took up his residence in Gæta, where he remained until April 12, 1850, when he returned to Rome.

in the name of the Council *pro humanitate, comitate, et hospitalitate,* which he had shown to all during the assembly. Bishop Portier was chosen to take the *Acta et Decreta* of the Council to the Holy Father, then in exile at Gæta, and to express to him the sorrow of the American prelates over all the evils which had come upon the Holy See and over the atrocious treatment the pope had received from his own subjects in the papal states. Bishop Portier was requested also to visit Lyons to thank the Society of the Propagation of the Faith for its great generosity to the American Church.

The third Solemn Session was held on Sunday, May 13. Pontifical Mass was celebrated by Archbishop Eccleston and the sermon was delivered by Bishop Hughes. Then followed the *Acclamationes.* It is interesting to note that the second of these was in honor of Mary's Immaculate Conception:

Beatissimae Virgini Mariae, sine labe originali conceptae, harum Provinciarium Patronae, honor aeternus.

Six decrees, to which a seventh was added convoking the First Plenary Council for 1850, were passed in this last Provincial Council of Baltimore. In the first decree, in response to the Encyclical Letter of Pius IX to the bishops of the world, requesting that they inform the Holy See on the status of the devotion of the clergy and laity toward the Immaculate Conception of the Blessed Virgin Mary, the Fathers of the Council replied that throughout the United States this devotion was practiced with great fervor; and the second decree contains the petition to the pope to define as an article of faith the dogma that from the first instant of Her conception, Mary was free from original sin.

With the creation of two more ecclesiastical provinces, a modification was asked in the method of nominating bishops. The names of the priests to be promoted to the episcopal office in any province were to be sent to the other archbishops, who were to inform the Holy See of their judgment on the character of the candidates. Propaganda issued a rescript on August 10, 1850, agreeing with this new arrangement,

> that for the future, over and above the previous prescriptions, the archbishop in whose province the vacancy occurs, will transmit to the other archbishops of the nation, the names proposed. Each archbishop will then send his observations on the priests recommended to the Holy See.[7]

The fourth decree stated that all churches and other ecclesiastical property donated to the Church or resulting from collections among the faithful should belong to the Ordinary of the diocese, unless it appeared by written documents that they belonged to some religious Order or Congregation. In the fifth decree, the regulation of former Councils was repeated, that no priest was to be permitted to go from one diocese to another unless it was certain that the other bishop would receive him, and no dismissorial letters were to be given unless it was clear that the bishop who was to accept the priest was willing to do so. In the sixth decree priests were strictly forbidden to marry those who had already been married by a non-Catholic minister or who intended so to be married. The final decree, as we have seen, stated that a National Council was to be held, with the authority of the Holy See, in 1850, "in order the better and more easily to provide for the advantage and benefit of religion in these States."

The decrees are signed by Archbishops Eccleston and Peter Richard Kenrick and by twenty-three suffragan bishops.

The letter to the Holy Father, Pius IX, dated May 13, 1849, expresses in the same noble strain as in previous Councils the love and loyalty of the Church in the United States for the Holy See. After thanking God for the marvelous advance of the Faith in the United States and for the piety and devotion of the priests and people, the Fathers submit the decrees of the Council for the pope's approbation, and at the same time deplore the calamities which had befallen him. The petition for the new

[7] *Concilia habita etc.*, 291.

archbishoprics is embodied in a separate letter of the same date. The Holy See decided that Savannah and Wheeling were to be suffragans of Baltimore, that St. Paul should be included in the Province of St. Louis, and that no change be made in the juridic status of the Diocese of Monterey. The letter to Vienna, of the same date, is a summary of all that the Church in the United States owed to the Leopoldine Association during the twenty years of its existence. Propaganda's letter (August 9, 1850) is a formal announcement of the erection of the new Sees and the appointment of their incumbents. Father Francis X. Gartland was selected for Savannah, Bernard O'Reilly for Hartford, Richard V. Whelan for Wheeling, Joseph Cretin for St. Paul, Joseph McGill for Richmond, and John Lamy for the Vicariate-Apostolic of Santa Fé. Bishop Joseph Sadoc Alemany, O.P., who had been consecrated at Rome on June 30, 1850, as successor to Bishop Garcia Diego, was not to be considered for the time being as a suffragan of Baltimore. The Mexican government had refused to permit the exercise of jurisdiction in Lower California on the part of the Bishop of Monterey, and Pius IX made the See subject immediately to the Holy See until the question of the province to which it belonged was settled.[8] Another decree from Propaganda (August 10, 1850) settled the question of the boundary lines between the Dioceses of Philadelphia and Pittsburgh.

Previous to Propaganda's action, the Holy See on July 19, 1850, erected the Archdioceses of New York, Cincinnati, and New Orleans, so that the Church in the United States by the close of that year comprised six ecclesiastical provinces—Baltimore, Oregon, St. Louis, Cincinnati, New York, and New Orleans. The number of suffragan Sees was twenty-seven, with two vicariates (New Mexico and Indian Territory). A tabular summary in the *Metropolitan Catholic Directory* for 1851 gives

[8] On July 29, 1853, in response to the suggestion of the First Plenary Council of Baltimore (1852), Pius IX erected the Province of San Francisco, with Monterey as a suffragan See, and Dr. Alemany became first archbishop of the new province.

the following statistics: churches, 1245; stations, 585; priests in the ministry, 1146; priests otherwise engaged, 157; seminaries, 28; clerical students, 322; colleges for young men, 36; academies for young girls, 65; charitable institutions, 108; and a total Catholic population of 1,334,500.

There is nothing in the *Pastoral Letter* of 1849 of interest to the history of canonical legislation.

Such, briefly, is the story of the canonical legislation of the seven (national) Provincial Councils of Baltimore between 1829 and 1849. From the ages occasionally given, it is evident that the prelates with few exceptions were men in the prime of life; and from what we know of them almost all were strong and vigorous. The fatigues of travel had become less and less as railroads increased, and nothing could measure the ineffable courage each prelate felt in these triennial assemblies with his colleagues. The Faith was increasing as in no other part of the world. The demands made upon our bishops to keep pace with the frontier movement westward through the erection of churches, schools, and welfare institutions were veritably colossal; but they went forward gallantly from year to year building the House of God in this country on foundations so strong that we of the present day must marvel at that profound trust in God which carried them through untold sacrifices and anxieties. Each Council seemed to be the harbinger of a new era of zeal and devotion for the Cause of Christ in the United States. Every problem, whether of external misunderstanding and opposition or of internal disorder and disobedience, was met firmly, honestly and without compromise. The consolidation of the work of our prelates in the three Plenary Councils of 1852, 1866, and 1884, was made possible by the canonical enactments of the provincial assemblies which had preceded them. To the nation at large, especially to those of other creeds, these seven Provincial Councils were in turn the occasion of an admiration and a consolation which was not allowed to pass in silence.

Amid the sectional hatreds, created by political, social and industrial conditions, the Catholic Church in the United States presented a strong bond of unity, practically the only stable unity, in the country. The nation was to benefit by that social asset during the dark days that followed the last of the Provincial Councils in 1849 up to the beginning of the fratricidal strife of the Civil War, and afterwards, when so little, except the force of arms, could be depended upon to keep America one and indivisible.

PART IV

THE PLENARY COUNCILS OF BALTIMORE

CHAPTER XV

THE FIRST PLENARY COUNCIL (1852)

THE reconstruction of the hierarchical divisions of the American Church between the last of the Provincial Councils (1849) and the First Plenary Council which began its deliberations on May 8, 1852, resulted in an ecclesiastical jurisdiction divided between six metropolitan Sees—Baltimore, Oregon, St. Louis, New York, Cincinnati, and New Orleans. To these were subject in provincial affairs twenty-six suffragan dioceses and two vicariates-apostolic, with the Diocese of Monterey for the time being subject directly to Rome.

An important, but highly jejune, chapter in the history of canonical legislation in the United States is the promulgation through diocesan synods of the Baltimore enactments between 1829 and 1849. After that date, or to be more precise, after July 19, 1850, when the Holy See created the three new provinces which gave us these six metropolitan Sees, our interest lies rather with the provincial councils held in these great divisions of the American Church. Before passing on to the First Plenary Council, the last of these diocesan synods directly affected by the Baltimore legislation may be chronicled. John Gilmary Shea was able to discover only three diocesan synods in the interim. What was probably the second Diocesan Synod of Cincinnati was held early in December, 1849, at which the dividing line between the Dioceses of Cincinnati and Cleveland was agreed upon.[1] There is a mention of an informal synod in Louisville under Bishop Spalding in July, 1850, at which statutes

[1] *Op. cit.*, IV, 181. Lamott, *History of the Archdiocese of Cincinnati (1821-1921)*, 209, mentions a first synod of 1837, but makes no mention of the Synod of 1849.

were drawn up for the better administration of the diocese.[2] The first Synod of California was convened at San Francisco on March 13, 1852.[3]

Doubtless, the American prelates were waiting for the First Plenary Council which, in 1849, they expected to see convened the following year. When the Council began its deliberations on May 8, 1852, all who were present sensed the fact that they were participating in one of the major events in the history of the American Church. The eyes of the entire nation were upon the stately procession that moved from the archbishop's house on the morning of Sunday, May 9, to the cathedral. The six archbishops and twenty-four prelates, robed in rich vestments, carrying their croziers and wearing miters, preceded by hundreds of priests, secular and regular, many of whom were to take part in the proceedings, made a picture of old-world beauty never seen before in the United States. To the prelates, officials, theologians, and those invited to sit in the Council, the dominant thought was the Church, its doctrine, worship, and discipline, and the problems which her leaders here were grappling with; problems far more complex than any that had been met in former conciliar assemblies. Few periods in our ecclesiastical history witnessed so marvelous an advance in progress as the three crowded years between the Councils of 1849 and 1852. By this latter year, the full force and weight of the tremendous immigration that had set in during the famine years in Ireland and the revolutions of 1848 throughout continental Europe were felt in all their serious portent for the future of Catholicism in the United States. How to control this vast inpouring

---

[2] *Constitutiones Dioecesis Ludovicopolitanae, a Reverendissimo ac Illustrissimo Domino Martino Joanne Spalding, Episcopo Ludovicopolitano, in Synodo Dioecesana prima, habita mense Julii 1850 in Ecclesia St. Josephi, Bardopoli, latae et promulgatae.* 20 pp. (Louisville, 1850). *Cf.* Spalding, *Life of Archbishop Spalding,* 141.

[3] Engelhardt, "The First Ecclesiastical Synod of California, March 19-23, 1852," in *Cath. Hist. Review,* I, 30-37, where the decrees are printed for the first time; they have mainly to do with the support of the clergy and mixed marriages.

of newcomers, how to mold them quickly and effectively to American ideals, how to provide for their ministration, especially for those on the frontier, how to curtail swiftly any tendencies to disturb the even and serene order created by the Provincial Councils—these were the principal ideas in the minds of our hierarchy. To the outsider, there was an added interest. Between 1844 and 1852, the Protestant Churches were splitting up into denominational and territorial divisions. The Methodist, Baptist, and Presbyterian Churches were losing their unity over the abolition problem—a unity never since recaptured; and with every social and religious institution in the nation straining and breaking under the dead weight of the slavery agitation, it was inevitable that to thousands of well-meaning men and women in the land, the question would arise: What action would the Catholic Church take in this crisis?

There was no more unity in Catholic ranks on the slave question than in those of the prominent Christian Churches at that time. It seemed inevitable that, with the whole nation roused to intense feelings, even as early as 1852, over the problem of slavery, Catholics and non-Catholics would expect the Council—the first of its kind in our history—to cast its voice either with slavery or with abolition. There had been passages at arms between our prelates of the North and of the South and between those of each section among themselves. All knew what the doctrine of the Church was, but all knew instinctively that this foremost political problem of the day had become too complex and was being too bitterly discussed to permit any hope that the moral distinction between slavery and the slave trade (as made clear by Gregory XVI in his letter of 1839 and by Dr. England's *Letters to Forsyth*) would be heeded. When, therefore, as the Council proceeded, it became evident that the attending prelates had decided to keep silent on the question, neither condemning nor condoning slavery, Catholics realized more acutely than ever the real meaning of the Church's place in American life, and non-Catholics appreciated the fact that here was a body of American spiritual leaders who meant to bring to the disturbed condition of the times the one asset the country needed: peace and calm. Silence was the only boon which alone would quiet the dissension and would permit the problem to be solved naturally. By their silence our prelates divorced this burning political question from Church affairs and gave to the deliberations of the Council that unity of Catholic outlook which was basic in the legislation that was passed.[4]

The greatest loss the Church here suffered between the two Councils was the death of Archbishop Eccleston on April 22, 1851. He had been the presiding officer over the last five Provincial Councils; he knew all the older members of the hierarchy intimately, had seen a new and younger generation of bishops arise to take their places, and had guided with uncommon tact and wisdom the legislation of the last score of years. From 1834 to 1847, as Archbishop of Baltimore, he was the supreme ruler, after the pope, of the Catholic Church in this country. His experience was of an exceptionally wide expanse in ecclesiastical affairs; and young as he was at the time of his consecration, no choice could have been more advantageous to the Faith here. During the seventeen years of his rule over the Province of Baltimore (1834-1851), an amazing increase of Catholic life and action was visible everywhere in the United States, especially in the West and Far West; and before his death he could look out over the Church here and recognize a growth scarcely to be surpassed in any period of ecclesiastical history. The primacy which the Council of 1849 had unsuccessfully solicited for him was his all through his episcopate by the common consent of his colleagues in the hierarchy.

His successor, Francis Patrick Kenrick, was then in the prime of life and was equally gifted with the virtues of leadership. His learning far exceeded that of any of his fellow bishops, and at the time he was selected by the Holy See as Eccleston's suc-

---

[4] Murphy, "Catholic Church in the United States during the Civil War Period (1852-1866)" *Records,* Amer. Cath. Hist. Society, XXXIX (Dec., 1928), 271-346.

cessor (August 3, 1851) his reputation for scholarship was internationally recognized.

The hierarchical development between 1849 and 1852 was an exceptional one. The erection of the Vicariate of the Indian Territory in 1851 left no part of the United States without its spiritual leader. The result was that as fast as the frontier was pushed westward, the Church kept pace with the movement, placing bishops at strategic points in all the territory west of the Mississippi. The consecrations of new bshops during these three years were not delayed, and ten priests were advancd to the episcopal order during this short interim and were to be found, when the Council of 1852 was convoked, in the fields assigned to them.

If we may accept as fairly accurate the survey given by the *Metropolitan,* a monthly Catholic magazine begun in Baltimore in February 1853, the statistics for 1852 contain the following: there were twenty-eight theological seminaries in thirty-four dioceses with three hundred and thirty-one students for the priesthood; the preparatory seminaries were five in number, with about two hundred students. From Georgetown College in the District of Columbia to Santa Clara College in California, twenty-five colleges for young men might be counted, with close to twenty-five hundred students. There were one hundred academies for young women. From the eighty churches in 1808, the number had increased to seventeen hundred and eleven in 1852. The clergy had grown from a little band of sixty-eight in 1808, to thirteen hundred and five by the time the Council of 1852 met in Baltimore; the number of Catholics in the nation was fast approaching the two-million mark; and the whole marvelous growth will seem to reach a climax in the Council itself when the decision is reached to place bishops in Portland (Maine), Burlington, Brooklyn, Newark, Erie, Covington, Quincy, Santa Fé, Natchitoches, and Upper Michigan, and to create San Francisco a metropolitan See.

The problems awaiting the deliberations of the prelates were more varied and complex than those of any previous assembly. There were few internal difficulties to settle, but the administration of Church affairs and the guidance of the faithful had become exceedingly perplexing owing to the almost unbelievable number of Catholic immigrants who came here during the previous decade and to the fact that the political temper of the country, through the Know-nothing movement, was coldly hostile to the great progress the Church was making.

The Seven Provincial Councils had succeeded in establishing a uniform system of ecclesiastical discipline in conformity to the general laws of the Church, and the Fathers of 1852 had before them the delicate task of consolidating that unity without in any way arousing latent variances of opinion in the racial divergencies or sectional sentiment. The success of the 1852 assembly in this respect was remarkable, if one compares it with the failure of the social, educational, and political agencies striving to accomplish the same end for the country at large. The internal domestic problems of the Church were also of serious import. These were: the parochial division of missionary labor in the dioceses, the defining of accurate geographical limits for the provinces and dioceses, the ever-present evils arising from mixed marriages, the problem of Catholic elementary education, the care of Catholics in the army and navy, uniformity of ritual observance, and the canonical status of pastors.

By the Brief *In Apostolicae Sedis fastigio* of August 19, 1851, Pius IX appointed Dr. Kenrick, then Archbishop-Elect of Baltimore, as Apostolic Delegate for the Council of 1852. The chief reason for the convocation of the Council, the Brief stated, was to bring about as far as possible a more complete uniformity of ecclesiastical order and discipline in the United States. Kenrick's thorough knowledge of canon law, his success in mastering the unhappy situation in Philadelphia, and his devotion to the Holy See were the causes for his elevation to the metropolitan See of Baltimore and for his election as Apostolic Delegate to preside over the Council.[5]

[5] *Concilia habita etc.*, 2d part, 4.

On November 21, 1851, Dr. Kenrick issued the letter of convocation, assembling the prelates for May 9, 1852. The object
for which the Council was summoned was:

By wise enactments and measures to promote discipline, and
enforce the sacred Canons; or to submit such modifications of them
as local circumstances may require, to the mature and enlightened
judgment of the chief bishop, who is divinely charged with the
solicitude of all the churches. We come together, brethren, not for
idle display of ceremonial pomp, but to take mutual counsel after
imploring divine guidance, for we watch, *as being to render an
account of your souls.* The power committed to us by Our Lord
is to be exercised for edification, for the building up of the body
of Christ, whose members should be closely joined in religious
communion.[6]

A preliminary meeting of the prelates was held on Saturday
evening, May 8, 1852, in the archbishop's house. There were
present the six metropolitans of the country: F. P. Kenrick,
F. N. Blanchet, P. R. Kenrick, Blanc, Hughes, and Purcell; and
twenty-three bishops, together with Bishop Alemany of Monterey whose presence the Holy See had specially requested: *quem
huic Concilio interesse voluit Sanctissimus.* Bishops de St. Palais
(Vincennes) and Cretin (St. Paul) had not arrived in Baltimore. There was present also Bishop Count de Charbonnel of
Toronto, who was in the city at the time.

The officials of the Council were selected at this meeting and
five committees were appointed for the dispatch of all affairs
coming before the prelates in the private or public congregations. The *Promoters* were Bishop Chanche and Father
Lhomme, then Vicar-General of the Archdiocese of Baltimore.
Father Damphoux was chosen as *Notary,* and the *Secretaries*
were the future bishops Rev. P. N. Lynch and Rev. Thomas
Foley. Father Francis Burlando, C.M., was made *Master of
Ceremonies,* and the *Chanters* were Father De Goesbriand and
Rev. Mr. John Dougherty. The committees selected were as
follows: 1. *Committee on Questions of Canon Law:* (Blanc,
chairman, Lefebre, O'Connor, Fitzpatrick, Spalding, Alemany

[6] Cited in *National Pastorals etc.,* 181.

and O'Reilly); 2. *Committee on the Administration of Church Property* (Hughes, *chairman*, Miles, O'Connor, A. M. Blanchet, A. Byrne, Timon, and Lamy); 3. *Committee on the Catholic Education of Youth and Allied Matters* (Purcell, *chairman*, Chanche, Whelan, McCloskey, Alemany, McGill, Neumann); 4. *Committee on the Ritual* (F. N. Blanchet, *chairman*, Loras, Odin, Vandevelde, Reynolds, and Rappe); and 5. *Committee on Contentious Cases* (Portier, *chairman*, Lefebre, Chanche, Henni, Whelan, Reynolds and Rappe).

During this preparatory meeting, the question of the erection of new Sees was broached, and it was decided that the suffragan bishops of the province where a new diocese was to be created should present the names of three priests deemed worthy of the episcopal order. These names would then be made known to the other archbishops in the private congregations devoted to that subject and the advice of all the bishops would be asked before selecting the names to be sent to the Holy See. The minor regulations as laid down by the Council of Trent were also agreed upon for the official procedure of the Council. Private congregations were to be held in the morning at ten o'clock, and at noon the prelates alone would take up the question of new Sees and their incumbents. Dinner was to be served each day at two o'clock in the afternoon in the archbishop's house. A chapter of the Holy Gospel was to be read at the beginning of the meal and the martyrology at the end. Conversation was permitted *ut recreentur animi, et dilectio foveatur.* The customary letters were then assigned to their writers. The letter to the Holy Father was confided to Bishop O'Connor (Pittsburgh); the one to the Society of Paris-Lyons to Bishop Portier (Mobile); a third, in German, to the Leopoldine Association, to Bishop Neumann (Philadelphia); the fourth, to the hierarchy of Ireland, to Archbishop Purcell; and the fifth, the *Pastoral Letter to the Clergy and Laity,* to Archbishop Peter Richard Kenrick. For the second time, a series of evening sermons in the cathedral was announced, those preaching being Archbishops Purcell and Hughes, Bishop McGill, Dr. Lynch, Father Charles Stonestreet, S.J., and Father William Murphy, S.J.

The first Solemn Session was held on Sunday, May 9, in the cathedral. Solemn Pontifical Mass was celebrated by the Apostolic Delegate, and Archbishop Hughes preached on Church unity as displayed by the Council itself. "You see before you," he said, "many of the first pastors of the Holy Catholic Church, coming from within limits extending from sea to sea—the most of them never met together before." [7] Among the forty-one *theologians* chosen by the respective bishops were the future prelates: Verot, O'Regan, Perché, Loughlin, James Roosevelt Bayley, Young, Conroy, and Quarter.

The Council was then opened with the ceremonies of the Pontifical, and the prelates in attendance for the first time took the customary conciliar oath. In the first private congregation (May 10) the questions brought up for discussion were: the ecclesiastical province to which the Diocese of Monterey should belong; the diocesan limits between Covington, Cincinnati, and Louisville; the extraordinary faculties of the bishops; and the controversy between Archbishop Blanchet and the Oblates. Bishops Timon, Alemany and A. M. Blanchet were appointed a committee to draw up a formula of prayers for the conversion of non-Catholics. The *Manual of Ceremonies,* compiled in 1840 by Bishop Rosati, and published by the John Murphy Company, of Baltimore, was given to the special Committee on the Ritual for examination. The fourth decree of the Council formally adopted the *Manual* for all the churches in the United States. The first public congregation (May 10) was devoted to the question whether it was expedient to publish the Tridentine decree on marriage. At the second private congregation (May 11) the Fathers debated over granting a decisive vote in their deliberations to the Abbot of the Trappist monastery of Gethsemane; at the public congregation that afternoon the problem of Catholic elementary schools was debated and an affirmative de-

[7] *Works,* II, 195.

cree was agreed upon, placing the whole question beyond debate in the future. In the third private congregation (May 12) the Fathers decided to petition the Holy See for the privilege of using the short form for baptism, either for twenty years or in perpetuity. Various questions were discussed in the next public congregation: secret societies, rebellious trustees, the legal incorporation of Church property, Catholic children in public schools, and freedom for Catholic worship in the army and navy. The legislation of the seven Provincial Councils of Baltimore was then solemnly promulgated anew and their decrees made applicable to the whole country.

The second Solemn Session took place in the cathedral on Thursday, May 13, when Bishop Chanche (who died shortly after the Council, on July 22, 1852) celebrated Pontifical Mass of Requiem for the happy repose of the souls of the bishops who had died since the Council of 1849 (Eccleston, Flaget, and Tyler). The sermon was preached by Bishop Spalding of Louisville, who was to preside as Apostolic Delegate over the Second Plenary Council of 1866.

At the fourth and fifth public congregations the *theologians* discussed the question whether it was expedient to extend a canonical status to pastors in this country. A committee was appointed (P. R. Kenrick, Blanc, and Hughes) at the fifth private congregation (May 14) for the purpose of ascertaining what dispensations from the Lenten fast might be accorded to the bishops of western Sees. Another committee (Reynolds, Timon, and Spalding) was named to settle the vexed question of a uniform Catechism in English, and Bishop Neumann was instructed to inform the Fathers of the best Catechism in German. It was also decided to restrict the privilege of publishing Catechisms enjoyed by Catholic publishers. A decree was also passed forbidding the burial of Catholics in unconsecrated ground, unless it were a case of necessity. At the next (sixth) private congregation the Bishops of Louisville, Philadelphia, and Monterey were selected to catalogue the changes, corrections and additions to be made in the *Manual of Ceremonies,* and the Holy See was to be asked to allow the American Church to use the Roman Calendar. The religious celebration of national holidays came up for discussion as did also that of the extraordinary faculties of the bishops for mixed marriages and for the first degree of affinity and the second degree of consanguinity. It was also decided not to promulgate for the Church at large the Tridentine decree on marriage. By a vote of twenty-three to seven, it was decided to insist upon the publication of the banns. Another vote (eighteen to thirteen) was passed to the effect that the Holy See would be petitioned to decide upon the extent to which the *Tametsi* was obligatory in the different American dioceses in order that some kind of uniformity might be agreed upon.

A third Solemn Session took place on Sunday, May 16, in the cathedral. Solemn Pontifical Mass was celebrated by Archbishop Blanchet and the sermon was preached by Bishop O'Connor of Pittsburgh. At the end of the Mass, all the decrees so far passed were publicly read and promulgated.

The seventh private congregation (May 17) decided to ask the Holy See for ample faculties for marriage cases; and the Fathers expressed the wish that, instead of an oath, a solemn promise by the two parties (Catholic and non-Catholic) in a mixed marriage should suffice. The curriculum of studies in the seminaries was brought up for discussion in the public congregation that afternoon, as were the questions of canonical parishes and the marriage of those without a domicile.

Reports from the standing Committees were heard at the eighth private congregation (May 18), and Bishop Alemany read a memorandum on the status of the Pious Fund. In the three final private congregations (May 19-20), the drafts of the conciliar letters were read and approved. A proposal to create a society for the support of the parochial schools was lost by one vote.

The fourth and last Solemn Session was held in the cathedral on Thursday, May 20, the feast of the Ascension that year, Pontifical Mass being celebrated by Archbishop Blanc and the sermon given by Bishop Fitzpatrick of Boston. Then followed the *Acclamationes,* the *Te Deum,* and the closing ceremonies as defined by the Pontifical.

The twenty-five decrees of the Council of 1852 may be viewed as the consolidation of the legislation which had been passed in all the national assemblies up to that year, and as the most important step so far made by the hierarchy for complete uniformity of Church life in the United States. The second decree in fact extended the decrees passed in the seven Provincial Councils to the entire country as the law of the American Church. In the first decree, the primacy and the supreme apostolic authority of the pope were solemnly acclaimed and the doctrines taught by the apostles and their successors, especially in the general councils and particularly in the Council of Trent, were solemnly acknowledged. To Pius IX, as the head of the whole Catholic episcopate, they offered their allegiance and reverence. The third decree ordered that the Roman Ritual, adopted by the Council of 1829, be followed as the uniform ceremonial of the Church here and be scrupulously observed in all the American dioceses; also that the *Manual of Ceremonies,* as ordered by the same Council and as approved by Gregory XVI (1841), be faithfully carried out in all the churches. The fifth decree repeated the words of the Council of Trent [8] regarding the residence of bishops; and the American prelates legislated for themselves that they were not to be absent from their dioceses without the permission of the Holy See, the metropolitan or the senior suffragan bishop. For just causes a bishop might be absent for three months without such a permission.[9] The bishops were exhorted by the sixth decree to choose a council of learned and prudent priests, who, as consultors, would assist them in the administration of the diocese, and the custom of a monthly

[8] Sess. XXIII, c. 2, *de. Ref.*
[9] Smith, *Elements of Ecclesiastical Law,* I: *Ecclesiastical Persons,* 308-310.

meeting with the Consultors was recommended. Apparently, since the Council merely advised the creation of this advisory board, few dioceses followed the injunction. The Second Plenary Council (1866) also advised it, but the Third (1884) found it necessary to command that the system be put immediately into practice.[10] The seventh decree considered favorably the necessity of constituting diocesan chanceries for the orderly arrangements of Church affairs as well as for a uniform official system of diocesan management. In the next decree the bishops were counseled to appoint a *Censor librorum*, especially for prayer-books and books of devotion. The custom of seeking an *imprimatur* of any other Ordinary than the one in whose diocese books were published was deprecated. Lest priests who were unknown or who were wanderers from place to place be too easily accepted, the prelates were warned to take precautionary measures for their reception, especially of those coming from Europe. Without explicit documents testifying to their character and merit, such priests in the future were to be refused diocesan faculties.

In the tenth decree, it was stipulated that missionary districts and parishes were to be given definite limits. The banns of marriage were to be proclaimed in all churches after Easter, 1853, and the bishops were ordered to grant no dispensation from the ruling, except in grave necessity.[11] Priests were instructed to institute catechetical classes in their parishes, and the duty of instructing the young in the doctrines of the faith was not to be delegated to others. The thirteenth decree is an advance upon similar enactments of the Provincial Councils regarding the establishment of parochial schools. The bishops were exhorted *per viscera misericordiae Dei* to begin these schools whenever possible in their dioceses, since Catholic boys and girls were in grave danger in educational institutions which were not directed by religious motives. Competent teachers

[10] Smith, *ibid.*, 465-466.
[11] Roberts, *The Banns of Marriage* (Washington, D. C., 1931), 45.

were to be provided out of the Church funds if necessary. The fourteenth decree urged the erection of a seminary in each diocese, and where this was not financially practicable, then the dioceses of a province should combine to create a provincial seminary for the training of the clergy. In the next decree the Fathers determined that the Ordinary, either personally or through a priest appointed for this purpose, exact an accounting of the administration of all Church property whether incorporated in the name of the clergy or laity. Although the evils of the trustee system had practically disappeared by 1852, the legal incorporation of ecclesiastical property was not a satisfactory one, and hence this decree was issued in order to safeguard ecclesiastical property from alienation or maladministration. Hence, also, the following decree distinctly forbidding lay persons from enjoying any right or privilege, without the consent of the Ordinary, in regulating the use of Church funds. Any usurpation of such rights or privileges was to be punished according to the Tridentine decree on the subject.[12] The seventeenth decree warned the clergy to eliminate all lay interference in Church affairs and to prevent the selection of lay trustees, lest any hindrance arise in the matter of the free administration of Church revenues.

The ritual for the Benediction of the Blessed Sacrament, as given in the *Ceremonial,* was to be strictly followed throughout the United States. The nineteenth decree brought out clearly a situation, now happily changed and not known to many at the time, the utter disregard for the religious rights of Catholic men in the American army and navy. The Society for the Propagation of the Faith of Paris-Lyons was to be established in all our dioceses,[13] and the faithful were also to be urged to become

[12] Godfrey, *The Right of Patronage* (Wash., D. C., 1929), 141.
[13] Statistics of the amounts contributed by the Catholics of the United States from 1840 on will be found in Hickey, *Society for the Propagation of the Faith* (Wash., D. C., 1922), 125. The amount contributed in 1851 was $600.00; in 1852, $16,026.41. Seven years later it was $37,730.81.

members of the Society for the Conversion of non-Catholics. The twenty-second and twenty-fourth decrees dealt with marriage cases, and a former decree regarding clandestine marriages was reënacted. The concession of using the shorter form for the baptism of adults was to be asked for in perpetuity. The last (twenty-fifth) decree stated that the decrees of the Council were to have force of law once they had been approved by the Holy See and printed by the authority of the Archbishop of Baltimore.

The decrees of 1852 were signed by the Archbishops of Baltimore, Oregon, St. Louis, New Orleans, New York and Cincinnati, by twenty-five of their suffragans, and by Bishop Alemany of Monterey.

The letter of the hierarchy to Pope Pius IX, dated May 19, 1852, describes the significant increase in the Church here since the last Provincial Council of 1849 and the encouraging spirit of devotion shown by priests and people throughout the country. The six archbishops and twenty-six bishops who participated in the Council were returning to their respective Sees filled with enthusiasm for the future of Catholicism in the United States. The loyalty of all to the Holy See is described, as is also the admiration of the American Church for the courage shown by Pius IX in the recent political disturbances in Italy.

Propaganda's letter (September 26, 1852) approved the decrees of the Council, but a private message was sent to Archbishop Kenrick regarding the growth of exceptions as well as the danger that lay in a too rigid *national* uniformity. Everything that tended by an accumulation of exceptions to give the American Church the semblance of a *national* Church was to be avoided. That same day a decree was issued granting the shorter form of baptism for adults for five years. An indult of September 5, 1852, sanctioned the formation of the Society of Prayers for the Conversion of non-Catholics and gave the prayer for the same. There is also a letter from Propaganda (October 23, 1852) containing instructions on the support of the bishops and on the method of receiving members of religious Orders into the United States.

The *Catholic Almanac* for 1854 gives a table (see p. 183) showing the *State of Catholicity in the United States in 1808, and Its Progress from That Time to the Present.*

Fourteen years were to pass before the Second Plenary Council was called in 1866; and the legislation of the Council of 1852, meager as it appears beside that of 1866 and of 1884, proved to be what the Church in the United States needed for guidance during those perplexing years which preceded the outbreak of the Civil War. Perhaps, the outstanding proof of the wisdom of our prelates lies in their silence over the slavery question, then dividing political parties and the Churches of other denominations into antagonistic groups which have never been wholly reconciled. Many expected at the time that this largest and greatest of all Catholic official assemblies in our history up to 1852 would take cognizance of the political debate on the slavery question and would issue a definite statement of the Church's position; but the hierarchy rejected the apparent demand for such a decision and refused to break with the traditional policy of the Church which excluded rigorously all discussions on political debate. The prelates were face to face with problems of far greater moment in their efforts to keep abreast of the tide of immigration to our shores. No other Church in the land, then as now, has realized the supreme need of keeping itself free from political questions; and no other Church has sympathized more profoundly with the basic American distrust of ecclesiastical interference in public life. It was this wisdom which served the Catholic body during the violence caused by Archbishop Bedini's visit the year after the Council closed (1853-1854),[14]

[14] *Cf.* Guilday, "Four Early Ecclesiastical Observers in America," *Ecclesiastical Review*, LXXXV (Sept., 1931), 249-254.

YEAR	1808	1830	1834	1840	1841	1842	1843	1844	1845	1846	1847	1848	1849	1850	1851	1852	1853	1854
Dioceses	1	11	11	16	16	16	16	21	21	21	†23	27	27	27	31	§32	32	41
Apostolic Vicariates								1	1	1	1	1			2	2	2	2
Bishops	2	*10	11	17	17	21	18	†17	25	25	26	27	26	27	32	32	32	39
Priests	68	232	316	482	528	541	561	617	683	737	834	890	1000	1081	1271	1385	1471	1574
Churches	80	230	299	454	512	541	560	611	675	740	812	907	966	1073	1245	1411	1545	1712
Stations				358	394	470	475	461	592	560	577	572	560	505	585	681	627	746
Eccles. Institutions	2	9	9	13	14	17	18	19	22	22	22	22	25	29	28	34	33	34
Colleges	‖1	6	6	9	10	11	11	11	12	14	14	14	15	17	18	19	20	20
Female Academies	2	20	20	47	49	49	48	48	63	63	63	74	86	91	87	100	102	112

This table shows that from 1834-44, the personal and material force of the Church in the United States increased at the rate of about 100 per cent; the number of dioceses, bishops, priests, churches, seminaries, colleges and female academies, having about doubled during that period. During the last ten years, nearly the same ratio is observable, except in the number of churches and priests: in these departments the ratio of increase has been about 170 per cent. * Archbishops and bishops are included in the same enumeration. † And eight bishops elect. ‡ The districts of Fort Hall, etc., in Oregon, are not included in this table. ‖ The figure of colleges expresses, as well as could be ascertained, the incorporated institutions. § Nesqually this year became an episcopal see.

as well as during the strident anti-Catholic movement of the Know-nothing party between 1854 and the Civil War.

As in previous assemblies, the legislation of the Council of 1852 should not be separated historically from the *Pastoral Letter* issued at the close of the meeting. The *Pastoral* opens with a noble statement of our allegiance to the Holy See and assures the clergy and the laity of their charge that "notwithstanding the diversity of origin, customs and language," a cordial union characterizes the Catholic body of the United States; a union exemplified by their docility and obedience and by their general fervor and devotedness in the exercise of the virtues of the Gospel. Episcopal authority is then defined and its source or channel, the Bishop of Rome and the Vicar of Christ, is described. The Fathers rejoiced at the occasion the Council gave them of proclaiming their "attachment to the centre of Catholic unity," and they exhorted all, priests and people, "to cherish a love for the Holy See, in which is preserved an unbroken succession of Pastors from the time of Christ to the present day." Certain causes for the breach of this unity in the past are mentioned, and among these is the interference of the laity in Church administration. The grave necessity of supporting the bishops in maintaining Church discipline is then proclaimed as an offset to the encroachment of evils in the ranks of clergy and faithful.

The needs of the Church "in this vast country, so rapidly advancing in population and prosperity," imposed upon the bishops, we read—"peculiar and arduous duties. We not only have to build up the Church, by the preaching of the Gospel, and the inculcation of all the virtues it teaches, but also to supply the material wants of religious worship in proportion to the unexampled rapidity with which our flocks increase. We have to establish missions in places where, but a few years since, none, or but few, Catholics were to be found, and where now the children of the Church cry with clamorous importunity for the bread of life. We have to build the Church where before

God's name was not publicly worshiped; and to multiply his temples where they no longer suffice for the constantly increasing wants of the faithful. We have to provide a ministry for the present and future wants of the country, and, in this matter, have to contend with difficulties which are unknown in countries where Religion has been long established, and where the piety and zeal of past generations have furnished ample means for this most important object. We have to provide for the Catholic education of our youth. Not only have we to erect and maintain the Church, the Seminary and the Schoolhouse, but we have to found Hospitals, establish orphanages, and provide for every want of suffering humanity, which Religion forbids us to neglect. We thank the Giver of all good gifts for the extraordinary benediction which He has hitherto bestowed upon our efforts, and those of the venerable men whose places we fill. We rejoice at having the opportunity of bearing public testimony to the generous assistance which we have received from our flocks in our respective dioceses. Much, however, as has been done, much still remains to be accomplished. Our churches are nowhere equal to the wants of the Catholic population, and in many places are far from being sufficiently spacious to afford one-half of our people the opportunity of attending Divine worship."

The education of priests, the great solicitude of the prelates over Catholic schools, the work of the Society of the Propagation of the Faith, and other questions are treated in this admirable *Letter*. Not unmindful of the constant attacks upon the Catholic body on the score of its spiritual allegiance to the Holy See, the Fathers admonished the faithful to show forth in their daily lives their attachment to the institutions of our beloved country by prompt compliance with all their civil duties, and by the cautious jealousy with which they would guard against the least deviation from the rules which were prescribed for the maintenance of public order and private rights: "Thus will you refute the idle babbling of foolish men, and will best approve yourselves worthy of the privileges which you enjoy, and overcome, by the sure test of practical patriotism, all the prejudices which a misapprehension of your principles but too often produces." The *Letter* closes with a touching appeal to the clergy, to the Sisterhoods and to the laity, to support the hierarchy in the tasks that lay ahead.

CHAPTER XVI

THE SECOND PLENARY COUNCIL (1866)

THE fourteen years between the First and Second Plenary Councils of Baltimore (1852-1866) are crowded with events of grave importance to American history as well as to the story of Catholic progress in the nation.

The intense propaganda of the Abolition movement, closely linked as it was between 1852 and 1860 with the anti-Catholic Know-nothing party, prepared both the North and the South for the fearful struggle of the Civil War. The outbreaks against Catholic persons and property between 1851 and 1855 revealed the fact that this anti-Catholic animus was stronger than at any time since Emancipation (1829). The shameless attacks upon Archbishop Gætano Bedini during his short visit to the United States in 1853-1854 and the unspeakable outrage at Ellsworth, Maine, upon Father John Bapst, S.J., in October, 1854, were preludes to the rioting in several cities, particularly in Louisville, the following year. From that time to the outbreak of the Civil War, the anti-Catholic and Abolition movements may be said to have walked hand-in-hand until the former was forgotten in the bitterness of the latter; but forgotten only while the War was on.

In spite of the vicious attacks of the Know-nothing element during the fifties and of the confusion in all aspects of social and political life during the Civil War, few periods present so steady a growth as that between the two Plenary Councils.[1]

In the interim, diocesan synods and provincial councils began to multiply. There were, as far as can be ascertained, diocesan

[1] *Cf.* Murphy, R., "The Catholic Church in the United States during the Civil War Period (1852-1866)," *Records,* Amer. Cath. Hist. Society, XXXIX (1928), 271.

synods in Philadelphia (1853, 1855, 1857), Pittsburgh (1858), Louisville (1858, 1863), Galveston (1858), Detroit (1859, 1862), St. Paul (1861, 1863), St. Augustine (1861), Mobile (1861), and Fort Wayne (1863). Provincial Councils were held in New York (1854, 1861), in St. Louis (1855, 1858), Baltimore (VIII Prov. Council, 1855; IX Prov. Council, 1858), and Cincinnati (1855, 1858, 1861). In the diocesan synods little was done except to enforce the Baltimore decrees, and of the Provincial Councils held during these years, those of Cincinnati were undoubtedly the most important. Spalding writes:

> These councils, over which the venerable Archbishop Purcell presided, are remarkable for the practical wisdom and thorough ecclesiastical spirit which characterize the decrees therein enacted. They show a perfect comprehension of the wants of the Church in the West, as well as of the proper manner of meeting them.[2]

Bishop Spalding of Louisville, who was to succeed Archbishop Kenrick in the metropolitan See of Baltimore in 1864, wrote the three *Pastorals* issued by these Cincinnati councils and they are among the most notable documents of this kind ever issued by our prelates.[3] Occasionally at the close of diocesan retreats, some Ordinaries issued *Statuta* based upon the Baltimore decrees, and others published *Pastoral Letters* on Lent, Jubilees and similar subjects, in which they stressed the legislation of Baltimore.

The year following the close of the First Plenary Council, the Holy See created a second ecclesiastical province on the Pacific Coast—that of San Francisco (July 29, 1853), with Archbishop Joseph Sadoc Alemany, O.P., as the first metropolitan, and Bishop Thaddeus Amat, C.M., as his suffragan in the Diocese of Monterey. That same year (August 12, 1853)

---

[2] *Op. cit.*, 200.

[3] *Acta et Decreta quatuor Conciliorum Provincialium Cincinnatensium (1855-1882), adjectis pluribus decretis, rescriptis aliisque documentis.* Cincinnati, 1866. *Cf.* Lamott, *op. cit.*, chap. VI (*Diocesan Synods and Provincial Councils*). The *Acta et Decreta* and the *Pastoral Letters* will also be found in the *Collectio Lacensis*, III, 183-232.

Propaganda informed Archbishop Kenrick of Baltimore that the new Sees asked for by the prelates of the Council of 1852 were created. The Diocese of Quincy, Illinois, to which Rev. Joseph Melcher was appointed, remained until 1857, under the administration of Bishop O'Regan of Chicago, owing to Father Melcher's unwillingness to assume the episcopal office. On January 9, 1857, this See was transferred to Alton and Rev. Henry Damian Juncker was appointed its first bishop. The Diocese of Natchitoches, cut off from that of New Orleans, was placed under the charge of Rev. Augustin Mary Martin, who was consecrated at New Orleans on November 30, 1853. To the Diocese of Brooklyn, comprising Long Island, was assigned as its first bishop Rev. John Loughlin, then Vicar-General of the Diocese of New York. The Diocese of Newark, embracing all of New Jersey, received its first bishop in the person of the convert, Rev. James Roosevelt Bayley, the nephew of Mother Seton, then secretary to Archbishop Hughes. The State of Vermont was detached from the Diocese of Boston and a See was established at Burlington, with Rev. Louis de Goesbriand as bishop. The States of Maine and New Hampshire were placed under Bishop David W. Bacon, as first Bishop of Portland, after the first appointee, Father Henry B. Coskery of Baltimore, had declined the post.

When the Diocese of Erie was separated from that of Pittsburgh, Bishop Michael O'Connor was transferred at his own request to the former See, and Father Josue M. Young, then a priest of the Cincinnati Diocese, was elected second Bishop of Pittsburgh. Bishop-elect Young was unwilling to accept this arrangement, and accordingly Bishop O'Connor was transferred back to Pittsburgh, and Dr. Young was consecrated (April 25, 1854) as first Bishop of Erie. The eastern part of Kentucky was detached from the Diocese of Bardstown-Louisville on July 29, 1853, and Father George A. Carrell, S.J., was consecrated first Bishop of Covington on November 1, that same year. Consecrated also at this ceremony was the celebrated Indian missionary, Frederic Baraga, who had been chosen Vicar-Apostolic of

Upper Michigan. Spiritual progress in the Vicariate-Apostolic of New Mexico was crippled by the action of some Mexican priests who remained in the territory after it had been detached from the See of Durango, and when Bishop Lamy, then Vicar-Apostolic, laid these conditions before Propaganda, it was decided to erect New Mexico into a diocese with the See at Santa Fé.

In 1857 the Diocese of Fort Wayne was erected with Rt. Rev. John H. Luers as first Bishop. That same year the Vicariates of Florida and Nebraska were created. Bishop Augustin Verot, S.S., was appointed to the former with his residence at St. Augustine. Later in 1861, Bishop Verot succeeded to the See of Savannah, and retained his administration of Florida. The choice of the Holy See for the Nebraska Vicariate was Rt. Rev. James O'Gorman, a member of the Trappist Order, who was consecrated at St. Louis on May 8, 1859. In 1857 the Vicariate of Upper Michigan became the Diocese of Sault Sainte Marie, with Bishop Baraga as its first incumbent. A few months before the outbreak of the Civil War, a second suffragan See in the Province of San Francisco was created, the Vicariate-Apostolic of Marysville, with Rt. Rev. Eugene O'Connell as its first Bishop.

With these additional Sees between 1852 and 1866, the hierarchy of the Church in the United States consisted of seven Provinces: Baltimore (1808), Oregon (1846), St. Louis (1847), Cincinnati (1850), New York (1850), New Orleans (1850), and San Francisco (1853). The number of suffragan Sees was forty.

The deaths in the ranks of the hierarchy during these twelve years were numerous, and in consequence the assembly at Baltimore in 1866 was practically made up of new men. Those who had passed away were: Bishops Chanche (1852), Barron (1854), Gartland (1854), Reynolds (1855), Vandevelde (1855), O'Reilly (1856), Cretin (1857), Loras (1858), Neumann (1860), Andrew Byrne (1862), Smyth (1865), Fitzpatrick (1866), Young (1866), and Bishop O'Regan of Chicago who was absent from the Council and who died at London, November 23, 1866. Archbishop Blanc of New Orleans died in 1860; Archbishop Francis Patrick Kenrick died in 1863; and Archbishop Hughes, shortly after New Year's, 1864. In all, the Church lost twenty prelates during the interim between the two Councils.

The seventh Archbishop of Baltimore, Martin John Spalding, at the time of his succession to the metropolitan See, was in his fifty-fourth year, and had been coadjutor and Bishop of Louisville since 1848. His publications, while in a different field from that of his predecessor, were popular and had attracted national attention. His *Evidences of Catholicity* (1845) was followed by a valuable biography, *Life, Times and Character of Benedict Joseph Flaget* (1852), and then appeared *Miscellanea: Reviews, Lectures and Essays on Historical, Theological and Miscellaneous Subjects* (1853), the *History of the Protestant Reformation* (1860), and other volumes. When he came to Baltimore,[4] Archbishop Spalding had not only the experience of the Seventh Provincial Council (1849) and the First Plenary Council (1852) to guide him, but had also what may be justly called the greater experience of the First (1855), Second (1858), and Third (1861) Provincial Councils of Cincinnati. It is this conciliar knowledge and experience which explains in a large measure the extraordinary work done by the prelates and their theologians in the Second Plenary Council of 1866. "In previous councils," writes Shea, "the decrees had been confined mainly to the establishment of uniformity of discipline and to the general management of Church affairs. It was now deemed necessary to enter into doctrinal definitions suited to the time and country. Protestant denominations no longer held to their old symbols, articles, confessions of faith, and vast num-

---

[4] See Spalding, J. L., *Life of the Most Rev. M. J. Spalding, D.D., Archbishop of Baltimore* (New York, 1878), 218, for the interference charged against the United States Government in his appointment.

bers were dropping from the influence of their organizations. Men began to question the very fundamentals of Christianity, often from the lack of any guide whom they could respect." [5]

There were many problems of a practical nature facing the Second Plenary Council of 1866, and chief among them was that of providing for the great increase in the Catholic population of the country from 1852 to 1866. The principal motives for holding a council, we read in Spalding's *Life*, were

first, that at the close of the national crisis, which had acted as a dissolvent upon all sectarian ecclesiastical organizations, the Catholic Church might present to the country and the world a striking proof of the strong bond of unity with which her members are knit together. Secondly, that the collective wisdom of the Church in this country might determine what measures should be adopted in order to meet the new phase of national life which the result of the war had just inaugurated; for, though the Church is essentially the same in all times and places, her accidental relations to the world and the state are necessarily variable. "The customs of men," says Benedict XIV, "vary, and circumstances continually change. That which is useful at one period may cease to be so, and may become even hurtful in another age. The duty of a prudent pastor, unless prevented by a higher law, is to accommodate himself to times and places, to lay aside many ancient usages, when by his own judgment and the light of God he deems this to be for the greater good of the diocese with which he is entrusted."[6] Thirdly, that an earnest effort might be made to render ecclesiastical discipline, as far as possible, uniform throughout the entire extent of the United States. The fourth motive I shall give in the words of Archbishop Spalding: "I think," he wrote, "that it is our most urgent duty to discuss the future status of the negro. Four millions of these unfortunate beings are thrown on our charity, and they silently but eloquently appeal to us for help. We have a golden opportunity to reap a harvest of souls, which, neglected, may not return." The bishops of the United States very generally agreed that the time was opportune for holding a Plenary Council, and that the interests of religion demanded that it should be convoked at as early a date as possible. Some few, however, seemed to hesitate, on the ground chiefly that the country was still in too unsettled a condition, and

[5] *History of the Catholic Church in the United States*, IV, 716-717.
[6] *De Synod Dioeces.*, lib. v, c. iii.

that public sentiment with regard to the Church, especially in the North, was as yet very uncertain. Then they feared, too, that unpleasant discussions might arise in the Council. Archbishop Spalding himself felt no anxiety on these points. The bishops were to meet to attend to their own business, and not to meddle with affairs of state; and he thought he understood the public sentiment of the nation well enough to feel confident that in doing this they could have nothing to fear. As to the other cause of uneasiness, he wrote to one of his brethren in the episcopate: "I see no reason why we should fear the discussion of agitating topics. The question is closed and need not be reopened." Pius IX, in his Letters Apostolic of February 16, 1866, after signifying his approval of the project of holding a Plenary Council, constituted Archbishop Spalding its president. "Wherefore," wrote the Holy Father, "having fully examined the subject, we, with our venerable brethren, the cardinals of the Holy Roman Church, who superintend the affairs of the propagation of the faith, have resolved to delegate you, venerable brother, whose piety, knowledge, and profound reverence for the Holy See are well known to us, to the office of convoking and presiding over that Council. . . . We command, besides, all and each of your venerable brother bishops of the United States, that they receive and accept you, whom we have deputed to call together this Council, as its president and director, and that they obey you, and support you." As the time for holding the synod had been left to the judgment of the American prelates, Archbishop Spalding, having first received their opinions on the subject, issued letters of convocation, calling all who, by right or custom, should take part in a council of this kind, to meet in Baltimore on the second Sunday of October, 1866.[7]

Once the Council was opened, the entire Church in the United States, priests, prelates, and people, realized the remarkable advance made by Catholicism during the fourteen years since the assembly of 1852. Shea's estimates, differing somewhat from the figures given in the *Catholic Directory* for these years, show the following growth:[8]

[7] Pp. 298-300.

[8] *Op. cit.*, IV, 715: "The great belt of Catholic activity and life thus extended from the Potomac and the southern lines of Kentucky and Missouri, and westward from the Atlantic to the Rocky Mountains, extending northward to the British frontier. In this belt the progress was especially notable in New York, Pennsylvania, Ohio, Kentucky, Illinois, Wisconsin, Iowa, Min-

	1852	1866
Catholic population	1,980,000	3,842,000
Priests	1,321	2,770
Churches	1,411	3,366
Stations	681	1,695

As Apostolic Delegate to the Council, Archbishop Spalding had plenary authority to guide the legislation necessary for the uniformity of discipline, the growth of diocesan organization, and the increase of the Faith among clergy and people. On March 19, 1866, he sent the letters of convocation to the other archbishops and bishops of the country, placing the date of the Council for the first Sunday in October of that year.[9] Meanwhile, the prelates were asked to write to him on all those questions which they deemed prudent to bring to the attention of the committees appointed to prepare the *agenda* of the Council: *Quatenus sapientibus monitis et suggestionibus, atque etiam formulis Decretorum et Fidei expositionis scripto exaratis.* These suggestions were to reach him before May 3, 1866. From the feast of the Assumption (August 15), on all Sundays, prayers were to be recited in the churches for the success of the Council, and the Friday before the opening of the Council was to be kept as a solemn fast. Attached to the letter of convocation went a

---

nesota, and the new Territories. South of this was the part which suffered so terribly by the Civil War, where the Catholics lost a large proportion of their churches and institutions, compared to the whole, and where in the poverty caused by the war and subsequent misgovernment, any attempt to recover lost ground was almost impossible, yet the dioceses of Wheeling and Mobile showed life and progress. In Louisiana, the Church held her own; in Texas, the growth was great. New Mexico gained steadily in priests and churches, and in the awakened devotion of the long neglected people. On the Pacific coast there was growth, in California, especially in the diocese of San Francisco, but in Oregon and Washington Territory the gain was slow. Throughout the country, besides the regular parochial churches and their work, much was done by missions given by the great religious Orders, the Jesuits, Redemptorists, Paulists, Dominicans, Benedictines, arousing the piety of the people and bringing back the tepid, indifferent, and careless. Such was the condition of the country when the Second Plenary Council of Baltimore convened."

[9] The letter will be found in the *Balt. Cath. Mirror*, XVII, (September 1, 1866).

copy of the Instruction sent by Propaganda (January 31, 1866) on the *agenda*.

Among the topics selected by the Sacred Congregation for discussion were: the spiritual care of the newly emancipated Negroes; new norms for the selection of bishops to vacant Sees; uniformity of Church discipline; *sacerdotes vagantes;* the erection of ecclesiastical seminaries; the observance of feasts and fasts; holydays of obligation in the United States; the legal security of Church property; problems of adjustment between the bishops and the regular Orders and Congregations on Church property ownership; and the increase of diocesan organization: Dubuque, Montana, and British Columbia being specially mentioned.[10]

In one of his letters at the time, Archbishop Spalding gives a digest of what he considered the most pressing business of the Council:

> I have thought of embodying in the Council a succinct exposition of doctrine, together with the condemnation of current heresies and errors, as well as suitable rules for the regulation of moral conduct and discipline. . . . I have thought, also, of making our approaching Council a complete repertory of our canon law, embracing, in systematic order, all our previous enactments in the Baltimore Councils, together with such canons of provincial and diocesan synods as we may wish to make of general application. In a word, of making it a sort of *corpus juris* for the American Church; throwing into an appendix all Roman rescripts and decisions which have reference to our affairs. . . . In order to carry out this plan, I shall need the active coöperation of the metropolitans.[11]

This was a departure from the method followed in all previous Councils of Baltimore, but it was not altogether an innovation. Some of the Provincial Councils of Europe had done so; the archbishop had, indeed, procured copies of a dozen or more of these assemblies, and he found that in comparison with their *Acta et Decreta* the Baltimore Councils appeared very meager, especially in doctrinal and moral exposition. "We

[10] *Conc. Plen. Balt. II,* xxiv-xxviii.   [11] Spalding, *op. cit.,* 301.

have very much to do," he writes, "to lay deeply and solidly the foundations of our canon law. Until now, we seem not to have advanced far beyond the rudiments." [12]

The main purposes of the Council, therefore, as Archbishop Spalding viewed it, were: the codification of all previous legislation; the shaping of new decrees so as to meet the needs of so many dioceses with their varied customs and tendencies, as well as to harmonize the racial differences in the Church at the time; and the exposition in clear unmistakable terms of the principal doctrines and disciplinary canons of the Church. A brief statement of the final *agenda* was sent to all those whose duty or right it was to be present at the Council, and all were requested to make any suggestions which they deemed worthy of deliberation in the assembly. When all these memorandums had been received, the archbishops formed a committee of the foremost theologians in the Church here to assist them in collating all the subjects selected by the members of the hierarchy and others who had been invited. Regulations were drawn up in accordance with the plan laid down by Pope Benedict XIV for the deliberations of the private and public congregations and for the ceremonies of the Sessions. A preliminary decree was then issued containing six sections: (1) The day of the opening of the Council was to be October 7, 1866, the feast of the Most Holy Rosary; (2) all prelates and synodal officials who had not yet taken the conciliar oath were to do so; (3) the question of precedence during the Council; (4) the religious exercises to be followed during the Council, the coöperation expected from all in problems concerning the good of the Church, and the order to be observed during discussions; (5) the conciliar officials and their duties—a *Chancellor* or custodian of all documentary reports, decrees, letters, etc.; a *Secretary* with his assistants; a *Notary* to handle all correspondence; two *Promoters* (one a bishop, the other a priest) to direct the deliberations of the congregations; *Judges* for contentious cases brought before

[12] *Ibid.,* 302.

the Council; and *Masters of Ceremonies, Prefects,* and *Chanters;* and (6) the rules regarding presence at all the meetings of the Council.

Preliminary meetings were held on Thursday, Friday and Saturday, October 4-6. The first was attended solely by the archbishops (Spalding, F. N. Blanchet, P. R. Kenrick, Alemany, Purcell, Odin, and McCloskey). Archbishop Spalding, as Apostolic Delegate, read the list of decrees as formulated by the committee of *theologians.* The officials of the Council were then selected.

The officers of the Council were as follows: *Promoters:* Rt. Rev. Dr. Lynch, Bishop of Charleston, Very Rev. Wm. O'Hara, D.D., V.G.; *Chancellors:* Rev. Thomas Foley, D.D., Rev. James Gibbons; *Secretaries:* Very Rev. James A. Corcoran, D.D., Rev. James Keogh, D.D., Rev. Thomas A. Becker, D.D.; *Notaries:* Rev. Francis Joseph Pabisch, D.D., J.U.D., Very Rev. Francis Sadoc Villarrasa, O.P., Rev. Michael Accolti, S.J., Very Rev. Michael Heiss, Rev. Wm. Wayrich, C.SS.R., Rev. John Foley, D.D., Rev. T. J. Butler, D.D., Rev. J. A. Healey; *Writers of Roman Letters:* Rt. Rev. Dr. E. O'Connell, V.A., of Marysville, California, Rt. Rev. Dr. Rosecrans, Auxiliary Bishop of Cincinnati; *Writers of Other Letters:* to the Leopoldine Association of Vienna, Rt. Rev. Dr. Luers, Bishop of Fort Wayne; to the Society of Munich, Rt. Rev. Dr. Henni, Bishop of Milwaukee; to the Propagation of the Faith, Rt. Rev. Dr. Verot, Bishop of Savannah; to the Society of the Holy Childhood, Rt. Rev. Dr. Martin, Bishop of Natchitoches; *Masters of Ceremonies:* Rev. Francis McNierney, Rev. Stanislaus Ferte, S.S.; and *Chanters:* Rev. P. P. Denis, S.S., Rev. John J. Dougherty, Rev. P. Chapon, S.S., Rev. J. J. Keane, Rev. Thaddeus J. Butler, D.D., and Rev. Charles Ziegler.[18]

---

[18] This list, from the volume entitled *Sermons delivered during the Second Plenary Council, etc.,* xliii-xliv, differs somewhat from that in the official *Conc. Plen. Balt. II,* lvi-lvii. The *New York Freeman's Journal* (October 26, 1866) claims to have printed the only correct list of the *Synodales* at the Council.

The following day, both metropolitans and suffragans met at the archbishop's house; again the list of decrees proposed was read, and the names of the officials chosen the previous day were announced for election by those present. A public meeting was held on Saturday morning in the cathedral at which the prelates and all those who had been invited were present. Archbishop Spalding again presided. The printed list of decrees was submitted and all were urged to discuss these with complete freedom. A list of all those whose duty and privilege it was to be present in the deliberations of the Council and the list of the committee of bishops and *theologians* chosen for each of the main questions to be discussed in the Council were then read. There were seven of these committees, the total membership being seven bishops and over one hundred priests. These committees were to meet every morning at nine o'clock and were to remain in session until their work was completed.[14] The parliamentary rules of the United States Senate were to be observed in these sessions, as well as indeed in all the meetings of the Council, especially in the private congregations where the hierarchy alone was present.

Four Solemn Sessions, eleven private congregations, five public congregations, one extraordinary private congregation, and the Mass for the prelates deceased since the last Council (1852) make up the entire series of official meetings and ceremonies of the Council.

The first Solemn Session took place on Sunday morning, October 7. Seven archbishops, thirty-eight bishops, three mitered abbots, and over one hundred and twenty *theologians,* marched in procession from the archbishop's house to the cathedral. The setting was likened to a pageant of the Middle Ages: "The whole city had crowded to behold the glorious scene. The streets around the Cathedral were thronged. Every window and available spot, even the housetops from which a view of the procession could be had, were filled with eager spectators, who looked

[14] The list of these will be found in the *Conc. Plen. Balt. II,* xliv-xlviii.

on in silent reverence." [15] One of the fine passages in the *Life of Archbishop Spalding* describes the effect of the Council upon the thinking people of the time:

The country had just come forth from a most terrible crisis, in which many ancient landmarks had been effaced, and the very ship of state had been wrenched from its moorings. House had been divided against house, and brother's hand had been raised against brother. The sects had been torn asunder, and still lay in disorder and confusion, helping to widen the abyss which had threatened to engulf the nation's life. Half the country was waste and desolate; the people crushed, bowed beneath the double weight of the memory of the past, which could no more return, and of the thought of a future which seemed hopeless. On the other side, there were the weariness and exhaustion which follow a supreme effort, and the longing for peace and happiness after so much bloodshed and misery. All were ready to applaud any power that had been able to live through that frightful struggle unhurt and unharmed; and when the Catholic Church walked forth before the eyes of the nation, clothed in the panoply of undiminished strength and of unbroken unity, thousands, who but a while ago would have witnessed this manifestation of her power with jealous concern, now hailed it with delight as a harbinger of good omen. Then it must be confessed, too, that during the war men had seen more of the Church, and, having learned to know her better, had come to love her more. There was not a village throughout the land where some brave soldier, not a Catholic, was not found to speak the praises of her heroic daughters, who, whilst men fought, stood by to staunch the blood.[16]

Solemn Pontifical Mass of the Holy Ghost was celebrated by the Apostolic Delegate, and the sermon was delivered by Archbishop McCloskey of New York, on the marks of the Church. "For us, Most Reverend Delegate Apostolic and Venerable Fathers of the Council," he said,

this is a moment of deep solemnity, of grave responsibility, as well as of religious joy. We are here as members of that Apostolic body, which has inherited the commission and received the promise. We are here not to decide any disputed points of doctrine or define any articles of faith—this belongs not to a Council such as this—much

[15] Spalding, *op. cit.*, 305.   [16] *Ibid.*

less are we here to discuss any mere secular topics of the day, to treat questions having a political complexion or tendency of any kind whatever. We are here to consult together and deliberate on those things which appertain exclusively to the proper discharge of the important trusts committed to us . . . of those things which concern the interests of a kingdom which is not of this world . . . to provide in season for the daily increasing spiritual wants of our vastly extended and rapidly expanding territory . . . to seek to multiply as far as in us lies all those means which may more effectually conduce to the diffusion and preservation of the faith, the improvement of morals, the establishment of sound discipline, to the increase of God's honor and glory and the salvation of souls. In this we rely, not on our own strength, but on that which cometh from above, not on any human lights of our own, but on the light of the Holy Ghost, which we have solemnly invoked at the altar. In the language of Solomon, we beg for understanding, that we may be able to judge aright and discern between good and evil. We beg for wisdom that sitteth by the throne of God, that he may send her out of His holy heaven and from the throne of His Majesty . . . that she may be with us and labor with us, that we may know what is good and acceptable in His sight. We beg him to bless us, to bless the shepherds and their flocks, to bless the pastors and bless the people, to bless the Church, to bless our Country, to bless our rulers, to bless us in His earthly city here, and make us blessed in the heavenly city above hereafter.[17]

At the close of the Mass, the names of those chosen to preach at the evening services were announced:

> Sunday, Oct. 7—Bishop Lynch (Charleston)
> Monday, Oct. 8—Bishop Rosecrans (Cincinnati)
> Tuesday, Oct. 9—Bishop Grace (St. Paul)
> Wednesday, Oct. 10—Rev. J. Lancaster Spalding
> Friday, Oct. 12—Rev. Patrick J. Ryan
> Sunday, Oct. 14—Bishop McGill (Richmond)
> Monday, Oct. 15—Bishop Wood (Philadelphia)
> Tuesday, Oct. 16—Rev. Isaac T. Hecker, C.S.P.
> Wednesday, Oct. 17—Bishop Elder (Natchez)
> Friday, Oct. 18—Bishop Duggan (Chicago) [18]

[17] *Sermons etc.*, 14-15.
[18] Their discourses are printed in *Sermons etc.*, liv-244.

The prelates present for the first time at a Council then took the conciliar oath. The list of those convoked to the Council was read publicly, the papal benediction was given by Archbishop Spalding, and the procession back to the archbishop's house was made.[19]

On Thursday, October 11, Solemn Pontifical Mass of Requiem was celebrated by Archbishop Blanchet and the sermon on the deceased prelates was delivered by Bishop Bayley of Newark.[20] After the absolution was given, Archbishop Alemany preached in Latin to the assembled prelates and conciliar officials on the dignity of the priesthood. The second Solemn Session took place on Sunday, October 14, in the cathedral. Solemn Pontifical Mass was celebrated by Archbishop P. R. Kenrick of St. Louis, the archdeacon being the future Archbishop Ryan, and the deacon, the future Cardinal Gibbons, then a priest five years. The sermon, delivered by Archbishop Purcell, was on the text: "No man can serve two masters." [21] The third Solemn Session was held on October 18 in the cathedral. Solemn Pontifical Mass was celebrated by Archbishop Alemany. On this occasion, Father James Gibbons was a deacon of honor to Archbishop Spalding. The sermon (in Latin) on Zeal for Souls was delivered by Archbishop Odin of New Orleans.

Our purpose does not lead us to enter into detail into all the deliberations of the private and public congregations nor is it necessary to discuss the changes in the original decrees contained in the special Instruction sent by Propaganda on January 24, 1868. The *Acta et Decreta* of the Council, published in 1868, form a large quarto volume of five hundred and twenty-six pages, with an index of twenty-eight pages.[22]

[19] For newspaper descriptions, cf. *Sermons etc.,* xii-xxii.
[20] *Sermons etc.,* 51-65. The sermon contains miniature sketches of some of the eighteen prelates who had passed away.
[21] *Sermons etc.,* 38-50.
[22] An appendix of almost one hundred pages contains thirty-four official documents from the Holy See on matters decreed by the Council and are printed as explanatory of the decrees themselves as well as of whatever

The decrees themselves are divided into fourteen titles (*tituli*):

  I. *De Fide orthodoxa, deque Erroribus Serpentibus*
 II. *De Hierarchia et Regimine Ecclesiae*
III. *De Personis Ecclesiasticis*
 IV. *De Ecclesiis Bonisque Ecclesiasticis tenendis tutandisque*
  V. *De Sacramentis*
 VI. *De Cultu Divino*
VII. *De Disciplinae Uniformitate promovenda*
VIII. *De Regularibus et Monialibus*
 IX. *De Juventute instituenda, pieque erudienda*
  X. *De Salute Animarum efficacius promovenda*
 XI. *De Libris et Ephemeridibus*
XII. *De Societatibus Secretis*
XIII. *De Novarum Sedium Episcopalium Erectione, deque Candi-
       tatorum Praesentatione*
XIV. *De Efficaciori Decretorum Baltimorensium Executione pro-
       movenda*

These fourteen sections are subdivided into chapters and the entire legislation is numbered from one to five hundred and thirty-four. There is much that is old in these decrees. All those enactments of the previous Councils of Baltimore which had given to the Church here canonical stability are repeated *verbatim* whenever it was found necessary. A number of rescripts and briefs from the Holy See, of Instructions from Propaganda, of the conciliar legislation of other lands, and of the provincial conciliar legislation in this country outside of Baltimore, find their way into the code of laws of 1866.

The whole tenor of the Second Plenary Council shows an increasing disposition in the American prelates to conform, wherever it

---

Propaganda found necessary to change before approval was given. Among these is a letter from Cardinal Barnabò, Prefect of the Sacred Congregation, to Bishop Amat of Monterey, dated November 13, 1867, giving his approval to a project of erecting an American College in Barcelona, Spain, for the Spanish-speaking missions of the United States. The letter of August 15, 1858, from Cardinal Barnabò, granting the "'prerogative of place" to the metropolitan See of Baltimore is also printed in this appendix.

is possible, to the general usage of the Church, and, indeed, to comply with certain wise provisions which, even in Catholic countries, have been allowed to fall into desuetude.[23]

The decrees of the Council are explanatory and hortatory as well as legislative.

The seven chapters under Title I, *De Fide Orthodoxa,* contain an explanation of certain doctrines of the Church—divine revelation; the meaning of *extra Ecclesiam nulla salus;* the nature and necessity of faith; Sacred Scripture; the Trinity; God the Creator, Redeemer and Sanctifier; eternal life; veneration and invocation of the Most Blessed Virgin Mary and of the Saints; and doctrinal error (sects, indifferentism, unitarianism, universalism, transcendentalism, pantheism, magnetism, and spiritism).

Title II, *De Hierarchia et Regimine Ecclesiae,* is divided into five chapters. Chapter I, "On the Roman Pontiff," repeats the first decree of the Plenary Council of 1852 wherein the Fathers express in the fullest and most explicit terms their whole-hearted devotion and reverence for the Holy See. The doctrine of papal infallibility had not then been pronounced, but the rest of this chapter shows unmistakably that it was in the minds of the prelates, some of whom four years later will oppose its declaration as inopportune. The following clause (n. 47) on the temporal power is significant on account of the political situation in Italy at the time:

Although the temporal power of the Roman pontiffs, or the patrimony of Peter, was not imparted by God in the beginning, and does not pertain to the essence of the primacy, it seems nevertheless most useful, and in the present state of affairs, to a certain extent, necessary, in order that the pontiff may independently exercise for the welfare of the Church the rights of his primacy. For the Catholic Church, founded and instituted by Christ for the eternal happiness of men, obtained by virtue of her divine institution the form of a perfect society, and therefore should enjoy that

[23] Spalding, *op. cit.,* 308.

liberty which will enable her to perform her office, without being subject to any civil power.[24]

The Fathers then enjoined that in all the churches of the United States an annual collection for the Holy Father be taken up on the Sunday within the octave of Saints Peter and Paul, in order to render him that assistance, so necessary owing to the sacrilegious spoliation of the greater and more fruitful part of his Patrimony. Chapter II, "On the Hierarchy of the Church," reiterates the divine authority of the Church to teach and to rule. Chapter III "On Provincial Councils," urges that these be held in accordance with the Tridentine decree and lays down regulations for their observance. Chapter IV, "On Diocesan Synods and Conferences," decrees that the Tridentine law be observed in this country, and the Fathers earnestly recommend the practice of regular theological conferences in each diocese. These, they say, will go far to supply the rare celebration of diocesan synods. They decree, therefore, that in cities the clergy should meet four times a year, and in the rural districts, twice a year. Chapter V is entitled "On Consultors, the Vicar-General, Archdeacon and Other Diocesan Officials." The burden of responsibility borne by our bishops was so great that the Fathers repeated the decree of the Plenary Council of 1852 that a group of priests, to be called councilors or consultors, be selected to assist them by their wise counsel. "In this manner the second sacerdotal order will give assistance to the first, and by the common consent and suffrage of all, the unity of administration will be made surer, and all will be done moderately and firmly, for the greater glory of God and the salvation of souls (n. 70)." It was decreed that the vicar-general constitutes one and the same moral person as the bishop and holds his authority from him. When the power of the bishop expires, by death, resignation, translation or otherwise, that of the vicar-general ceases also. The duties of the other diocesan officials (vicars-forane,

[24] Smith, *Notes on the Second Plenary Council of Baltimore* (Baltimore, 1874), 44-48.

rural deans, secretary, chancellor, notary, clergy examiners, ecclesiastical judges, etc.) are then described, and the bishops are urged to make such appointments for the proper administration of diocesan affairs.

Title III, *De Personis Ecclesiasticis,* is divided into seven chapters. Chapter I, "On Metropolitans," defines the extent of the jurisdiction enjoyed by the archbishop within the province over which he presides, and five special duties are given, chief of which is the right to hear appeals from a diocesan court to that of the metropolitan. Chapter II, "On Bishops," deals with the episcopal power of orders and jurisdiction.[25] The bishops are urged in the words of the decrees of the previous Councils of Baltimore not to promote any candidates to sacred orders, except such as are capable of serving on the missions, and who have beforehand taken the mission oath of perpetually dedicating themselves to the mission assigned to them. Also, the Fathers petitioned the Holy See to issue a declaration forbidding ecclesiastics in sacred orders and ordained *titulo missionis,* as well as all diocesan priests, from entering a religious Order or Congregation without the written consent of the Ordinary. The remainder of the chapter is devoted to the selection of administrators *sede vacante* and of their rights and duties.

Chapter III, "On the Election of Bishops" is a further attempt to stabilize the method of nominating bishops to vacant Sees in this country. Many changes had occurred since the extraordinary privilege granted by Pope Pius VI to the priests of the young Republic to elect their first bishop (John Carroll). The Council of 1833 had decreed with the approval of the Holy See that when a See became vacant, the votes of the other bishops of the province were to be taken. In 1850 Propaganda required the metropolitan of the province to send the names of candidates to the other metropolitans, who were to send their opinions

---

[25] A useful commentary on this part of the decrees is given in the *Archiv für katholisches Kirchenrecht* (XXII, 117) ; cf. Smith, "Cathedral Chapters," *Amer. Cath. Quar. Review,* III (1878), 262.

on the same to the Holy See. In 1859 it was decreed by a rescript from the Holy See that in the election of a metropolitan, the other archbishops had a deliberative vote. In 1861 each bishop was required to send triennially to Propaganda and to the metropolitans of the provinces the names of eligible candidates for the episcopate. The Fathers of the Second Plenary Council reënacted these decrees and rescripts, and enjoined upon the prelates whose privilege it was to recommend to the Holy See priests for any vacant See the duty of holding a special meeting to discuss the qualifications and abilities of those proposed. The question of whether, as in Ireland, the priests of the diocese should have a share in the election of their bishop was not settled in the private congregations of the Council of 1866, although it was known that Archbishop Spalding and other prelates were in favor of this privilege,

so as, in some way, to give the second order of the clergy a voice in the presentation of candidates for episcopal office. He would have given the diocesan councillors the right to present a list of names to be sent to Rome with that of the bishops. He thought that the episcopal council in this country should be looked upon as a quasi-chapter, and that the giving them a vote would bring us nearer the general discipline of the Church in this matter. Indeed, he was in favor of introducing the canonical chapter, as an element in our Church polity, whenever this could be done. The Plenary Council does not seem, however, to have entered upon the discussion of this subject.[26]

The chapter closes with a list of the questions to be answered regarding the candidates' ability and worthiness for the episcopal dignity.

Chapter IV, "On Priests Having the Care of Souls" takes up the question of parochial rights, the immovability of parish priests, the manner of their appointment, the examination for parishes, etc. The Fathers repeat the injunctions of the Provincial Councils of Baltimore on these questions, and after warning the bishops to be on their guard against vagrant priests (*magis*

[26] Spalding, *op. cit.*, 311-312.

turpis lucri quam animarum zelo ducti), they considered it desirable that in accordance with the Tridentine regulation regarding canonical pastorates, there should be parish priests in the proper sense of the term (*parochi proprie dicti*) in the United States as in other Catholic countries; but "our circumstances are such as will not at the present conjuncture admit of this. It is, however, the sincere desire of the Fathers of this Plenary Council, that gradually and as far as circumstances will permit, our discipline should in this respect conform to that of the entire Church" (n. 123). They legislated for the determination of parish boundaries, and while granting to the priest in charge parochial or quasi-parochial rights, they made it clear that they did not intend to grant immovability to pastors. All priests had to stand an examination before the bishop and two assistants before being appointed to a parish, and they must have labored in the diocese five years before being eligible for the same. Priests appointed to parishes before the end of the five-year term were to be merely administrators, until they became eligible for examination.

Chapter V, "On Preachers of the Word of God" is an excellent summary on sacred eloquence. Chapter VI, "On Clerical Life and Conduct," speaks of clerical dress, conduct in public, plays and other public amusements, the wearing of the cassock in the rectory and in sacred ceremonies, the prohibition against practicing medicine, card-playing and gambling, and of having recourse to civil courts of law without permission of the Ordinary. The chapter has also an earnest admonition to all clerics to flee idleness and to devote themselves to ecclesiastical studies, and to avoid hankering after riches. Priests are forbidden to conduct banks or to receive money on deposit from their people without permission of the bishop. Rules are laid down for the decorum of the priest's house. Chapter VII, "On Ecclesiastical Seminaries," reënacts the legislation of the previous Councils of Baltimore on the subject. Each diocese, if at all possible, was to have its own seminary, and where this was impracticable, each province should support one for its own Sees. Preparatory seminaries were also advocated, and boys of twelve and over with the desire of becoming priests are to be instructed in these institutions. The curriculum of studies was outlined and examinations were to be public. In all those dioceses where there were many German Catholics, care should be taken that the young aspirants to the priesthood be instructed in that language.

Title IV, *De Ecclesiis Bonisque Ecclesiasticis tenendis tutandisque,* has a single chapter containing twenty-two decrees in which the history of the canon law in this country on the holding of Church property is explained and new legislation enacted to offset the recurrence of the evils of trusteeism. After repeating all the statutes on the problem from previous Councils of Baltimore, the Fathers decreed that, since in practice the civil tribunals scarcely ever carry out the provisions of the common law which fully recognizes the laws of the Church, the bishops should protect all Church property by legal means. Administrators, whether ecclesiastical or lay, of Church property are bound to give an annual financial report to the Ordinary on the same. Nor is the property of the religious Orders and Congregations exempt from this law.

Title V, *De Sacramentis,* has ten chapters on the sacraments in general, on each of the seven sacraments in particular, on indulgences, and on the sacramentals. The enactments of previous Councils on the Roman Ritual, on the use of Latin in all ceremonies, in parochial registers, and on the manner of entering baptisms and marriages are repeated. Pastors were forbidden to baptize children not belonging to their own parish. The decree about baptizing children of non-Catholic parents as stated by the Council of 1829 was reënacted. Rules were made regarding sponsors. Baptism was never to be administered in private houses, unless grave necessity demanded it. The ceremonies of adult baptism, that is, the use of the formula of infant baptism, are given, and the permission to retain this privilege was to be asked from the Holy See. The method of receiving converts into the Church is explained. The churching of mothers after childbirth was urged as a worthy and laudable practice. Rules regarding sponsors in conferring the Sacrament of Confirmation were laid down, and each child was to have a sponsor. In case this cannot be done easily, there should be two godfathers for the boys and two godmothers for the girls. The Lateran precept of the Paschal Communion is given. Children are to be well instructed for their First Holy Communion. No definite age is set down for this, but the Fathers say that as a general rule, none "should receive this Bread of Angels before the age of ten; nor should It be refused to any one who is otherwise disposed, after the age of fourteen" (n. 261). Regulations are made for administering Holy Communion to the sick. Decree of previous Councils on confession and confessionals are reënacted and further regulations are laid down for the worthy administration of the Sacrament of Penance. The chapter on indulgences explains the Catholic doctrine on that subject, and priests are warned to recommend those indulgences which the people can gain more easily and frequently and with greater fruit. The doctrine of the Sacrament of Extreme Unction is fully set forth as are also the ceremonies used in conferring this sacrament.

The chapter closes with the announcement that the Bishop of Savannah (Verot) has offered to the Abbot of the Cistercian Monastery of Gethsemane a piece of ground near the city of St. Augustine for the production of olive oil, wine and candles to be used in Church services. In the Chapter on Holy Orders, the doctrine of the priesthood is explained. A decree is enacted that each diocese have at least three examiners of the clergy who will test the ability of all candidates for Holy Orders. Priests had to be ordained with some title, patrimony, benefice or of religious poverty. In this country the *titulus missionis* was to be generally used. The Fathers of the Council asked that the Holy See dispense with the oath of serving perpetually on the missions, but this was not granted. The indissolubility of the marriage contract is asserted, the proclamation of the banns more strictly insisted upon, mixed marriages are more strongly condemned, and marriage before non-Catholic ministers severely condemned. The Fathers settled the much discussed question whether the Tridentine decree on clandestinity was promulgated throughout the United States, and they renewed the decree of the Council of 1843, which stated that such promulgation was inopportune, and the *Tametsi* should bind only in the Province of New Orleans. This petition to the Holy See to allow the general discipline then prevailing to become a law, was refused.[27] A final chapter on the sacramentals of the Church closes this fifth title.

Title VI, *De Cultu Divino,* has three chapters on the Sacrifice of the Mass, on the Benediction of the Most Blessed Sacrament and the Forty Hours' Devotion, and on Vespers. The obligation of celebrating Mass on Sundays and festivals for the people is placed upon pastors. The regulations concerning stipends and the foundation of perpetual Masses are then discussed. Rules are given for the frequency of the Benediction of the Blessed Sacrament, and the conditions for gaining the plenary indulgence during the Forty Hours' are explained. A final decree orders the celebration of Vespers on Sundays and holy days.

Title VII, *De Disciplinae Uniformitate promovenda,* is concerned with uniformity of discipline regarding feasts and fasts, dispensations, burial in non-Catholic cemeteries, and days of prayer and thanksgiving set apart by the civil authorities. The Holy See was petitioned to grant a universal dispensation from the fast on the Saturdays of Lent, but the reply was that each bishop should make his own petition, stating his reasons for the dispensation. The difficulty of observing the law forbidding

---

[27] "As the Fathers of Baltimore (in T. t. V, c. IX, n. 340) have requested that in all the provinces of the United States, except New Orleans, the impediment of clandestinity should be declared as abolished, the Most Holy Father has thought fit by no means to accede to such a demand." Smith, *Notes etc.,* 270; *Conc. Plen. Balt. II,* cxlv. *Cf.* "Die französichen und amerikanischen Synoden über die Civilehe," *Archiv für katholisches Kirchenrecht* (**XXXV**, 432-446).

servile work on holydays of obligation generally observed at the time was discussed and the problem of uniformity involved left unsettled. The Fathers asked and obtained that the feast of the Immaculate Conception be made a holy day of obligation in all the American dioceses.

Title VIII, *De Regularibus et Monialibus,* consists of two chapters devoted to the religious Orders and Congregations of men and women. The important decrees concern the support of religious houses and the relations between the Ordinary and religious having charge of schools, colleges, and churches. The Fathers stipulated that these relations be expressed in writing. The nature of the vows taken by nuns is then discussed, as is also the law of enclosure.

Title IX, *De Juventute instituenda pieque erudienda,* contains three chapters, in the first of which pastors are exhorted to build and equip parochial schools throughout the United States. Catechism classes were to be held regularly for all Catholic children attending the public schools, especially in preparation for First Holy Communion and Confirmation. Children who have reached the age of seven should begin going to Confession, and those over that age who discern properly what Holy Communion means may be permitted to receive. Industrial schools or reformatories are especially praised and the bishops are urged to build and equip these wherever they are found necessary.[28] The third chapter deals with the proposed Catholic university. One of the first subjects in connection with the Second Plenary Council which suggested itself to Archbishop Spalding's mind was the creation of a national Catholic university. His biographer tells us that the deep interest he took in this project is seen in his Irish and Belgian correspondence, in which he seeks for information concerning the establishment of the Universities of Dublin and Louvain. The question as submitted to the Fathers of the Second Plenary Council was this: Whether the

[28] *Cf.* Shea, "What Can Be Done for the Orphans," *Amer. Cath. Quar. Review,* XI (1886), 81-88.

time had not come for founding a university which would give the Church here ampler means for bringing the truths of our Faith before the more intelligent class of Americans in a manner that could not but arrest their attention. Spalding believed that no time should be lost, and that the project should be begun immediately "to create an American Catholic literature, irreproachable both in thought and style, which would deal with all the living problems of the age, and thus furnish a Catholic solution for the doubts by which thousands of those outside the church, who think, are tortured." To attain this end, he was of the opinion that nothing would be more likely to contribute "than a great central seat of Catholic learning, encircled by the halo of illustrious names, to which the eyes of Catholics from every part of the Union might turn with pride and reverence." The time, however, as his biographer writes, when the great work "of founding a Catholic university in the United States was to be begun, had not yet come, though the Fathers of the Second Plenary Council of Baltimore express their most ardent desire to see such an institution established here; and their words concerning the plan of studies which should be pursued in higher ecclesiastical seminaries plainly show the urgent want of a Catholic University in this country." [29] The American Colleges of Rome and Louvain and All Hallows College in Ireland are praised for their high standards of clerical training. After the close of the Council a private letter was sent by Archbishop Spalding and Bishop Wood to the hierarchy making an appeal for an endowment fund for the American College in Rome. [30]

Title X, *De Salute Animarum efficacius promovenda*, has four chapters: The first, on zeal for souls, describes the qualities necessary in the priest and on special dangers to the piety of the flock. The second chapter urges the custom of holding Missions and lays down rules for the missionary fathers. The third chapter urges the spread of Sodalities and Confraternities and

[29] Spalding, *op. cit.*, 313-315.
[30] Brann, *Hist. of the American College etc.*, 435-440.

those specially praised are the Confraternities of the Most Blessed Sacrament, of Perpetual Adoration, of the Sacred Heart of Jesus, of the Blessed Virgin, of the Rosary, of St. Joseph, of the Holy Angels, of the Apostleship of Prayer, and of the Society for the Conversion of non-Catholics. Likewise, the bishops are urged to promote the Society of the Propagation of the Faith and the Holy Childhood. The Society of St. Vincent de Paul is also commended. Rules are given regarding the erection of these Societies and Confraternities. A fourth chapter deals with the spiritual care of the Negroes, and the Bishops are urged to give this pressing question serious attention in diocesan synods and provincial councils, wherever the number of Negroes is large enough to need special legislation.

Title XI, *De Libris et Ephemeridibus,* deals with the necessary ecclesiastical permission to print and publish books treating of religion and divine worship. Censors are to be chosen in each diocese to examine all Catholic books before publication, especially in those dioceses where Catholic printing establishments exist. The Catholic Publication Society for the Dissemination of Catholic Literature is commended, and rules are laid down for the composition of prayer-books for the faithful. Catholic newspapers are recommended as a barrier to the evils of the daily press.

Title XII, *De Societatibus Secretis,* treats of secret societies, the Freemasons, Odd Fellows, and Sons of Temperance being specially mentioned.[31]

Title XIII, *De Novarum Sedium Episcopalium erectione, deque Candidatorum Praesentatione,* contains the list of the New Sees called for by the Fathers of the Council:

   I. *Province of Baltimore*—Wilmington, Scranton, Harrisburg, Vicariate-Apostolic of North Carolina
   II. *Province of Oregon*—Vicariate-Apostolic of Idaho
   III. *Province of St. Louis*—Green Bay, Lacrosse, St. Joseph, Omaha,

[31] Coppens, "Laws of the Church with regard to Secret Societies," *Amer. Cath. Quar. Review,* V (1880), 275.

Vicariate-Apostolic of Montana, Vicariate-Apostolic of Colorado and Utah, Vicariate-Apostolic of Arizona
IV. *Province of Cincinnati*—Columbus
V. *Province of San Francisco*—Grass Valley
VI. *Province of New York*—Rochester

The Fathers asked also that the Sees of Philadelphia and Milwaukee be made archbishoprics.[32]

Title XIV, *De Efficaciori Decretorum Baltimorensium Executione promovenda,* urges the bishops to leave no stone unturned (*ut nullum non moveant lapidem*) during the canonical visitation of the dioceses as well as in the conferences of the clergy to see that the decrees of the Council be carried out. It was decreed that once the approval of the Holy See was obtained the *Acta et Decreta* of the Council would be printed in book form so that the decrees might be studied in seminaries.[33]

The wisdom and prudence which characterized the decrees of the Council were everywhere recognized.

We find here [says Spalding] evidence of that American good sense, eminently exact and practical, which, in dealing with lofty things, seizes them principally by their positive side, and which, without losing sight of principles, yet adapts them to times and circumstances. If doctrine is greatly represented in this volume,

---

[32] On the meaning of the *praerogativa loci* granted to the metropolitan See of Baltimore in 1858, *cf.* "Das zweite Plenarconcil von Baltimore," *Archiv für katholisches Kirchenrecht* (xxii, 98).

[33] An interesting controversy arose after the publication of the *Acta et Decreta* of the Council of 1866, over the manner in which the Holy See had approved the same. In his *Elements of Ecclesiastical Law* (New York, 1877), Dr. Smith maintained (74-77) that the decrees had not been approved *in forma specifica* and that it was allowed to appeal from them to the Congregation de Propaganda Fide. Indeed in the fourth edition of this work (New York, 1881), Dr. Smith averred that "a careful study of the subject would seem to show that the Second Plenary Council of Baltimore was not confirmed by the Holy See in any form, not even in *forma communi,* but merely revised and corrected" (77, note 30). A strong exception to this statement was made by Rev. P. F. Quigley, Professor of Canon Law in St. Mary's Seminary, Cleveland, Ohio, in a series of articles printed in the *Catholic Universe* and published under the title *Points in Canon Law* (Cleveland, 1878). Dr. Smith replied with *Counter-Points in Canon Law* (Newark, 1879), later embodying his arguments in the three-volume edition of his *Elements* (New York, 1882-1888).

mere speculation occupies but small space. Above everything else, the Council has aimed to be a work of organization. . . . No superfluous details, no useless erudition; everything bears the seal of legislation soberly but firmly motived, wherein nothing is omitted that can enlighten and convince the mind, and nothing is allowed to lengthen what should be short, or complicate what is simple. It is a majestic monument of simple and severe proportions, in which art seems neglected, but is by no means wanting.[84]

Cardinal Cullen expressed his opinion of the Second Plenary Council in the following letter to Archbishop Spalding:

When last writing, I thanked you for the copy of your Plenary Synod which you so kindly sent me. Since then I have been able to consult it frequently, and I find that it is a mine of every sort of knowledge necessary for an ecclesiastic. I congratulate you most warmly on your success in bringing out a work which cannot fail to be of the greatest value to the church of America, and, indeed, to every other church.[85]

The closing ceremonies of the Council, the fourth and last Solemn Session, were held in the cathedral on Sunday, October 21. Solemn Pontifical Mass was celebrated by Archbishop Odin of New Orleans, and Father James Gibbons was the deacon. A sermon on *The Apostolic Ministry, the Divinely Constituted Witness of the Faith* was delivered by Archbishop Kenrick of St. Louis. No reference apparently was made in the sermon to the presence of President Johnson, his secretary, Colonel Robert Johnson, and the mayor of Washington, Mr. Wallach. As senior Archbishop, Dr. Purcell addressed the Apostolic Delegate, Archbishop Spalding, thanking him for the dignity, impartiality and learning with which he had conducted the Council. Archbishop Purcell said:

Most reverend and honored brother! In accordance with an ancient custom, I, as the oldest bishop, wish to address you in the name of the prelates and priests here assembled, before our departure. You represent here the Head of our Church, the Vice-Gerent of Christ, and it is impossible for us to give expression to all the

[84] *Op. cit.,* 317-318.   [85] *Ibid.,* 318.

emotions of veneration and respect which we feel. We feel that the Holy Father was inspired from above when he selected you for the difficult task of presiding over our deliberations, for in your choice we recognize the finger of God, the work of the Holy Ghost. You were born in Kentucky, the land of all gentlemanly feelings and instincts and were then transferred to the East to expand and fortify the Church in this nation. We look about us and are witnesses of the results of your efforts as we see the mitred host of venerable prelates. But in addition to these proofs of your brotherly endeavors we know the books you have published, the sermons you have preached and the many virtues you have practiced. We are of the opinion that the deliberations of this Council under your leadership will be among the most important if not the most important in the annals of the Church. We cannot but testify that the American clergy under your leadership in the results of its work stands second to the clergy of no nation, not even excepting France and Germany. We pray to the Almighty God that you may long lead us through your wisdom, your talents and your holy zeal.[36]

In reply, Archbishop Spalding said:

What I have just heard—which I know expresses the feelings of all my venerable brethren—compensates me more than an hundredfold for whatever little labor I have undergone in preparing for this Council. I feel and say from my heart that I am unworthy of the eulogy which the partiality of my venerable brother has passed upon me. I can lay claim only to industry and earnestness. The true secret of all this, I am sure, is that I am the voice or the shadow of him who represents divine unity and authority on this earth; that I am invested, however unworthy, with the authority of Pius IX, through whose voice Peter speaks, and through Peter, Christ. Herein consists the simplicity, and the beauty, and the sublimity of our faith. We are but the last link in a golden chain, the first of which was Peter, and he was bound to the rock, which is Christ. Never were the unity and the unearthly character of the Church shown more strikingly than in this Council. Here we have venerable prelates from all parts of this great and vast Republic, some of whom have come five or six thousand miles—have come at my voice, because in my voice they recognized the voice of Peter and of Christ. They have come together with one heart and one soul, intent only on the great object of beautifying the house of

[36] Niedermayer-Perine, *The Council in Baltimore etc.*, 39-40.

God, of proclaiming his truth and his holiness, and of promoting the salvation of men. All other considerations have been wholly forgotten. During the two weeks of the Council, while we were in session from six to eight hours a day, not one word has been breathed on or one allusion made to the stirring topics of the day. Our kingdom is not of this world; we have higher aims—glory to God in the highest, peace on earth to men of good will. We came together to devise ways and means to carry out the purpose for which Christ died on the cross—to save men, to bind them together in unity and charity, and to make them lead holy lives. Absorbed in this great object, we have soared far above the region of storms and clouds, into the pure atmosphere of God, where no controversy or contention is stirred up by human passion; and men, sprung from various nations, have in this Council lost sight of all differences of nationality and temperament, and have been blended into that beautiful unity and harmony which the Catholic Church alone can exhibit.[37]

Then followed the *Acclamationes,* to which was added for this occasion:

Almae nostrae Republicae, pax summa, prosperitas plena, ac Dei Omnipotentis superfluens benedictio!

To our great and cherished Republic, supreme peace, full prosperity, and the overflowing benediction of Almighty God!

The *Te Deum* was then sung and the recessional to the archbishop's house took place.

The following morning, a group of the prelates held an extraordinary private congregation on the affairs of the American College at Rome, on certain reserved cases of the Sacrament of Penance, and on the missionary work to be done among the Negroes. At this meeting the *Pastoral Letter to the Clergy and People* was read and approved.

With so elaborate a code of laws for the American Church, then emerging from the catastrophe of the Civil War, it is logical to suppose that the *Pastoral Letter,* issued by the Council on October 22, 1866, would be proportionately broad-visioned in its scope. The influence of the *Pastoral Letter* of the Third Provin-

[37] Spalding, *op. cit.,* 319-320.

cial Council of Cincinnati (1861), written by Archbishop
Spalding while Bishop of Louisville, is visible in its arrangement. There are thirteen topics: authority of plenary councils;
ecclesiastical authority in general; relations of Church and State;
aid for the pope; matrimony; books and newspapers; Catholic
education; Catholic industrial schools; vocations to the priesthood; the laity; the clergy; the emancipated slaves; and religious
communities.

The *Pastoral* was the second official utterance of the archbishops and bishops of the United States assembled in a plenary
session. It was spoken of at the time as "the herald of that full
legislation which in a few months will be promulgated for the
Catholics of the United States," and as containing "the outlines
of that legislation traced with a rapid pen." [88] The primary
object of the *Pastoral* was undoubtedly to impress upon the
minds and hearts of American Catholics the necessity of authority and of cheerful obedience to the divinely constituted order
of the Church. In emphatic language the cardinal principles and
duties of the faithful are explained, and their relations to society
and civic government are clearly defined. The section on the relations of the Church to the State was a noble utterance at a time
when politically the country was in a turmoil and when Reconstruction plans and projects were somewhat at the mercy of a
bitter and vindictive group of leaders. Several sentences stand
out boldly: among them, the following: "In prescribing anything contrary to God's law the Civil Power transcends its authority, and has no claim on the obedience of the citizen." The
prelates recognize that, "except in some brief intervals of excite-
ment and delusion," the State had hitherto never interfered with
our ecclesiastical organization or civil rights, but they assert that
in many of the States "we are not as yet permitted legally to
make those arrangements for the security of Church Property
which are in accordance with the canons and discipline of the
Catholic Church"; and attention was called to laws recently

---

[88] *Catholic World*, IV (1866), 425-426. An excellent digest of the *Pastoral* is in the *Archiv für katholisches Kirchenrecht* (XXXV, 446).

passed in Missouri for the taxation of ecclesiastical property, the avowed object of which was "hostility to the Catholic Church." After describing the afflicted condition of Pope Pius IX, the *Pastoral* urges upon the faithful the necessity of supporting the pope financially in his distress; and they legislate for the foundation of the annual collection already spoken of. In the section devoted to the Sacrament of Matrimony, the faithful are warned against

successive polygamy, no less opposed to the unity and stability of Christian marriage than that simultaneous polygamy which, to the scandal of Christendom, is found within our borders. No State law can authorize divorce, so as to permit the parties divorced to contract new engagements; and every such new engagement, contracted during the joint lives of the parties so divorced, involves the crime of adultery.

Considerable interest was aroused at the time by the strong approbation given in the *Pastoral* to the project of the Paulist Fathers who, under Father Hecker's leadership, had established a Catholic Publication Society (for the distribution of tracts and books on Catholic doctrine) which the Fathers called "second to none in importance among the subsidiary aids . . . for the diffusion of Catholic Truth." The admonition of the First Plenary Council in regard to the establishment and support of parochial schools is repeated in stronger terms; and, although no direct moral obligation is placed upon Catholic parents by the *Pastoral* to send their children to Catholic schools, the results of a non-religious education in the common or public schools are clearly defined. Less severe in its condemnation of non-Catholic education than the *Pastoral Letter* of the Provincial Council of Cincinnati (1861), the *Pastoral* of 1866 leaves no room for doubt that the American Church was fast reaching a decision in this important part of Catholic life.[39]

The section devoted to the emancipated slaves has been variously interpreted. Among the motives brought forward for the

[39] Jenkins, T. L., *Christian Schools* (Baltimore, 1889), 34-35. It is interesting to note that the *Catholic Directory* (Sadlier) for 1867, begins a separate section under each diocese for the parochial schools.

necessity of the Second Plenary Council was the urgent duty of discussing the future status of the more than four million unfortunate beings who were silently but eloquently appealing for help.[40] All that the *Pastoral Letter* did, or could do, in fact, was to recommend this "new and most extensive field of charity" to the faithful. "We could have wished," the prelates wrote,

that in accordance with the action of the Catholic Church in past ages, in regard to the serfs of Europe, a more gradual system of emancipation could have been adopted, so that they might have been in some measure prepared to make a better use of their freedom, than they are likely to do now. Still the evils which must necessarily attend upon the sudden liberation of so large a multitude, with their peculiar dispositions and habits, only make the appeal to our Christian charity and zeal, presented by their forlorn condition, the more forcible and imperative. We urge upon the Clergy and people of our charge the most generous coöperation with the plans which may be adopted by the Bishops of the Dioceses in which they are, to extend to them that Christian education and moral restraint which they so much stand in need of. Our only regret in regard to this matter is, that our means and opportunity of spreading over them the protecting and salutary influences of our Holy Religion, are so restricted.

Finally, the *Pastoral* sums up the work of the Council in these words:

We have taken advantage of the opportunity of the assembling of so large a number of Bishops from every part of our vast country, to enact such decrees as will tend to promote uniformity of discipline and practice amongst us, and to do away with such imperfect observance of the rites and approved ceremonies of the Church as may have been made necessary by the circumstances of past times, but which no length of prescription can ever consecrate, and thus to give to the services of our Religion that beauty and dignity which belongs to them, and for which we should all be so zealous.

So closed the most important ecclesiastical assembly ever witnessed in the United States up to that year.

[40] Timon to Spalding, August 23, 1865, cited by Theobald; "Catholic Missionary Work among the Colored People of the United States (1776-1866)," *Records,* American Catholic Historical Society, XXXV (1924), 342.

CHAPTER XVII

THE THIRD PLENARY COUNCIL (1884)

IT will be a perennial regret to American Catholic historical writers that the fourth volume of John Gilmary Shea's *History of the Catholic Church in the United States*, which he finished on his deathbed in 1892, closes with the Second Plenary Council of Baltimore in 1866. No scholar of his time knew the intervening years between that date and the Council of 1884 so well as he; and with his passing and the consequent dispersion of his papers, much valuable information was lost to all who succeed him in this last phase of the history of our national canonical legislation. Shea's 1879 edition of the DeCourcy-Shea *History* of 1854 and O'Kane Murray's centennial *History* of 1876 are of minor worth for the interim between 1866 and 1884. The late Bishop Thomas O'Gorman's volume, *A History of the Roman Catholic Church in the United States*,[1] covers these years, but the pages he devotes to them contain only a short summary of the progress made by the Church; of the Third Plenary Council there are but a few lines.

To attempt an historical account of the progress of the Church in the United States during these exceptionally crowded eighteen years (1866-1884) would carry the narrative beyond the subject of this volume: canonical legislation. Events of the greatest importance to Catholicism occurred during these years.[2] The assemblage of prelates who met in Baltimore in November, 1884, was composed of almost an entirely new group of leaders.

[1] New York, 1907.
[2] *Cf.* Guilday, "The Church in the United States (1870-1920): a Retrospect of Fifty Years," *Catholic Historical Review*, VI (1921), 533-547.

Of the six archbishops who signed the decrees of the Council of 1866, Archbishop Spalding, Blanchet, Purcell and Odin had passed away, and of the thirty-seven bishops whose signatures are found in the same list, twenty-two had gone to their reward. Besides these, twenty-two other members of the American hierarchy died during these years, among them Archbishops Bayley and Wood. Three of our bishops died abroad in the interim: Bishops Chabrat, Rese and De la Hailandière.

As a result of the Council of 1866, the Dioceses of Columbus, Green Bay, Harrisburg, La Crosse, Rochester, St. Joseph, Scranton and Wilmington (Delaware), and the Vicariates-Apostolic of Marysville, North Carolina, Arizona, Idaho, Montana, and Colorado-Utah were added to the American Church. In 1870, the Dioceses of Springfield (Massachusetts) and of St. Augustine were created. The Dioceses of Ogdensburg and Providence were erected in 1872, and between that date and the opening of the Council of 1884, the following additions to our hierarchical organization were made: the Dioceses of San Antonio, Peoria, Kansas City, Davenport, Grand Rapids, Trenton and Manchester, and the Vicariates-Apostolic of Brownsville, Northern Minnesota, Indian Territory and Dakota. Meanwhile the provincial divisions were multiplied. Boston, Milwaukee, Philadelphia, and Santa Fé became metropolitan Sees in 1875 and in 1880, the Province of Chicago was created. John McCloskey, second Archbishop of New York, had been made a Cardinal in 1875.

The numerical growth of the Church in the United States between the two Councils was almost beyond the counting. The *Catholic Directory* for 1866 and for 1867 gives no general summary of the number of priests, people, churches and institutions, probably because the disturbed state of the country made it impossible to secure exact returns. Shea has estimated the total Catholic population at 3,842,000 in 1866; [3] and there is no

[3] *Op. cit.*, IV, 715.

doubt, although the *Directory* of 1884 gives some vital statistics as a basis for estimating the Catholic population without attempting to decide upon the same, that the Catholic population had almost doubled during these eighteen years (1866-1884).[4] In his retrospect of July, 1884, written in preparation for the Third Plenary Council, Shea has not attempted to give us the numerical growth during the interim, but is satisfied to sketch on large lines the progress of Catholicism at the time.

In this year [he writes], the year of the Third Plenary Council, there are summoned to it: a cardinal, the Archbishop of New York, eleven other archbishops, besides the Apostolic Delegate, fifty-eight bishops, six mitred abbots, and heads of more religious Orders than can now be found in many countries. They will convene as the ecclesiastical superiors of at least seven thousand secular and regular priests, charged with the care of more than eight millions of souls.[5]

In the Apostolic letter of Leo XIII (January 1, 1884) selecting the city of Baltimore for the sessions of the Third Plenary Council, the pope likewise appointed its archbishop, James Gibbons, as the presiding officer and Apostolic Delegate of the assembly, owing to the inability of Cardinal McCloskey, who was then seventy-four years old, to accept the post. Cardinal McCloskey celebrated the golden jubilee of his priesthood on January 12, 1884, and it was realized by all that any other public ceremony would be too great a tax upon his physical powers. Although he was represented in all the preliminary deliberations by his coadjutor, Archbishop Corrigan, the venerable first Cardinal of the United States was looked to by the other prelates, particularly by Archbishop Gibbons, for guidance and counsel in the work to be done by the plenary meeting of 1884.[6]

[4] Shaughnessy, *Has the Immigrant Kept the Faith?* (New York, 1925), 162-167.
[5] "The Progress of the Church in the United States, from the first Provincial Council to the third Plenary Council of Baltimore," *Amer. Cath. Quarterly Review*, IX (1884), 495.
[6] Farley, *Life of John Cardinal McCloskey: 1810-1880* (New York, 1918), 364.

The letter of convocation was addressed by Archbishop Gibbons to the American hierarchy on March 19, 1884. No one could deny, he wrote, how many and how permanent were the blessings which had accrued to the Catholic Church here from the deliberations and the decrees of the Council of 1866. Nevertheless, in the eighteen years which had passed since that assembly, the marvelous increase in the number of the faithful and the unprecedented growth of the institutional life of the Church had created many problems which needed careful and mature consideration. For that reason, the Council was convoked in order that any abuses which may have crept into American Catholic life be eliminated and that uniform standards of discipline be strengthened by common counsel. The prelates were then requested to be in Baltimore for the month of November following for the opening sessions.

Among the new problems present was one in which the Council of 1884 succeeded so brilliantly that its decretal legislation won the admiration of the whole Catholic world, particularly in Australasia, England and Ireland: a summary of the doctrinal basis of Catholic belief. Nothing is said in the published *Acta et Decreta* of the Council of the preliminary meetings held in Rome in November-December, 1883, for the purpose of deciding, with the guidance of the Holy See, the questions which should, or should not, be permitted to come before the conciliar legislators. The inner history of these Roman meetings as well as that of the private congregations of the Council itself has not yet been written; nor is this the time or the place to do so. There was some opposition among the leaders of the American Church to holding the Council in what was a presidential year, and opinion was divided on the place for its sessions. The committee called to Rome by Leo XIII in October, 1883, represented fairly well the different attitudes. After their deliberations began in Rome, there arose also several perplexing questions which were settled by our representatives in a frank and thoroughly American fashion. Chief among these was freedom in the selection of the problems which were to come before the Baltimore assembly.[7]

The first practical matter which arose was that of hospitality for the many prelates invited to attend; but with their usual openheartedness, Baltimore Catholics and non-Catholics found no difficulty in providing for the comfort of the visiting archbishops and bishops. On Thursday, November 6, at five in the afternoon, the archbishops met as guests of Archbishop Gibbons in an informal discussion of the matters which were to be brought up in the Council; and the following morning, in the *aula maxima* of St. Mary's Seminary, all the prelates met for the purpose of deciding upon the method to be followed in the meetings. After a word of greeting from Archbishop Gibbons, they were made familiar with all that had thus far been accomplished in Rome and in Baltimore for the prompt and complete dispatch of the business before the Council. His biographer has written that the organization and guidance of the Council "was the greatest constructive project" upon which Gibbons ever embarked.[8] All received in printed form the *schematismus* of the Council, the list of the committees and of the conciliar officials, and those decrees which had already been put into canonical form in order that all might be ready for the discussion of the same.

The division of the Council's labors into distinct sections under the charge of committees of bishops and theologians was more elaborate than in any previous assembly. Three episcopal committees were appointed: one for new business (Archbishops Williams, Heiss, and Feehan); one on the Catechism (Archbishop Alemany and Bishops de Goesbriand, Ryan (C.M.), Dwenger, J. L. Spalding, Kain and Janssens); and a third for

[7] *Cf.* Guilday, "Retrospect etc.," *Cath. Hist. Review,* IV, 533-547. The Council was hailed at the time as the "most important Council of the Church in America and among the largest in ecclesiastical history" (*Balt. Cath. Mirror,* XXXV, September 27, 1884); *cf.* "The National Catholic Council," *Cath. World,* XL (1884-85), 708-714.

[8] Will, *Life of Cardinal Gibbons* (New York, 1922), I, 234.

the conciliar letters. Archbishop Gibbons was selected to write the letter to the Holy Father; Archbishop Corrigan, with the aid of Bishops O'Farrell and Keane, was selected to write the *Pastoral Letter to the Clergy and Laity;* and Archbishop Seghers and Bishop Moore, the one to the Society of the Propagation of the Faith.

There were twelve committees of *theologians* to whom was entrusted part by part the entire decretal legislation already agreed upon as a basis for discussion. Each of these committees had as its chairman an archbishop, and was composed of several bishops, a notary, and a selected number of *theologians.* Among these last were many whose names were then well-known in the American Church or who later reached prominence in ecclesiastical circles—Fathers Sabetti (S.J.), Dumont (S.S.), Richard Burtsell, Joseph Cataldo (S.J.), Bishop Curtis, Cardinal Farley, Bishop Ludden, Fathers Edward Sorin (C.S.C.), James Corrigan, Bonaventure Frey, (O.M.Cap.), Francis X. Weniger (S.J.), Alphonsus Magnien (S.S.), Isaac Hecker (C.S.P.), Bishop Keiley, Monsignor Lee, Bishop Harkins, Bishop Bonacum, Archbishop Katzer, Father Dyer (S.S.), Rev. S. B. Smith, Monsignor Brann and others.[9]

Rules were agreed upon for the sessions of these committees as well as for the private and public congregations. The committees of the *theologians* were to meet every day except Sundays, Tuesdays and Fridays at four o'clock in the afternoon. Six of these were to assemble in the archbishop's house, the others in St. Mary's Seminary. Two public congregations were to be held each week, on Tuesdays and Fridays at four P.M., and all were to be vested according to rank. The private congregations of the bishops were to be held every day except Sundays and Thursdays in the *aula maxima* of St. Mary's Seminary. The solemn sessions were to take place on Sundays and Thursdays at 11 A.M., and on November 13 the Mass of Requiem for the dead prelates was to be celebrated. A procession was to begin

[9] The order followed is that given in the *Acta et Decreta*, xxvi-xxxiv.

the first of the Solemn Sessions, weather permitting. By a special indult of the Holy See, all who participated in the Council were granted a plenary indulgence on the ordinary conditions, and the papal blessing was to be given at the Solemn Sessions. The order to be observed was already outlined in the little *Praxis* which was published the previous year.[10] Parliamentary rules were also made. Among these were the following: a majority of those entitled to a decisive vote should constitute a quorum, and all questions were to be decided by a majority vote, except when these rules forbade it. No proposition once negatived by the Council could be renewed, unless a majority of those voting should so decide. Then the list of those chosen to preach in the cathedral was published.[11] Two other preachers were selected to give sermons in German in St. Alphonsus Church during the Council. Telegrams of felicitation were sent to Leo XIII and to Cardinal McCloskey. It was decided to send a letter to the German hierarchy, then suffering for the Church through the anti-Catholic animosity of the Kulturkampf. Bishop Kain of Wheeling proposed that the Council issue a formal protest against the spoliation of the property of the Sacred Congregation de Propaganda Fide, and it was decided to do so in the *Pastoral Letter*. The Italian government had passed laws in 1866 and 1873 confiscating the property of Propaganda, including the American College, the title of which was in the name of the Sacred Congregation, but which had been created and maintained from 1859 by the contributions of American Catholics. When the danger of a new confiscation arose again in 1884, the American hierarchy succeeded in arousing the interest of President Arthur and the College was saved.[12]

The first public congregation was held on Saturday, Novem-

[10] There was also published in anticipation of the Council a popular *Manual of the Public Ceremonies of the Third Plenary Council of Baltimore for the Use of the Faithful.*

[11] Twenty-one of these sermons are printed in the *Memorial Volume of the Third Plenary Council of Baltimore* (Baltimore, 1885).

[12] Brann, *History of the American College, Rome* (New York, 1910), 149-196; Will, *Life of Cardinal Gibbons*, I, 246.

ber 8, and Archbishop Gibbons spoke on the diversity of spiritual gifts in the Church (I Cor. xii. 4), urging all who were members of the Council to recognize that divisions of opinion were inevitable in such a large group, but assuring all that the freedom and frankness of the discussions would in no way harm the splendid unity they all possessed, one with another. Strict silence to outsiders on the questions brought before the Council was enjoined.

The first Solemn Session, the actual opening of the Council, was held in the cathedral on Sunday, November 9, with a procession from the archbishop's house, followed by Solemn Pontifical Mass, sung by Archbishop Peter Richard Kenrick, and a sermon on "The Church in Her Councils" was delivered by Archbishop Patrick John Ryan of Philadelphia. There were present fourteen archbishops, fifty-seven bishops, seven archabbots, three diocesan procurators, one diocesan administrator, seven domestic prelates, three monsignori, thirty-one superiors or provincials of the religious Orders and Congregations, eleven presidents of theological seminaries, and eighty-eight priests who acted as *theologians* to the hierarchy. Besides Cardinal McCloskey, six bishops were absent on account of illness, and seven other ecclesiastics were excused for various reasons. There was present also at this session, Bishop Peter Maria Osouf, Vicar-Apostolic of northern Japan.[18]

The officials of the Council were then publicly appointed. As *Promoters* were selected Bishops Kain, Janssens, Loughlin, De Goesbriand, William McCloskey and Fink, O.S.B. Monsignor Robert Seton was named *Notary*. The *Secretaries* were Rev. James Corcoran, Very Rev. Henry Gabriels, Very Rev. Sebastian Messmer, and Very Rev. Denis J. O'Connell. The *Chancellors* were Fathers George Devine and John Foley. As *Masters of Ceremonies* Fathers James McCallen (S.S.), Michael Kelly, and

---

[18] The *Balt. Cath. Mirror* (November 8, 1884) records the presence of Bishops Lynch and O'Mahony of Toronto, Bishop Walsh of London, Ont., Bishop Cleary of Kingston, Ont., and Rt. Rev. J. H. Tabert of Ottawa.

Thomas Broydrick were chosen; and as *Chanters*, Fathers André (S.S.), Bartlett, O'Keefe, Lammel, Cassidy, Drennan, and Marr. The profession of faith was then made by all present, and papal benediction was given by the Apostolic Delegate.

The official *Acta et Decreta* do not contain all the proceedings of the public and private congregations held during the month which followed. These documents, now in the Baltimore Cathedral archiepiscopal archives, are so numerous and varied that a whole volume would be required to deal with their contents adequately. Accordingly, it has been considered more practical to treat the Council solely from the excerpts printed in the official volume; these are from the documentary material of the private congregations only. Among these excerpts are: the petition of the Fathers of the Society of Jesus for the introduction of the Cause of beatification of the first Jesuit Martyrs of North America and of Catherine Tekakwitha, the Iroquois virgin; the decision to found a Catholic University for higher studies in the United States, for which an executive Board was named; the support of the two American Colleges at Rome and Louvain, for which advisory and executive committees were created; the publication of an authentic English version of the Bible; and the question of the incorporation of all ecclesiastical property in the possession of the religious Orders.

The decrees of the Council follow the method of division inaugurated in the Council of 1866. They are divided into *Tituli*, of which there are twelve. In the preliminary Title, it was decreed that all the enactments of the Second Plenary Council, except those changed or abrogated by the Council of 1884, should remain in force. The eleven Titles which follow, treat the following subjects:

   I: *The Catholic Faith*
  II: *Ecclesiastical Persons*
 III: *Divine Worship*
  IV: *The Sacraments*
   V: *Clerical Education*

VI: *Education of Catholic Youth*
VII: *Christian Doctrine*
VIII: *Zeal for Souls*
IX: *Church Property*
X: *Ecclesiastical Trials*
XI: *Christian Burial*

A final Title concerns the promulgation of the decrees and of the more efficacious means of applying the enactments of the Council to all parts of the provinces and dioceses of the American Church. Each Title is subdivided into chapters and each chapter into decrees, numbered from 1 to 319.

Title I, *The Catholic Faith,* consists of a single chapter, divided into ten parts, containing a statement of the principal doctrines of the Faith, giving special attention to the dogmatic constitutions of the Vatican Council, adopting reverently the definitions of that Council on Reason, Revelation, Sacred Scripture, and Infallibility, and condemning all errors, especially those signalized by the *Quod Apostolic muneris* (on socialism), the *Diuturum illud* (on political government), and the *Arcanum* (on Christian marriage), issued by Pope Leo XIII.[14]

Title II, *Ecclesiastical Persons,* contains nine chapters. Chapter I on "Bishops" reached what was for many years to come the final stage in the evolution of the method of nominations to vacant Sees up to the promulgation of the Code (1918). The various systems agreed upon by our prelates in former Councils or as ordered by the Sacred Congregation de Propaganda Fide had not been entirely satisfactory, especially to the priests who believed that they should be given a more deliberative voice in the selection of candidates for the episcopate.[15] The system of cathedral chapters was occasionally put forward by Rome as more consistent with the general laws of the Church, and during

[14] *Cf.* Wynne, John J., S.J., *Great Encyclical Letters of Leo XIII* (New York, 1903).

[15] *Cf.* Corrigan, P., *Episcopal Nominations* (New York, 1883); id., *What the Catholic Church Most Needs in the United States, or, the Voice of the Priests in the Election of Bishops* (New York, 1884); Peries, "Episcopal Elections," *Amer. Cath. Quarterly Review* (January, 1896), 61-91.

the preliminary meetings of November-December, 1883, there
was a temporary deadlock between our representatives and
Propaganda on the question, a compromise being reached eventually by the system of diocesan consultors through whom the
clergy might voice their opinions on the matter. The new legislation for filling vacant Sees arranged the selection in a practical
way. Within thirty days after the vacancy, the consultors and
irremovable rectors were to meet under the presiding metropolitan or senior suffragan and select three candidates whose names
would then be submitted to the bishops of the province. Where
a metropolitan was to be selected, the senior suffragan bishop
or his deputy was to preside. Within ten days after the meeting, the suffragan bishops were to meet for discussion on the
candidates so selected, and they had the right to approve or dis-
approve any or all of these candidates. Other rules were made
for a selection of a coadjutor-bishop or for electing a bishop to
a newly erected diocese.[16] Other topics mentioned in this chapter are: the dignity of the episcopal office; loyalty and reverence
toward the Holy See; the obligation of the diocesan visitation at
least every three years; and the administration of the Sacrament
of Confirmation. Chapter II on "Diocesan Consultors" stipu-
lates that there should be at least four of these officials, six being
the maximum number. Two, however, would suffice, in case of
necessity. One half were to be chosen by the bishop; the other
half to be nominated by the clergy, and each priest voting was
to present three names for each choice. The matters which
came within the privilege of the consultors were: the convocation of a diocesan synod; the division of parishes; the appointment of religious to a parish; the choice of examiners for the dio-

[16] *Cf.* McCarthy, "Historical Development of Episcopal Nominations in
the Catholic Church of the United States (1789-1884)," *Records,* American
Catholic Historical Society, XXXVIII (1927), 297-354. *Cf.* Smith, *Elements, etc.,* I, 149-160; Corcoran, "The Decrees of the Third Plenary Council," *Amer. Cath. Quarterly Review,* XI (1886), 344-356; Nilles, *Commentaria in Concilium Plenarium Baltimorense Tertium,* pars II, *Decreta
Concilii* (Innsbruck, 1890) ; "Das dritte Plenarconcil von Baltimore," *Archiv
für katholisches Kirchenrecht* (LVII, 418, written by Bellesheim).

cesan seminary; the choice of certain diocesan officials; the administration of Church property where the sum to be expended exceeded five thousand dollars, and the cathedraticum.[17] The consultors were elected for three years and were irremovable except for grave causes. *Seda vacante,* the administrator of the diocese was obliged to consult them in all matters falling under their canonical jurisdiction. They were to meet at least twice a year. Chapter III is on the "Examiners of the Clergy." There were to be six of these officials, whose duty it was to examine the junior clergy and to preside over the concursus for irremovable rectorships. Chapter IV deals with "Rural Deans" or "Vicars Forane." Their appointment was recommended to the bishops, and their duty consisted in expediting matters of minor importance within a given district of the diocese. They were to be the *oculi et aures* of the bishop, *discrete vigilantes* and *paterne monentes* over the conduct of the clergy and faithful.[18] Chapter V on "Irremovable Rectors" contains eight sections, describing the conditions under which they may be appointed. Ordinarily, one-tenth of the pastors of a diocese should be so honored; and the candidates were to be chosen from those who had been in the ministry for at least ten years and who had successfully passed the concursus. The removable causes are given: disobedience in grave matters; public criticism of the Ordinary in the matter of Catholic education and of Church property administration; fraudulent returns in the annual report; public scandal; or incapacity in Church administration. Chapter VI describes the "Concursus" in nineteen sections. The examination for irremovable rectorships was to take place before the Ordinary (or the Vicar-General) and three examiners, and the *materia examinis* covered the major theological subjects, together with ability in catechetical instruction and in preaching. Chapter VII on the "Diocesan Clergy" is divided into four parts: on the ordination of priests for the diocese, the incardination of priests, sick and infirm priests, and *de sacerdotibus lapsis.* The

[17] Smith, *op. cit.,* I, 464-495.   [18] *Ibid.,* 388-389.

legislation of this chapter bound priests by oath to remain in the diocese for which they were ordained, and required a probation of three to five years for incardination.[19] A Clerical Fund was to be organized in each diocese for sick and infirm priests by a tax imposed on each parish or on the salaries of the clergy in case the bishops should approve this method; otherwise, an annual fee should be paid by the priests of the diocese for this purpose, and every priest was urged to become a member of this clerical aid society. The treatment to be accorded to unworthy priests is explained. They had no claim for support from the bishop, but those who showed signs of repentance should be given every opportunity of amendment.[20] The Fathers of the Council expressed their profound gratitude to the superiors of certain religious Orders who had agreed to care for those priests who voluntarily subjected themselves to a disciplinary penance, and in particular to the Abbots of Gethsemane, New Mellaray and St. John's, to the Rector of the Passionist Monastery (Hoboken), and especially to Archabbot Wimmer of St. Vincent's, Beatty, Pennsylvania, who agreed to care for these unfortunates in houses specially set aside for that purpose. Chapter VIII on "Clerical Life and Manners" has ten sections which repeat to a large extent the enactments of 1866. Priests were ordered to make a retreat at least once every two years, to spend some time each day in study and reading, and to avoid everything in their conduct which might give cause for scandal; attendance at horse races and theaters being especially condemned. The Roman collar was made obligatory. They were forbidden to bring civil action against their fellow priests

[19] This legislation was rendered superfluous by the special rescript of November 22, 1885, by virtue of which a priest ordained for any diocese was permitted to serve the missions in another diocese within the same province without renewing the missionary oath. *Cf.* Corcoran, *l.c.*, 348.

[20] This, as well as other cognate disciplinary questions, had been brought to the attention of the American Church by a lengthy discussion, entitled *Jura Sacerdotum Vindicata: The Rights of the Clergy Vindicated, or a Plea for Canon Law in the United States,* by Rev. William Mahoney (New York, 1883), xi-442.

without the Ordinary's written permission and were ordered to dress as became their station in life. Their presbyteries were to be regulated wisely and according to the rules of the Church, and in their private lives they were to see that there was nothing hindering their spiritual perfection. They were also to refrain from all political questions both in the pulpit and in public.[21] Chapter IX on the "Regular Clergy" asked for and obtained the extension to the United States of the regulations for harmony and mutual understanding between the Ordinaries and the regular clergy on the missions laid down in the Constitution *Romanos Pontifices* of Leo XIII (1881),[22] and all controverted points of jurisdiction were to be referred to the Prefect of the Sacred Congregation. Rules are also given for the control of religious Institutes within the diocese, and bishops are ordered to see that the laws of enclosure be strictly enforced. "Precautions are to be taken lest Sisters should go about begging at all times and in all places, to the scandal of the faithful, and to their own possible spiritual detriment. In some parts of the country this had become such an intolerable abuse that it needed to be checked with an iron hand." [23] Later in Title IX there is a stringent warning to all foreign superiors of religious communities and to foreign bishops against permitting clerical beggars (*mendicaturi*) to come here for the purpose of collecting funds. Ordinary and extraordinary confessors of nuns were to be appointed for a term of three years, and the extraordinary confessor was obliged to hear the confessions of nuns at least twice a year. Those who have taken vows in the religious

[21] The Fathers cite here (n. 93) the following words from the Pastoral of the Ninth Provincial Council of Baltimore (May 9, 1858): "Our clergy have wisely abstained from all interference with the judgment of the faithful, which should be free on all questions of polity and social order, within the limits of the doctrine and law of Christ. . . . Leave to worldlings the cares and anxieties of political partizanship, the struggles for ascendancy, and the mortifications of disappointed ambition. Do not, in any way, identify the interests of our holy faith with the fortunes of any party."

[22] The text of the *Romanos Pontifices* will be found in the Appendix to the *Acta et Decreta*, 212-230.

[23] Corcoran, *l.c.*, 349.

Brotherhoods, whose rule forbade them to aspire to the priesthood, could, after leaving these communities, be accepted by the
Ordinary without a dispensation from the Holy See.

Title III, *Divine Worship*, has four chapters: on bination; on
uniformity of feasts and fasts; on the Sunday observance; and on
sacred music. The necessity of celebrating two Masses on Sundays and holydays of obligation was recognized on account of
the number who were obliged to hear Mass, and the bishops by
a special Instruction of Propaganda (1870) were permitted to
extend this faculty to their priests.[24] Without the expressed
permission of Rome, however, no priest was to be allowed to
accept a stipend for the second Mass. The number of holydays
of obligation was fixed at six: The Immaculate Conception,
Christmas, Circumcision (New Year's Day), Ascension, Assumption, and All Saints. Dr. Corcoran, the chief secretary of
the Council, gives us a curious reflection on this part of the
chapter:

> As to fasting [he writes] the difference of climate, the lack, in
> many places, of food suitable to one who keeps the abstinence, the
> physical needs of the laboring classes, and other considerations
> made it nearly impossible to attain anything like uniformity in this
> vast country of ours. Whatever uniformity is attainable, must be
> local to a great extent, limited to a few coterminous States, and
> agreed on in Provincial Councils.[25]

Sunday observance was particularly stressed because difficulties
in this matter had arisen with those immigrants whose ideas
regarding Sunday rest differed from that which prevailed here.
Church music was to be carefully chosen, and the Fathers of the
Council urged that Gregorian Chant be taught in the parochial
schools.

Title IV, the *Sacraments*, is confined to two chapters on the
baptism of converts and on marriage. A careful investigation of
a probable former valid baptism of each convert was to be made

---

[24] *Conc. Plen. Balt. III*, 233-243.
[25] *L.c.*, 349; *cf.* Shea, "The Church and her Holydays," *Amer. Cath. Quarterly Review*, xi (1886), 462-475.

before conferring the sacrament and the ritual prescribed for the same was to be scrupulously followed.[26] Catholics were reminded that no authority on earth can dissolve the bonds of valid marriage. Any who attempted marriage before a non-Catholic minister incurred the pain of excommunication reserved to the bishop. Mixed marriages were not to be performed unless the customary promises were made beforehand, and no dispensation from these was to be given. Pastors had the grave duty of ascertaining afterwards whether these promises were being kept. It was also agreed that a chancery tax might be imposed for all dispensations for mixed marriages.

Title V, *Clerical Education,* has five chapters on preparatory seminaries, major seminaries, on the *Seminarium Principale* or university, on the examination of the junior clergy, and on the regular quarterly conferences of the clergy. The studies in the preparatory and major seminaries are given in detail. In the minor seminaries the students were to be instructed in a foreign language (German, French, Italian, Spanish, Polish or other Slavic tongues) as diocesan needs required. In the major seminary, Catholic philosophy was to be taught according to the method of St. Thomas Aquinas, the patron of Catholic schools. Six years must be given to the study of philosophy and theology. Sacred eloquence was to form a serious part of the training of the candidates for the priesthood. The philosophical and theological branches are described in this chapter as are also the method of examinations and the spiritual and financial administration of the seminary.[27] The Fathers of the Third Plenary Council became the founders of the Catholic University of America by decreeing that the time had come for the creation of one central school of higher learning, and a commission was appointed for the purpose of instituting the means necessary for its foundation. It is true that the Council did not legislate specifically for the immediate establishment of a central Catho-

---

[26] The ceremonies to be followed were those given in the *Acta et Decreta* of the Council of 1866, 231-293.
[27] Cox, *Administration of Seminaries* (Washington, D. C., 1931).

lic university, but its formal action in appointing a committee for this purpose may be said to be the corner stone of the university which was eventually opened in November, 1889. Students were still to be sent, however, to the Universities of Rome, Louvain, and Innsbruck.[28] Five times, in five successive years, unless grave cause were present, the junior clergy were to undergo a written examination in the principal theological branches, and the papers were to be preserved in the episcopal archives for future reference. The quarterly conferences (semiannual in rural districts) were to be attended by all priests having charge of the *cura animarum*.

Title VI, *Education of Catholic Youth,* has two chapters: one on parochial schools and one on high schools. The legislation of the Synod of 1791, of the Seven Provincial Councils (1829-49), and of the First (1852) and Second (1866) Plenary Councils had marched forward steadily toward the explicit stand taken by our hierarchy in 1884 on the question of Catholic education. The Council of 1866 gave us an emphatic statement on the inevitable remedy the Church would be obliged to apply to the risk and the danger Catholic boys and girls were encountering in the common schools. Whenever possible parochial schools were to be erected, and a strong plea was made to religious communities and teaching orders to devote themselves to the work. Between the two Councils (1866-1884) the public school system had made great progress in the United States, but step-by-step with that progress went an increasing abandonment of religious teaching and influence. There is no doubt that during these years the problem of Catholic children in these schools was the dominant anxiety of our prelates and clergy. Some of the Provincial Councils which had been held between 1852 and 1866 [29] had legislated for an outright system of Catholic parochial school training. This was particularly true of the Pro-

[28] *Cf.* Shea, "The proposed Catholic University of America," *Amer. Cath. Quarterly Review,* X (1885), 312-325; Erbacher, *Catholic Higher Education for Men* (Washington, D. C., 1931).
[29] New York: 1854, 1860, 1861; Baltimore: 1855, 1858; St. Louis: 1855, 1858; New Orleans: 1855, 1861; and Cincinnati: 1855, 1858, 1861.

vincial Councils of Cincinnati in which the zeal and sacrifice of the German parishes were held up as a model to all others in this respect. There was some discussion on the question, owing to the financial outlay involved; and eventually the matter was taken to Propaganda. As a result, on November 24, 1875, the Sacred Congregation issued a celebrated Instruction [30] in which the general principle was enunciated that both the divine and natural law forbade the presence of Catholic children in schools in which their Faith was in jeopardy. The consequence of this letter was that parochial schools began to spring up in all parts of the United States. The Council of 1884 "surpassed all preceding Councils on American soil in the number, importance and cogency of its regulations on the subject of education," [31] and the general law was passed binding the clergy and laity, whenever possible, to establish parish schools. The words of the decree (n. 196) are as follows:

Therefore, we not only exhort Catholic parents with paternal affection, but we *command* them with all the authority in our power, to procure a truly Christian education for their dear offspring, given them by God, reborn to Christ in baptism and destined for heaven; and further, to defend and secure all of them from the dangers of secular education during the whole term of their infancy and childhood; and finally, to send them to Catholic, and especially parochial, schools, unless, indeed, the bishop of the diocese judge that in a particular case other provision may be permitted.

Parents were, however, not bound under pain of mortal sin to send their children to Catholic schools, and pastors were warned to avoid all excessive zeal (*immodico zelo*) in the matter, lest the freedom permitted by the Sacred Congregation in 1875 and by Leo XIII in 1884 be violated. This freedom was, however, to be granted at the discretion of the Ordinary. Where permission was granted by the Ordinary for Catholic children

[30] The Instruction will be found in Latin in the *Acta et Decreta* of 1884, 279, and in English in Jenkins, *Christian Schools* (Baltimore, 1889), 128-133.
[31] Jenkins, *op, cit.,* 134. Almost one-fourth of the decrees of the Council are devoted to the subject of Catholic education.

to frequent the common schools, no one, layman or cleric, should presume to denounce or condemn such an action, much less should pastors make it a pretext to refuse the sacraments to the children or to their parents (n. 198). Parochial schools were to be multiplied as quickly as possible, and their curriculum should be perfected, so that no Catholic parent should any longer have an excuse for not supporting them. The Council was determined to raise the standards of the schools so that they would become "the honor and ornament, the hope and strength both of the Church and of the republic." [32] Nothing is overlooked or forgotten in this section that would tend to create a more perfect system of Catholic education. Teachers and studies, schools and administration, and methods are all dealt with in detail. High schools, as we now understand the term, were in their infancy in 1884; but the Council recognized the necessity of multiplying Catholic high schools, academies, and colleges, and legislated to the effect that every effort should be put forward by priests and people to create a complete system of Catholic training which would protect the Catholic youth of the land at every stage of its education. "God grant our fondly cherished hope," the prelates wrote, "of seeing matters so arranged that these desires may be fully accomplished by facilitating the advancement of Catholic children by regular ascent from the elementary to the superior Catholic schools." [33]

Title VII, *Christian Doctrine,* treats in four chapters the office of preaching, catechetical instruction, prayer-books, and books and newspapers. The qualities of a good sermon are given. Again, priests are warned not to bring politics into the pulpit and care must be taken to avoid a too frequent mention (*praesertim asperiori modo*) of money. One of the most interesting, albeit perplexing, pages of American Catholic history lies beneath the enactments (nn. 217-219) on the Catechism. The desire for a uniform Catechism was never absent from the

---

[32] *Acta et Decreta,* n. 207, 110.
[33] *Ibid,* n. 208, 111; Jenkins, *op. cit.,* 147.

thoughts of our spiritual leaders from the days of John Carroll. Challoner's *Abridgement of Christian Doctrine* (1772) was used here in the early days of our organized Church, although other Catechisms, such as Father Molyneaux' (1785), Butler's (1788), Maréchal's (1818), England's (1821), Flaget's (1825) and others were in circulation. A uniform Catechism was urged in the Council of 1829, but nothing was done until the First Plenary Council (1852) and a commission was appointed for that purpose. This Catechism was unsatisfactory and the Second Plenary Council (1866) again discussed the problem and a committee was appointed to examine a Catechism by Rev. Dr. John McCaffrey, then President of Mount St. Mary's College, Emmitsburg, Maryland, but no formal approval was given. The desire for such a Catechism grew stronger in the interim between 1866 and 1884, and a commission was appointed for that purpose; with the result that the *Baltimore Catechism* was approved by Archbishop Gibbons in 1885. This was criticized by theologians and catechists and never won general favor.[84] The chapter on prayer-books (*quorum infinitus prope est numerus*) defines the regulations which should govern the compilation and publication of these volumes. None should be published without the permission of the Ordinary, and compilers were urged to use the prayers of the Missal, Breviary and Ritual. A commission was appointed to prepare a Manual of Prayers. In the matter of objectionable books and newspapers, the Fathers state that it is not sufficient to condemn them; they should be met by a Catholic literature adapted to non-Catholic minds, and the Catholic press should be supported and multiplied. There should be one Catholic newspaper in each province, and diocesan papers were also commended. It was the opinion of the Council that in each large civic center there should be a Catholic daily of equal influence with the best newspapers of the city. It was not necessary that it bear the name

[84] Nilles, *Commentaria in Concilium Baltimorense Tertium*, II, 188, 265 (Innsbruck, 1888). *Cf.* Guilday, *England*, I, 314.

Catholic. Catholics were warned that not all newspapers being printed under presumably Catholic editorship were equally orthodox or sufficiently reverential to episcopal authority and to Catholic tradition.

Title VIII, *Zeal for Souls,* with three chapters, treats especially of the care which must be taken to instruct immigrants in their own tongue. Priests should be appointed for all the large ports to minister to the newcomers, and special guidance should be given to young women and girls (*quae saepe, nullo comite, nullo custode aut tutore, iter faciunt*) who often run grave danger to their virtue. Praise is given in this section to the welfare societies (Mission of Our Lady of the Rosary and the St. Raphael Society) which were then at work in New York City caring for the immigrants. The need of an organized effort to preserve the faith of the Catholic Negroes and Indians had been felt since the close of the Civil War, and the Council of 1884 appointed a permanent commission for this purpose: "The Commission for Catholic Missions among the Colored People and the Indians." [25] A special annual collection was ordered to be taken up for this purpose in all the churches on the first Sunday of Lent and the funds were to be distributed at the discretion of the Commission. The third chapter has to do with societies of various kinds. Secret societies were censured and the faithful warned not to become members of such groups; a commission of the bishops was to pass upon all societies of this kind in order that a uniform discipline be sustained. All Catholic societies, especially those for the spread of temperance, which have received the approbation of the Church, were to be encouraged. Societies for the young, for the distribution of Catholic literature, for the care of those in prison, and for other charitable ends were to be instituted. The Society of the Propagation

[25] Corcoran writes: "They will continue to use their best efforts to undo the last traces of the anti-Catholic policy of Hiram Ulysses Grant and his spiritual adviser, Rev. Mr. Newman, who without scruple sent out Methodist agents and missionaries to rob Catholic Indians of their supplies and their religion," *l.c.,* 352.

of the Faith was to be established in all the dioceses. Under the
caption of Temperance Societies, all Catholics engaged in the
manufacture or sale of intoxicating liquors were warned to use
every influence to avoid creating occasions of sin for those who
indulged in the same; they should keep their saloons closed on
Sundays and should refuse to sell to minors. As far as possible
their places of business should not become the scene of blas-
phemy or scurrilous talk.

Title IX, *Church Property,* explains the doctrine of the right
of the Church, being a perfect society, to possess temporal goods,
and repeats the regulations of former Councils. Bishops are the
supreme administrators of all ecclesiastical property in the diocese, and pastors are their representatives in this regard. Lay
trustees, if appointed, must be Catholics of standing in the community and of sterling loyalty to the disciplinary enactments of
the Church; and when elected are to be appointed by the pastor,
with the bishop's approval. The deeds to all Church properties
should be in the name of the Ordinary and all should be safe-
guarded as well as possible by the civil laws of the state. The
last chapter of this Title treats of prohibited methods of collecting Church funds. The practice of collecting seat-money at the
doors of the church was an abuse which should be suppressed
as soon as practicable. Certain parts of the church should be set
aside for the poor; unobtrusively, however. All extraordinary
means (picnics, excursions, fairs, etc.) are to be conducted in
such a way that all abuses be eliminated. Balls, with dancing
and banquets, for pious purposes are stamped with the Council's seal of reprobation. In a very special way the Fathers condemn a custom, the existence of which had been rumored (*quae
utinam inanis et mendaxque sit!*) of refusing the sacraments to
those among the faithful who were not supporting the parish.
The question of stole-fees was to be properly arranged by the
bishop in diocesan synod.[36] Another abuse condemned in this

[36] Cf. Kremer, *Church Support in the United States* (Washington, D. C.,
1930), 91-93; Ferry, *Stole Fees* (Washington, D. C., 1930).

chapter was what the Fathers called the detestable method of advertisements which offered Masses in return for financial support toward church buildings or other pious works.

Title X, *Ecclesiastical Trials,* instituted an ecclesiastical court in each diocese to bé governed by the Instruction of Propaganda of 1884, with major officials: a judge, diocesan attorney, attorney for the accused, and a chancellor or notary, and a number of minor officers.[37] The entire procedure is given, according to the tenor of the Instruction of July 20, 1878.[38]

Title XI, *Christian Burial,* contains a single chapter which mitigates to some extent the rigid ruling of former Councils regarding the burial of Catholics, especially converts, in non-Catholic cemeteries. Catholic cemeteries were to be properly and decently cared for, lest their neglected condition should inspire Catholics to avoid the burial of their dead in the same.

The last Title declares that all the decrees of the Council were binding in conscience as soon as their approbation had been obtained from the Holy See and were promulgated by the Apostolic Delegate, Archbishop Gibbons, without waiting for the same to be done through provincial councils or diocesan synods.

An Appendix of one hundred and seven pages follows the decrees in the officially printed *Acta et Decreta* of the Council. This contains the important documents referred to in the decrees. Among these are: the letter of Leo XIII regarding the American College at Rome (October 25, 1884); Propaganda's Instruction on the visit *ad limina* (June 1, 1877); the oath to be taken by bishops-elect; the Instruction on the *concursus* for irremovable rectorships (October 10, 1884); Propaganda's Instruction on the *titulus* of ordination (April 27, 1871); the

[37] Smith, *Elements etc.,* II (*Ecclesiastical Trials*), 128-140; Porter, "The Decrees of the Council of Baltimore," *Month,* LVII (June, 1886), 153-165.

[38] Printed in *Conc. Plen. Balt. II,* 287-292; the knowledge of which, writes Corcoran, "would be sufficient to knock on the head most of those appeals that for several years back have been floating backward and forward, shadowlike, without shape, color or substance, between Rome and this country, puzzling alternately both sides and even finding their way to our secular tribunals," *l.c.,* 355.

Romanos Pontifices of May 8, 1881; various Instructions on matrimonial cases; the Instruction of 1875 on the public schools; and Instructions on cases of clerics brought before the diocesan courts.

During the month the Council deliberated on all these problems, four Solemn Sessions were held. The first of these has already been described. The second Session occurred on Sunday, November 16, with Solemn Pontifical Mass sung by Archbishop Williams of Boston; Archbishop Elder of Cincinnati preached on the priesthood. The third Solemn Session was held on November 23, when Solemn Pontifical Mass was sung by Archbishop Feehan of Chicago and a sermon on the Sacrifice of the Mass delivered by Bishop Fitzgerald of Little Rock. The fourth Solemn Session was held on November 30, when Bishop Loughlin of Brooklyn celebrated Mass and Bishop Hennessy of Dubuque preached on the Sanctity of the Church. The final Solemn Session was held on December 7, Solemn Pontifical Mass being celebrated by Archbishop Corrigan; and, in place of Archbishop Riordan who had become ill, Bishop Spalding of Peoria preached.

The customary Mass of Requiem was sung on November 13 by Archbishop Alemany, assisted by the future prelates, Archbishops Messmer and Denis O'Connell and Bishop Henry Gabriels. Eight archbishops and thirty-three bishops who had passed away since 1866, were remembered by Archbishop Corrigan who preached their panegyric.

A Solemn Mass of Thanksgiving was offered up on November 27 (Thanksgiving Day) by Archbishop Lamy of Santa Fé, the sermon being preached by Bishop Spalding.

The Council of 1884 cannot be viewed as a separate and distinct canonical legislative body. A study of its decrees shows that its legislation is a carefully planned codification of all the laws enacted since the Synod of 1791. But apart from this, the *Acta et Decreta* of 1884 made a profound impression upon the Church in general. Nilles' *Commentaria in Concilium Plenar-*

ium Baltimorense Tertium (Innsbruck, 1890) as well as lauda-
tory reviews of the legislation of 1884 in leading Catholic
periodicals abroad made known to Europe and Australasia what
the chief secretary of the Council, James Corcoran, signalized as
the wise and prudent provisions of its decrees, the same wise
and zealous spirit in which they were conceived and the immense benefit they would be to the Catholic Church in the
English-speaking world. Another canonist, Rev. George Porter,
S.J., in the London *Month*, recommended to all, cleric and lay,
the perusal of the printed decrees of 1884:

> We find so much comprehensiveness [he writes], so much large-
> heartedness in the legislation; so much foresight and thought and
> experience brought to bear on the work; such a thorough-going
> practical American character stamped on every line, and, lastly, such
> a spirit of priestly holiness breathing through it all, that it is impos-
> sible to resist the thought—a great blessing will follow to America
> from the Council.[39]

Bellesheim, known to many in the English-speaking world
through his well-written histories of Catholic Ireland and Scotland, wrote also of the value of the Baltimore decrees for the
entire Church.[40]

The *Pastoral Letter to the Clergy and Laity*, issued at the
close of the Council (December 7, 1884), surpassed all similar
documents by its sublime eloquence and by the variety of topics
it treated. The sincerely patriotic attitude of our prelates on all
questions affecting American life and ideals won for the *Pastoral*
the profound respect of leaders in all parts of the country and
of many other creeds. Commenting on the remarkable changes
which had taken place since 1866 in the material and spiritual
growth of the nation, especially in the "land of the far West
. . . once so desolate and impassable," a particularly moving
passage runs as follows:

[39] "The Decrees of the Council of Baltimore," LVII (June, 1886), 165.
[40] "Das dritte Plenarconcil von Baltimore," *Archiv für katholisches Kirchenrecht*, LVII, 87.

The wilderness has exchanged its solitude for the hum of busy life and industry; and the steps of our missionaries and Catholic settlers have invariably either preceded or accompanied the westward progress of civilization. Forests have given away to cities, where Catholic temples re-echo the praises of the Most High, where the priceless perfume of the "Clean Oblation," foretold by Malachi, daily ascends to heaven, and where the life-giving sacraments of Holy Church are dispensed by a devoted clergy. In view of this great progress of our holy religion, this marvellous widening of the tabernacles of Jacob, it has been judged wise and expedient, if not absolutely necessary, to examine anew the legislation of our predecessors, not with any purpose of radical change, much less of abrogation, but to preserve and perfect its spirit by adapting it to our altered circumstances. And as every day gives birth to new errors, and lapse of time or distance of place allows abuses to gradually creep into regular discipline, we have judged it the duty of our pastoral office to check the latter by recalling and enforcing established law, and to guard our flock against the former by timely words of paternal admonition.

The presence of so many of our prelates at the Vatican Council (1870) which "during its short session of seven months, gave solemn authoritative utterance to some great truths which the Church had unvaryingly held from the days of Christ and His Apostles," is commented on as one of the most important events in Catholic American history. The good sense of the American people can always be depended upon, the Fathers write, to understand the Church's attitude on political questions which seem to put Church and State in opposition. "We think," they say

we can claim to be acquainted both with the laws, institutions and spirit of the Catholic Church, and with the laws, institutions and spirit of our country; and we emphatically declare that there is no antagonism between them. A Catholic finds himself at home in the United States; for the influence of his Church has constantly been exercised in behalf of individual rights and popular liberties. And the right-minded American nowhere finds himself more at home than in the Catholic Church, for nowhere else can he breathe more freely that atmosphere of Divine truth, which alone can make him free. We repudiate with equal earnestness the assertion that we need to lay aside any of our devotedness to our Church, to be true Americans; the insinuation that we need to abate any of our love for our country's principles and institutions, to be faithful Catholics. To argue that the Catholic Church is hostile to our great Republic, because she teaches that "there is no power but from God"; because therefore, back of the events which led to the formation of the Republic, she sees the Providence of God leading to that issue, and back of our country's laws the authority of God as their sanction—this is evidently so illogical and contradictory an accusation, that we are astonished to hear it advanced by persons of ordinary intelligence. We believe that our country's heroes were the instruments of the God of Nations in establishing this home of freedom; to both the Almighty and to His instruments in the work, we look with grateful reverence; and to maintain the inheritance of freedom which they have left us, should it ever—which God forbid—be imperilled, our Catholic citizens will be found to stand forward, as one man ready to pledge anew "their lives, their fortunes, and their sacred honor."

Among the principal topics dealt with in the *Pastoral* are the following: the education of the clergy; the rights of pastors; Christian education; the Christian home (marriage, indissolubility of marriage, home virtues, good reading, the Sacred Scriptures, and the Catholic press); the observance of Sunday; forbidden societies; Catholic societies; and home and foreign missions.

It was explained to the clergy that, while it is the spirit of the Church to preserve inviolable the rights of pastors, it was equally obvious that "in countries like our own, where from rudimentary beginnings our organization is only gradually advancing toward perfection, the full application of these laws is impracticable; but in proportion as they become practicable, that they should go into effect." This vexed question of the general introduction of canonical parishes in this country was a legacy from the long past; and the Fathers of 1884 did not settle it because the conditions of Church organization here prevented conformity with the common law.

In the matter of elementary Catholic education the *Pastoral* reflects the strong and emphatic legislation of the decrees of the Council. "Two objects therefore, dear brethren, we have in view, to multiply our schools and to perfect them":

We must multiply them, till every Catholic child in the land shall have within its reach the means of education. There is still much to do ere this be attained. There are still thousands of Catholic children in the United States deprived of the benefit of a Catholic school. Pastors and parents should not rest till this defect be remedied. No parish is complete till it has schools adequate to the needs of its children, and the pastor and people of such a parish should feel that they have not accomplished their entire duty until the want is supplied. But then, we must also perfect our schools. We repudiate the idea that the Catholic school need be in any respect inferior to any other school whatsoever. And if hitherto, in some places, our people have acted on the principle that it is better to have an imperfect Catholic school than to have none, let them now push their praiseworthy ambition still further, and not relax their efforts till their schools be elevated to the highest educational excellence. And we implore parents not to hasten to take their children from school, but to give them all the time and all the advantages that they have the capacity to profit by, so that, in after life, their children may "rise up and call them blessed."

A frequently quoted passage on the value of good reading merits inclusion here:

Train your children to a love of history and biography. Inspire them with the ambition to become so well acquainted with the history and doctrines of the Church as to be able to give an intelligent answer to any honest inquiry. Should their surroundings call for it, encourage them, as they grow older, to acquire such knowledge of popularly mooted questions of a scientific or philosophical character as will suffice to make them firm in their faith and proof against sophistry. We should be glad to see thoroughly solid and popular works on these important subjects, from able Catholic writers, become more numerous. Teach your children to take a special interest in the history of our own country. We consider the establishment of our country's independence, the shaping of its liberties and laws as a work of special Providence, its framers "building better than they knew," the Almighty's hand guiding them. And if ever the glorious fabric be subverted or impaired it will be by men forgetful of the sacrifices of the heroes that reared it, the virtues that cemented it, and the principles on which it rests, or ready to sacrifice principle and virtue to the interests of self or party. As we desire therefore that the history of the United States should be carefully taught in all our Catholic schools, and have directed that it be specially dwelt upon in the education of the young ecclesiastical students in our preparatory seminaries; so also we desire that it form a favorite part of the home library and home reading. We must keep firm and solid the liberties of our country by keeping fresh the noble memories of the past and thus sending forth from our Catholic homes into the arena of public life not partisans but patriots.

One of the best summaries of the *Pastoral Letter,* that printed in the *Catholic World* for February, 1885, does not hesitate to claim that its pages reveal a fact of supreme importance—"the hierarchy of the Catholic Church in the United States share the conviction that American political institutions are in advance of those of Europe in helping a man to save his soul, and that they promise a triumph for Catholicity more perfect than its victory in medieval times; and they do not hesitate to express their convictions." Looking backward over the years when the legislation of 1884 was, with the direction of the Holy See, the guiding influence over our Church (1884-1918), it may well be granted that the Fathers of the Council succeeded admirably in giving the Church here a diocesan organization which attracted the admiration of the entire English-speaking world. How far that legislation has influenced the Churches of England, Ireland, Scotland and Australasia cannot be easily gauged; and how far the decrees of 1884 found their echo in the legislation of the Code of 1918 is a question our canonists have not yet fully probed. It has been said, however, by one of our best informed canonists that "to one who follows our bishops from Council to Council and knows what they did and said, the Code appears as the completion of their work." [41]

[41] Creagh, John T., *Code of Canon Law and Church in the United States* (privately printed, 1919).

PART V

SUMMARY OF THE CONCILIAR LEGISLATION OF BALTIMORE

(1791–1884)

FOREWORD

AT the time the Code of Canon Law went into effect (Pentecost, May 19, 1918), it was generally believed that, apart from some new legislation, the transition from the older canonical regulations under which the American Church had lived for over a generation would be an almost imperceptible one. The principal changes or additions to our laws were embodied in a slender supplementary volume [1] to the *Catholic Encyclopedia.* Whatever adjustments needed to be made are directed by the general principles set down in canons one to six of the Code. Father Stanislaus Woywod's *The New Canon Law: A Commentary and a Summary,* which appeared shortly after the Code went into effect,[2] makes no mention of the lines of coalescence between the twenty-four hundred and fourteen canons of the Code and the Baltimore legislation which prevailed here in the United States. But a careful perusal of his commentary reveals the fact that the legislation of the Third Plenary Council of Baltimore (1884) not only anticipates some of the important changes in the new legislation but has had an appreciable effect upon this general canonical revision of the law of the Church. The School of Canon Law erected at the Catholic University of America in 1923 has already published over sixty doctoral dissertations in many of which the relationship between the Baltimore legislation and that of the Code is treated.

A summary of the legislation passed in all our national assemblies between the Synod of 1791 and the Plenary Council of 1884 in which assembly the decrees of the previous convocations were so judiciously codified will enable us to appreciate the wisdom, the knowledge and the prudence which governed the

[1] Pp. 82 (New York, 1918).   [2] New York, 1918.

minds and hearts of our legislators during that century of Church organization in the United States.

A summary of this kind is not easily made. The number of topics dealt with formally in these assemblies which have been described in these pages, is large and varied. The Synod of 1791 presents the most practical legislation from that date to the Council of 1866, with the exception of the Council of 1829, when the decrees were arranged in a more logical order. The haphazard method of the decretal enactments of 1833, 1837, 1840, 1843, 1846, and 1849 will scarcely permit these assemblies to be taken as models for such a summary. The logical sequence of the decrees which appears first in the Council of 1866, was brought to perfection in that of 1884; and this latter Council may well be taken as a norm for the outline of an historical summary of the legislative advance made between 1791 and 1884. Moreover, the outline of both the 1866 and 1884 legislation approaches, though it never exactly coincides with, the division of Church law accepted by the canonists who framed the Code of 1918.

The main sections of the Code are: Persons, Sacred Things, and Canonical Trials; and to a large extent these divisions, while not expressly stated, are those of the conciliar legislation of 1884. Apart from the first Title of the decrees of 1884 on Faith, the ten Titles which follow, fall logically into the framework of the Code of 1918. The principal topics, therefore, of this summary may be given as follows: (1) Catholic Faith, Sacraments, Christian Worship, Feasts and Fasts; (2) Clerical Discipline, Ecclesiastical Property, New and Vacant Sees; and (3) Catholic Education and Social Welfare.

CHAPTER XVIII

CATHOLIC FAITH, SACRAMENTS, CHRISTIAN WORSHIP, FEASTS AND FASTS

I. CATHOLIC FAITH

Apart from specific declarations on matters of faith, such as obedience to the Holy See, devotion to the Blessed Virgin Mary, and the desire to see the doctrine of the Immaculate Conception defined as dogma of the Church, it is only in the Councils of 1866 and 1884 that we find a section devoted to a general statement of Catholic belief. Both Councils have as their first Title the heading *The Catholic Faith*. That of 1884 is more ample since it sums up the definitions of the Vatican Council (1870) on Reason, Revelation, the Holy Scriptures, and Papal Infallibility, and expresses the mind of the Fathers as in perfect concord with the teachings of the Encyclical Letters of Pope Leo XIII. This section of the decrees of the Council of 1886, however, goes more into detail on the prevalent doctrinal and moral errors of the day. This change, or addition, which is visible in the *Pastoral Letters* for these two Councils, was

by no means necessary; for all Catholics had years ago adhered to these definitions. But it is not out of place. Let it stand as a witness of the loyalty of the American Church to Christ's Vicar on earth which will condemn our children's children if ever they deliberately shut their eyes to the light and rise up in rebellion against the truth, as happened three hundred years ago. Let it stand there as a beacon and wholesome warning to remind those who are outside of the Church and yet glory in the name of Christian, that the Catholic Church is the only teaching body left that maintains unchangeably the reverence due the Scripture and its inspiration, and that defends, in defending Christian marriage and the sacred

255

bond of the family, the last prop of human society and Christian civilization.[1]

It is the lofty and sublime tone of these introductory Titles of the Councils of 1866 and 1884, and their firm attitude in the presence of a disintegrating Christian faith outsde the Church, which gained for our hierarchy the admiration of the Catholic world.

II. THE SACRAMENTS

1. *Baptism.* The first decree of the National Synod of 1791 concerns the re-baptism *sub conditione* of those the validity of whose former baptism could not be ascertained with moral certitude, and the grave duty of the priest to act cautiously in such cases. In the Meeting of 1810, the prelates ordered that in the future baptism should not be conferred in private homes unless grave necessity demanded it. The Council of 1829 recognized the difficulty in country districts, where there were few churches, of obeying this law; but it urged the clergy to insist upon the erection of baptisteries, no doubt with the hope that the faithful wherever possible would be thus compelled to build churches. The same Council ordered that the names taken in baptism be those of saints. Baptismal registers were made obligatory in 1791; the admonition was repeated in 1810; and the law reënacted in 1829. After that time, apparently, there was no difficulty in this respect. Sponsors are mentioned in 1791, and the requisition was made in 1810 that where no sponsor could be had the ceremonies were to be omitted and baptism administered privately. In 1829 the rule that the sponsors must be Catholics is given, and non-Catholic children in danger of death were to be baptized. The baptism of adults presented a difficulty in the earlier years of our canonical legislation. The Synod of 1791 stated that in the reception of converts who had been validly baptized, the ceremonies need not be supplied. The Council of 1829 decreed that the Holy See would be asked to

[1] Corcoran, *l.c.,* 345.

permit the continuance of the permission to baptize adults with the form used in the baptism of infants. This petition was embodied in the letter sent by the Council to Pius VIII and was granted (June 28, 1830) for twenty years. In the Council of 1852, an extension of the privilege was asked, either for another twenty years or in perpetuity. Propaganda asked the Holy See for five years only and this was permitted. The same petition was renewed in the Council of 1866 without any general extension being granted. The Council of 1884, after repeating the warning to ascertain the status of any previous baptism, instructs priests to receive converts into the Church by the Instruction of 1859 as given in the Appendix of the *Acta et Decreta* of 1866.

2. *Confirmation.* A general rule is given in the Synod of 1791 that this sacrament is not to be conferred upon children who had not attained the use of reason and who were not capable of going to confession intelligently. The Council of 1829 places the age of reception at seven, unless the child be in danger of death. The use of cards, in case of a large number to be confirmed, on which the names taken are to be written, was ordered; and they were to be handed to the bishop during the conferring of the sacrament. Bishops are requested in the Council of 1866 to confer the Sacrament of Confirmation as often as was found necessary during their visitations of the diocese; and pastors are ordered to prepare the candidates by a thorough drilling in the Catechism. The bishop or a priest of his choice should examine the children in Christian doctrine before conferring the sacrament. The Council of 1884 enters into the theological explanation of the sacrament and speaks of the necessity (*pracepti*) of receiving confirmation especially for those surrounded by enemies of the Church or living in the midst of temptations. The rubrics are to be strictly observed, and no child under seven should be confirmed. Sponsors should be present, at least two for the boys and two for the girls.

3. *Holy Eucharist.* The earliest legislation (1791) reminds the faithful of the need of an ever-increasing devotion to the

Sacrament of the Altar; they are to be warned frequently that everything about the altar should be spotlessly clean and also of their obligation to support the Church in order that everything the Ritual commands be carried out in a proper and dignified manner. This is repeated in the decree of 1829. The Council of 1852 prescribes the manner of giving the Benediction of the Most Blessed Sacrament and the decrees of 1884 also speak of the strict observance of the Ritual for this august ceremony. The regulations for the Forty Hours' Devotion are given by the Council of 1884, and pastors are urged to form Sodalities whose members are to take turns in adoration during the exposition of the Blessed Sacrament. A whole chapter [2] of the Council of 1884 is devoted to the doctrine and the laws of the Church on the Holy Eucharist, especially frequent communion, the communion of the sick, the paschal precept, and the First Holy Communion of the young.

4. *Penance.* The doctrine of the Sacrament of Penance is given but once in the canonical legislation from 1791 to 1884 —in the Council of 1866, where a special chapter is devoted to the qualities necessary for a good confession and to the duties of the confessor. The Synod of 1791 is concerned mainly about the canonical safeguards for faculties for confession. The bishops are exhorted in the Council of 1829 to use great caution in conferring faculties upon priests who come from outside their dioceses; members of religious Orders and Congregations enjoyed, however, their own privileges as granted by the Holy See. The immediate suspension of faculties is urged in all cases where priests are not obedient to Church law, especially in the matter of abetting lay interference. In 1833 the difficulty caused by unknown or wandering priests induced the Fathers to abrogate their mutual agreement of 1810 for the use of faculties in neighboring dioceses. From that date, no priest could exercise the ministry without the authority of the diocesan Ordinary. Confessionals were ordered to be erected in the Councils of

[2] Title V, Chapter V.

1829 and 1843, and these two assemblies also gave direction for the confessions of women and young girls. The Council of 1866 repeated the injunctions of these two Councils and admonished the bishops not to place difficulties in the way of religious women who asked for an extraordinary confessor. This injunction was repeated in the Council of 1884, and the regulation was made that such confessors should not hold office for more than three years. Extraordinary confessors were to hear the confessions of all the nuns two or three times a year. Great care should be shown in the selection of these confessors who were to be priests of a mature age, learned, pious, and known for their saintly lives.

5. *Extreme Unction.* The Synod of 1791 ordered that this sacrament should be administered to children in danger of death, providing they had reached the use of reason. Nothing is said in any of the Councils which follow, until the assembly of 1866, when the doctrine of the sacrament, its liturgy and the rules for its administration are given.

6. *Holy Orders.* The first mention of this sacrament occurs in the Council of 1837, when the bishops were warned to ordain *titulo missionis* only those candidates for the priesthood who had taken the Mission oath. This was by virtue of an indult from the Holy See; in 1852 this indult was extended for five years, and the regulations for priests who desired to enter a religious Order or Congregation were again outlined. A whole chapter devoted to the Sacrament of Holy Orders in the Council of 1866 contains the doctrine of the sacrament and gives in detail all the regulations on the same (312-23). The legislation of 1866 regarding ordination *titulo missionis* is repeated in 1884.

7. *Matrimony.* The Baltimore legislation from 1791 to 1884 on the subject of marriage occupies a major share in the deliberations and decisions of the Councils. The principal topics dealt with by the Fathers are: Christian marriage in general; banns; nuptial Masses; mixed marriages; clandestinity; registra-

tion of marriages; dispensations; divorce; and the matrimonial court.

(*a*) *Doctrine.* The Synod of 1791 exacted from those about to be married a knowledge of the fundamental truths of the Catholic faith and urged pastors to dissuade Catholics from marrying those outside the true fold. At the Meeting in 1810, the hierarchy hesitated to give any general rules regarding marriage, merely stipulating that all Catholic nuptials be performed in the church, and pastors were told to insist gradually upon the observance of this rule. The Council of 1829 legislated for the proper dispositions for marriage, and warned pastors not to join in the holy bonds of matrimony those who were unworthy to receive the sacrament. No further legislation of a general nature occurs until the Council of 1866, when several paragraphs are devoted to the indissolubility of Christian marriage, and the current errors of free love and polygamy are decried. Those about to be married should prepare themselves by the Sacraments of Penance and Holy Eucharist, and the decree of 1829 is reënacted in this respect. The decretal portion of the Council of 1884 is a lengthy one. The encyclical *Arcanum* of Leo XIII on Christian marriage which had but recently appeared (1880) had naturally a profound effect upon the legislation of 1884. The decretal section is a succinct summary of the encyclical.

(*b*) *Banns.* The triple proclamation of the banns was ordered by the Synod of 1791 for *vagi et peregrini*. No further legislation occurred until 1846, when the law was made that as soon as each bishop deemed it advisable, banns should become the normal procedure in the Church here, and Propaganda insisted on them for mixed marriages also. Evidently, the law was not generally observed; and in 1852, it was decreed that on and after Easter Sunday, 1853, the proclamation of the banns was obligatory in the American Church. This legislation was repeated in the Council of 1866, as "a most salutary discipline."

(*c*) *Nuptial Mass.* The sole mention is that of the Council of

1866 where pastors are exhorted to introduce the custom in all the Churches here.

(*d*) *Registers*. These are not mentioned in the Synod of 1791, but in the Meeting of 1810 pastors were sternly reminded of their obligation to keep baptismal, matrimonial and burial records in special books for that purpose. This is repeated in the Council of 1829, and in that of 1866; and priests, while not asked to follow the formulas of the Roman Ritual in inscribing names, were given practical instructions how to keep these registers. Among the many duties of the pastors, as described by the Council of 1884, that of keeping accurate registers was insisted upon.

(*e*) *Clandestinity*. Of all the legislative enactments of the Baltimore Councils, that of clandestinity or the invalidity of a marriage attempted before any other than the parish priest or his delegate and two witnesses, as decreed by the *Tametsi* of the Council of Trent, gave rise to considerable confusion owing to the fact that the Tridentine decree was binding only in such places where it had been formally promulgated. Prior to the Council of 1884, it was uncertain where and where not the decree obtained. In 1843 the Fathers decreed that the *Tametsi* bound only in the city of Detroit and nowhere else in the United States, except in those dioceses where it was known to have been formally promulgated. They also decided to ask the Holy See to exempt Detroit. The ruling of the Council of 1849 was an indirect application of the Tridentine decree, as was that of the First Plenary Council of 1852, and the Fathers of 1852 debated the question of passing, with the approval of the Holy See, a uniform ecclesiastical law on the subject, without however reaching a definite conclusion. The Council of 1866 admitted the existence of the confusion over the matter of the geographical extent of the *Tametsi* in the United States, and requested unsuccessfully the Holy See to confine the Tridentine law to the Province of New Orleans. At the request of the Holy See, the Council of 1884 made a thorough investigation of the whole question of formal and virtual promulgation of the *Tametsi*. It was decided that the Tridentine decree did not obtain in the Provinces of Baltimore, Philadelphia, New York, Boston, Oregon, Milwaukee, Cincinnati (except the diocese of Vincennes), St. Louis (except the city of St. Louis itself, St. Genevieve, Florissant and St. Charles), and Chicago (except Kaskaskia, Cahokia, French Village, and Prairie du Rocher in the Diocese of Alton).

(*f*) *Mixed Marriages.* The regulations for mixed marriages, as set down by the Synod of 1791, contain essentially all the legislation passed by our bishops up to the Council of 1884. The grave reluctance of the Church in permitting mixed marriages is stated in the Synod, and the Council of 1840 made clear in its first decree the antipathy of the Church for these unions, urging priests to use all legitimate means to prevent Catholics marrying non-Catholics on account of the many evils which arise from such marriages. The Council of 1866 is even more outspoken: *Matrimonia Catholicorum cum haereticis semper detestata est Ecclesia.* The legislation of 1840 is repeated, although priests are warned not to be so rigid in the matter that the Catholic party be turned away from the Church. The decrees of 1884 reiterate the abhorrence of the Church for these unions.

(*g*) *Dispensations* are spoken of only in the Council of 1866 and 1884, the latter basing its action on an Instruction of Propaganda (May 9, 1877) on the valid causes for granting the same.

(*h*) *Divorce* is spoken of for the first time in the doctrinal part of the decrees of 1866, and the Council of 1884 repeats the salient passages of the *Arcanum* of Leo XIII on the same subject. The growing evil of divorce had entered Catholic circles, and pastors were urged to preach from time to time on this grave subject. Moreover, without ecclesiastical permission, Catholics were forbidden to appeal to the secular courts for separation *a thoro et mensa.*

III. CHRISTIAN WORSHIP

The devotional life of the Catholic faithful in the United States has been of gradual growth from the years immediately following the birth of the nation and the cessation of the old English penal laws up to the present, when it has flourished into a remarkable outpouring of love and veneration for Our Blessed Lord, the Blessed Virgin, the saints, martyrs and confessors of this and other lands. The subjects dealt with under this head in the Baltimore Councils are many and varied: attendance at Mass; First Holy Communion; Church music; bells; cemeteries; litanies; indulgences; missions; the Ritual and Ceremonial; devotion to the Blessed Virgin Mary, to the Sacred Heart, and to the Blessed Sacrament; prayers; Vespers and Benediction of the Most Blessed Sacrament; the use of Latin in the administration of the sacraments; frequent communion; the Viaticum of the sick and dying; and the liturgy in general. Devotion to the Blessed Virgin Mary under the title of her Assumption was instituted by the Synod of 1791, when that day (August 15) was made the national Catholic feast of the Diocese of Baltimore then coterminous with the republic, in gratitude for Bishop Carroll's consecration on Assumption Day the previous year. The Council of 1846 asked and obtained that the Blessed Virgin Mary under the title of her Immaculate Conception be proclaimed the Patroness of the Church in the United States; and the Council of 1849, in its second decree, asked that the Supreme Pontiff declare the Immaculate Conception to be a dogma of faith. The Council of 1866 has a chapter devoted to the doctrinal basis for the devotion to the Immaculate Queen of Heaven, and cites in its decrees pertinent passages from the *Ineffabilis Deus* of December 8, 1854. Devotion to our Lady was urged as part of the training of the aspirants to the priesthood by the Council of 1884. Devotion to the Blessed Sacrament is especially urged by the Council of 1866, and the *Pastoral Letter* of 1884 recommends this devotion together with the devotion to the Sacred Heart of Jesus. The principal duties of the Catholic, of attendance at Mass on Sundays and holydays, and the counseling of their presence at Vespers and Benediction of the Most Blessed Sacrament are frequently mentioned in the Baltimore decrees. Benediction is first mentioned in the Council of 1852 when a uniform ritual was enjoined upon the dioceses; and in the Council of 1866 a separate chapter is given to Benediction and to the Forty Hours' Devotion. All through the Baltimore legislation the Roman Ritual and the Ceremonial are insisted upon, as is also the use of Latin in the administration of the sacraments. As we have seen, the Council of 1829 legislated for an English edition of the *Ceremonial,* conformable to the Roman Ritual, and this volume was eventually published in 1841, with the approval of the Holy See. The Council of 1866 gave a chapter to the subject of an approved prayerbook, repeating the admonitions of the Council of 1829 on the subject, and issued regulations for the composition of such books. The Council of 1884 appointed a committee to prepare an official prayer-book which appeared the following year; this has remained until the present the official Catholic Prayer Book of the United States.

IV. FEAST AND FASTS

The nascent Church in the United States at the time of the creation of our hierarchy (1789) inherited its laws of abstinence and fasting and its special feast days from England. The Synod of 1791 legislated for the complete ritual on Sundays and holydays of obligation, wherever it was possible to have High or Solemn Mass. The feast of the Assumption was made at the same time the national Catholic holyday. The Council of 1837 asked for a dispensation from the obligation of hearing Mass on Easter Monday and Pentecost Monday; this was granted by Pope Gregory XVI on September 2, that year. This same council asked for a dispensation from the fast on Wednesdays and Fridays of Advent, and the same was granted for Wednesdays but not for Fridays. The Council of 1840 asked a dispensation for the Saturday abstinence; this was granted for twenty years. A petition for a dispensation from the fast on the vigil of the feast of Saints Peter and Paul was also requested, but the Holy See transferred celebration of the feast to the Sunday within the octave, and bishops were informed that the mind of the Sacred Congregation was to hold the faithful to the fast on the preceding day. The First Plenary Council of 1852 requested the Holy See to permit the use of the Roman Calendar as a norm for Church feasts in this country. The Sacred Congregation in its reply recognized the necessity of more uniformity, but warned the hierarchy that such uniformity was not to be gained through a minimizing of Church discipline. The holydays of obligation in 1852 were: the Circumcision, Epiphany, Annunciation, Ascension, Corpus Christi, Assumption, All Saints, and Christmas Day. By 1884, the feast of the Immaculate Conception had been added, and in the Council of 1884, for the sake of uniformity, six feasts were made obligatory throughout the United States—the Immaculate Conception, Christmas, Circumcision, Ascension, Assumption, and All Saints. Moreover the same Council asked that the obligation to abstain from servile work on these days, in case they did not fall on a Sunday, be abrogated. The Council of 1866 did not make a uniform law for the entire country for abstinence and fasting; and in the last Council (1884) the Fathers agreed that owing to difference of climate, the lack of suitable food in many places, and the physical needs of the laboring classes it was almost impossible to reach a uniform norm for all our dioceses. The question was left to the discretion of diocesan synods and provincial councils.

CHAPTER XIX

CLERICAL LIFE AND DISCIPLINE, ECCLESIASTICAL PROPERTY, NEW AND VACANT SEES

I. CLERICAL LIFE AND DISCIPLINE

As the analysis of the twelve formal assemblies of our bishops has undoubtedly shown, few subjects for discussion and deliberation so occupied the minds of the prelates as the private and public life of the clergy. No aspect of that life is overlooked in the sum total of almost a thousand decrees from 1791 to 1884. These decrees are concerned mainly with clerical duties in general, the virtues of the priesthood, especially sanctity, knowledge and zeal, obedience to the bishops, the relations of the regular clergy with the diocesan Ordinary, financial affairs, especially methods of raising money for Church support, mutual relations between the priests themselves, the care of sick and infirm priests, relations with the laity, particularly the trustees, clerical dress, the priest's household, sacerdotal faculties, the work of preaching, of catechizing and instructing the faithful, and of preparing the children for the reception of First Holy Communion and confirmation, the keeping of parochial registers, unworthy members of the cloth, and all those things which were unbecoming in the life of a priest. The noblest and most courageous of all our conciliar documents is the *Pastoral Letter to the Clergy* of 1829, the sole message of its kind between 1791 and 1884, although all the *Pastorals* contain paragraphs of special direction and exhortation to our priests. Apart from legislating for the control of those priests (mainly from abroad) who found it irksome to live according to canonical rules and regulations and for the delicate problem of the clergy's relations with the laity, especially during the trustee epoch, there is little that is new in all these enactments. The unstable conditions of life in the growing West and Far West almost up to the Council of 1884 gave rise in some of the Councils to rigorous enactments; but as the Church here assumed a compact canonical discipline, whatever evils or disturbances there were became less and less; so much so that, apart from the problem of the canonical rights of pastors, there was little that was calculated to swerve the clergy from the fast and rigid line of duty and obedience.

This is an unwritten chapter in the history of the Catholic Church in the United States—the story of its priesthood; but once written in the light of the Baltimore decrees, there will be revealed a magnificent epic of a courageous devotion to the people and of a serene and noble obedience to Church authority of which any country may well be proud. Our bishops, too, while legislating for their priests, were exemplars all through these years of strict conformity to the spirit of the laws governing sacerdotal perfection.

II. ECCLESIASTICAL PROPERTY

The method of tenure of Catholic Church property in the United States from Bishop John Carroll's day to the present has undergone many serious vicissitudes; chief of which has been the problem of harmonizing with civil law the fundamental principles of the sanctity of all property devoted to the service of God and of the Church's innate and sovereign right of acquiring and possessing property, real, personal and mixed. On account of the diversity of State law, there has never been any uniform system in the nation for safeguarding these rights. The long, and at times, tragic, history of the system of protection, commonly called *trusteeism,* which stretches across the pages of our canonical legislation from the Synod of 1791 to the last Plenary Council of 1884, is filled with unfortunate conflicts and schisms, the results of which are still to be seen in some parts of the American Church. The Synod of 1791 permitted the selection of two or three laymen (*tamquam curatores*) in each parish to assist the pastor in financial matters. But evils soon arose from this permission, when unworthy men were made trustees or when the pastor, or the bishop, lacked that prudence which local circumstances required for a harmonious coöperation between the clergy and the laity. These evils were condemned by the *Non sine magno* of Pope Pius VII (August 22, 1822), but the extraordinary ramifications of the disturbances caused by the system reached such a stage that the Council of 1829 passed a stern ruling for the future, to the effect that, owing to the abuses of lay trusteeship, no church should be erected in the future without being legally deeded to the bishop, wherever the laws of the respective States permitted it. Bishop England's constitutional form of temporary government in the Diocese of Charleston was formally exempted by the Council from this law. A further decree denied to the trustees the *jus patronatus* or any semblance of the same. The Council of 1833 is silent on the question. That of 1837 decreed that all ecclesiastical property in each diocese be secured as soon as possible by the best means the civil law afforded, and those who violated the Church's law were warned of the penalties inflicted by the Council of Trent in such cases.

The Council of 1840 went a step further, urging the bishops to have recourse to the civil law for incorporation whenever these laws allowed it. Where this was not possible, each bishop was to protect diocesan property by a last will and testament to that effect. Priests were henceforth forbidden to retain in their own names any property given by the faithful for Church purposes. By this year—the golden jubilee of the American hierarchy (1790-1840)—the system had changed from lay trusteeship to that of incorporation in the name of the diocesan Ordinary. The Councils of 1843 and 1846 are silent on the matter, and that of 1849 merely repeats the ruling of 1840, making an exception, however, for all property held by religious Orders and Congregations in their own names. The First Plenary Council of 1852 passed a decree strictly excluding the laity from any part in the administration of Church property without the express consent of the Ordinary, and invoking the sanctions of the Council of Trent on all offenders against this regulation. The Second Plenary Council of 1866 devoted a separate Title to the question of safeguarding Church property rights, repeating the admonition of the Provincial Councils of 1829, 1837, 1840, 1849, and the First Plenary Council of 1852. Its own special legislation upholds the legal basis for the Church's possession of property against the action of several State legislatures which had passed laws aimed against the incorporation of ecclesiastical property in the name of the bishop and against their power to transmit by will such property to their successors. The Council of 1866 again legislated for such transmission by a last will and testament, regardless of the system of tenure permitted by the respective States. So many difficulties had arisen from this system—practically speaking of holding Church property in fee simple—that the confidence of the priests and people in episcopal management had become somewhat shaken. "Business worry, legal complications, bankruptcy . . . had proved instructive, so that the Third Plenary Council (1884) only tolerated the fee simple title in bishops when no other tenure was possible." Title IX of the *Acta et Decreta* of the Council devoted five chapters to Church temporalities and the heart of its legislation is contained in the decree which reads:

In the States in which a civil legal incorporation of parishes or ecclesiastical bodies, such as accords with church law, does not exist, the bishop himself will be able to become a corporation-sole before the law to hold and administer the property of the whole diocese; or the property of the diocese by a similar law may be committed to the bishop in trust that he may hold it in the name of the diocese and administer it according to the wish of the church; or as a last resource the bishop may hold the temporal goods of the diocese and administer them in his individual name, under that absolute title of law which in English is called fee simple; in which case let the bishop be always mindful, that, although the full ownership of ecclesiastical property is given him by the civil law, nevertheless according to the admonition of the sacred canons he is not the owner of it but only the administrator.

A full historical treatment of the conciliar legislation of Baltimore during these years (1791-1884) on the question of Church property rights and incorporation would carry this summary beyond its logical limits, were even a tentative outline to be attempted on this thorniest of all problems in Church administration. The Baltimore legislation of 1884, culminating in a quasi-compromise between the system of lay-trustees and that of fee-simple tenure on the part of the bishops, has not since that time assured the Church everywhere of a safe system of legal protection; and it remains to be seen how far the Code will enable the Church here, under our uneven legal conditions, to arrive at a definite method, agreeable to the Church and to the civil law.

III. NEW AND VACANT SEES

There are two aspects to the problem of episcopal nomination in this country; one is the canonical status of the nominators and the nominees; the other is the evolution of the legislation either passed by the Baltimore Councils or decreed by the Holy See for safeguarding this very important aspect of jurisdiction in the American Church. The extraordinary action of the Holy See in permitting the priests who then constituted the American clergy to elect their own bishop (1788) stands apart from this historical development. The action of the Sacred Congregation de Propaganda Fide in permitting Bishop Carroll to select his own coadjutors (Lawrence Graessl, 1793; Leonard Neale, 1795), as well as the method of selecting the first members of the American hierarchy (Cheverus, Egan and Flaget) in 1808, are likewise exceptions to the canonical history of episcopal nominations. The Synod of 1791 and the Meeting of 1810 passed no legislation on the question of episcopal succession; but in the second set of regulations drawn up at the Meeting of 1810, we find the following:

Nomination of Bishops

In case the Holy See will graciously permit the nomination to vacant Bishopricks to be made in the United States, it is humbly and respectfully suggested to the Supreme Pastor of the Church to allow the nomination for the vacant diocese to proceed solely from the Archbishop and Bishops of this ecclesiastical Province.

The story of the confusion caused by domestic and foreign meddlers from 1810 to 1829 need not be described here. The Council of 1829 is silent on the problem of the manner in which our new and vacant Sees should be filled. Certain irregular methods had been used; and in the next Council (1833), the Fathers proposed a sane fixed system which met with the approval of the Holy See, and which placed the power of nomination in the hands of the bishops of the Province of Baltimore (i.e., the United States). This legislation prevailed from 1834 to 1850. The Council of 1840 decreed that "it was not expedient that the Bishop ordinarily be selected from those priests who were not citizens of the United States." The Council of 1846 asked for a change in the oath of consecration and the request was granted; it suggested also that in the selection for new and vacant Sees a knowledge of the languages commonly used in the diocese be given serious consideration in the selection of nominees. The legislation of 1833-1846 was practical, so long as the United States constituted one ecclesiastical province. The Fathers of the Council of 1849—there were then three provinces—realized that a new method was necessary, and the suggestion they made was accepted by Propaganda (August 10, 1850). This decree widened the scope of the nominating body, giving all the archbishops the right to decide upon the nominees for all dioceses in the country. The First Plenary Council (1852) revealed the fact that this method had not met with much favor among the clergy who believed they should have a more effective voice in the selection of their superior officers. The Council urged the formation of a body of consultors through whom the priests might express their preferences. This was again recommended in the Second Plenary Council (1866), though no strict legislation was formulated to this effect. The ruling of 1850 was changed by Propaganda in 1856 and again in 1859, but up to the Third Plenary Council (1884), the power of nomination lay practically in the hands of the bishops. Whatever privileges the clergy had were merely a concession from the respective Ordinary. Propaganda issued an Instruction on January 31, 1866, ordering the bishops to send triennially a list of eligible candidates to the Holy See; but the purpose of this regulation was rather for prompt action when a See fell vacant. This Instruction became a law through the conciliar decrees of 1866. It too was not wholly satisfactory either to the Holy See which wished to have the canonical practices of Europe followed in the American Church, or to the clergy who felt they should be given a right to the choice of their bishops. The opposition of our prelates to the creation of cathedral chapters and Propaganda's insistence upon the recognition of the common law of the Church resulted in a compromise in the Council of 1884, in the legislation which required the creation of a board of consultors in each diocese, through whom the clergy would be heard. These decrees while not limiting the nominating power of the bishops, gave the clergy the privilege they had long desired. All, bishops and priests, knew that their selections were merely recommendations. The Holy See assumed no obligation to appoint any of the nominees, though usually the selection was made from the official lists sent to Rome. This law represented the final stage of the development in episcopal nominations up to the Code of 1918. The story of how it met the complex conditions of Church life here from 1884 to 1918 does not come within the scope of this summary.

CHAPTER XX

CATHOLIC EDUCATION AND SOCIAL WELFARE

I. CATHOLIC EDUCATION

It is evident from Bishop Carroll's *Pastoral Letter* of 1792 that the question of Catholic education was discussed in the Synod the previous year. Our elementary school legislation begins formally with the decree of the Council of 1829, where the Fathers state that they judge it absolutely necessary that schools be established for the moral and religious training of the young. The Council of 1833 appointed a committee of three Catholic college presidents for the purpose of revising the non-Catholic textbooks in use in our schools. The Council of 1840 warned pastors to protect the rights of Catholic children who were attending the public schools, lest they be induced or forced to read the Protestant Bible, to sing Protestant hymns or to recite Protestant prayers. The First Plenary Council of 1852 adopted a decree exhorting the bishops, in view of the very grave evils arising from the defective spiritual education given in the common schools, to establish Catholic schools in connection with all the parishes of their dioceses, and to provide for their support from the revenues of the churches. The movement toward parochial school education received its greatest impetus from the Provincial Councils of Cincinnati between 1852 and 1866, and when the Second Plenary Council (1866) was convened it was hoped that a nation-wide effort toward a Catholic school system would be supported. Comparatively little, however, was accomplished by the Council since the Fathers were satisfied merely to restate the decrees of previous Councils. However, recognition of the dangers of non-religious

273

education of Catholic children in the public schools was keener than ever, and our hierarchy was prepared for the Instruction from Propaganda in 1875, urging bishops to create a Catholic educational system for the United States. The Instruction formed the basis of the legislation of the Third Plenary Council of 1884, and the Committee on Schools, of which Archbishop Feehan, Bishops Spalding (Peoria), Flasch (La Crosse) and Cosgrove (Davenport) were members, came to the decision that the time was opportune to insist upon parochial schools wherever they could be supported. Within two years of the Council a school was to be erected alongside each parish church, and all Catholic parents were obliged to send their children to these schools, unless excepted by legitimate authority. Moreover, the problems of managing these schools, of training teachers, and of creating the proper relationship between the priests and the people for their successful development were to be made the subject of special instructions to the candidates for the priesthood. Catholic secondary and higher education was not overlooked by the Councils of 1866 and 1884, and to the latter assembly belongs the credit of the decision to create a central house of higher learning which eventually (1889) brought about the opening of the Catholic University of America.

II. CATHOLIC SOCIAL WELFARE

Apart from passing references to the necessity of Catholic charity for educational, religious and welfare purposes in Carroll's *Pastoral Letter* of 1792, and the warning by the hierarchy in their Meeting of 1810 against the frequenting of dangerous amusements and "the promiscuous reading of all kinds of novels," the graver problems of Catholic social welfare hardly arose before the peak of immigration had been reached in the forties. It is true the ordinary means of alleviating distress had grown in number and in efficiency of organization before this time. As Dr. O'Grady has shown in his recent *Catholic Chari-*

ties in the United States (Washington, D. C., 1931), orphan asylums, hospitals, homes for the poor and the aged, and charitable societies were not lacking in any of our dioceses; but the earliest formal legislation for social welfare is that of the First Plenary Council of 1852, although already in the Council of 1840 the evils of drunkenness are stigmatized as the cause of scandal to Catholics and non-Catholics, and total abstinence is praised as a worthy state in all cases where it is deemed necessary.

The Council of 1852 calls attention to the intolerance which unfortunately prevailed in the American army and navy and urged the bishops to take means to protect the rights of Catholic soldiers and sailors who were being forced to attend Protestant services. Evidently, in spite of the efforts of our hierarchy, discrimination against religious equality in the army and navy had not wholly disappeared, since the Second Plenary Council (1866) found it necessary to repeat the decree of 1852. The number of Catholics in both branches of the service had grown owing to the Civil War, and besides there were thousands of orphans of Catholic soldiers, killed during the combat, who needed attention. Orphanages and Protectories were to be established wherever needed to cope with the situation; a situation which grew worse instead of better, for, outside of open violence, no other aspect of Protestant propaganda reached the same depravity as that which was making Catholic orphan boys and girls its victims.

The Council of 1866 urged especially the growth of Missions, or weeks of spiritual exercises for each congregation; and anyone familiar with the zealous work done by the priests in charge of these extraordinary times of grace realizes how much social welfare and betterment goes hand-in-hand with the reawakening of religious fervor. The same Council legislated for the spread of Catholic societies, confraternities and sodalities, and added to the security of social peace by forbidding Catholics to become or to remain members of secret societies. The emancipation of the Negroes and the aftermath of the War brought out an acute situation among the Catholic colored population of the South, and the Council of 1866 devoted a chapter to the subject, emphasizing also the need of social and religious work among the Negroes in its *Pastoral Letter.* Clergy and people were exhorted to coöperate with the bishops of the dioceses where the colored people were. The coming of the Mill Hill Fathers to Baltimore in 1871 represented the first organized effort to win the souls of the Negroes to the Faith; and by the time the Third Plenary Council was convened in 1884 the work had become firmly established.

The Council of 1884 placed the Missions among Negroes and Indians upon a national basis. A permanent Commission was named with Archbishop Gibbons as chairman, and an annual collection was ordered for the first Sunday of Lent to support the work. The development of the welfare work among the Negroes and Indians has not proceeded along the design of the Council of 1884; and while there is to-day some confusion in the scope of the work of the three boards which are now directing its field, the legislation of 1884 brought permanent order into this important part of Catholic American action.

Another problem which was met courageously by the Councils of 1866 and 1884 was the growing intemperance in the ranks of the faithful. Both within and without the Catholic Church, the spirit of temperance had been fostered by societies of different kinds, and while the tendency of the non-Catholic groups was toward total abstinence through legal prohibition, Catholic leaders, even in the presence of the great wave of enthusiasm for total abstinence aroused by Father Theobald Mathew in this country (1849-1850), never failed to stress the virtue of temperance. Our leaders were, however, in favor of the total abstinence societies which sprang up as a result of his celebrated visit, and they saw with satisfaction the amalgamation of these societies into a national body in 1871, under the name: The Catholic Total Abstinence Union of America, especially because the Union disavowed any tendency to depend solely upon legal means for the suppression of the evils arising from intemperance. But they did not deem it necessary to legislate on the same. There is no mention of temperance or total abstinence societies in the list of confraternities recommended by the Council of 1866, and only a fleeting reference in the *Pastoral Letter* of that year. The Council of 1884 discusses temperance societies, and after carefully distinguishing between lawful and unlawful groups, states that temperance societies are a blessing to each community when they are truly Catholic and are not led

by artful demagogues, headstrong men, rebellious to the Church, not caring for the observance of the Decalogue, nor afraid of the other deadly sins, but priding themselves on their outward works, and especially their abstinence from drink, which can no more save their souls than could pompous fasting save the Pharisees who hated Christ.

The care of the immigrants did not receive the united attention of our conciliar legislators before the Council of 1884. There was no lack of care of the immigrants up to this time. Charitable societies existed as far back as 1737, and the Hibernian Society of New York, founded in 1790, was of great assistance to the Church in watching over the newcomers. Savannah, Charleston, Philadelphia and other ports of entry had such welfare groups. The Mission of Our Lady of the Rosary, founded in New York in 1881 for the protection of Irish immigrant girls, and the St. Raphael Society, founded in 1861 in Germany for the protection of emigrants which later (1889) established the Leo House in New York, are responsible for much of the social welfare work of this kind and were commended by the Fathers of the Council of 1884.

CONCLUSION

Needless to say, many other aspects of Catholic welfare, some of a passing and others of a permanent nature, are considered in the deliberations of these eleven assemblies of the Catholic hierarchy of America.

The means taken at the close of these meetings to reach the minds and hearts of the clergy and faithful—the *Pastoral Letters*—were effective in stressing every phase of Catholic action. Bishop Carroll's *Pastoral* of 1792 dwells particularly upon the social effects of a Catholic education for the establishment of "a prevailing purity of manners." Obedience to God, as taught by Catholic instructors, instills in a supernatural way obedience to civil government. A reverential love and fear of God in the heart of the citizen heightens the realization of the brotherhood of all men in Christ and creates those habits of virtue which are essential to social well-being and happiness. If special stress is placed by our first bishop upon devotion to the Mother of God, it is again under the social value of the preservation through Her intercession and patronage of an integral faith in Christ upon which morality must be based in order to exist. In the two *Pastorals* of 1829, it is the "vast tide of immigration which has rolled across the Atlantic during the half-century just elapsed" which occupies the attention of our prelates; and in the midst of the problems created by this great influx they see clearly the social, as well as the religious, import of our loss-and-gain problem, and rightly they call attention to the solution of the problem as found in the social and political convulsions of Europe at the time. Here for the first time, also, do we find the warning of the evil effects of anti-Catholic attacks and of the supreme value of the Catholic press in keeping the nation on the steady keel of religious equality. The necessity of a social bond of union among Catholics—"the knitting together of our members into compact unity"—despite the prevailing violent political antagonisms is described in an eloquent page that might well be repeated every year since it was first written. Against the dangerous social tendencies of false liberalism, chief of which is a lessening of respect for the supreme place of religion in daily life, the faithful are cautioned in terms that every Christian must accept. Nor is the social value of a life of perfection on the part of those whom the Master called the Light of the World forgotten in the *Pastoral to the Clergy* that same year. That which struck at the heart of the social bond between clergy and faithful—scandals—are again viewed in this same light. The *Pastoral* of 1833 has a more profound note reflecting the financial conditions of the day— the meaning of life itself, based on the text: "What does it profit a man to gain the whole world, if he lose his own soul?" And within the doctrine itself, the place of supernatural grace, of prayer and supplication, is explained. The *Pastoral* of 1837 could not avoid a topic on the lips of every Catholic at the time —the increasing animosity to the Church; and this again is de- plored from the social viewpoint on account of its inevitable effect upon the faith of all Christians. Civic and national peace and security were at stake, and Catholics were cautioned to help preserve them by patience in their tribulation and by a Christ- like spirit of magnanimity toward their enemies. So also are vile and anti-Catholic books and pamphlets viewed by our lead- ers; and again do we find emphasized the necessity of the Catho- lic press in this regard. By the year 1840, so many practical problems of organization in Church progress had presented themselves that we find this national note of social and civic security somewhat subdued in the *Pastoral* of that year; but one factor in Catholic social welfare is mentioned in strong terms— the danger of mixed marriages. There may be a more obvious connection than is apparent in the paragraph which follows on the danger of riches. Intemperance is first mentioned in the *Pastoral* of 1840, and there is no doubt that it has a large share in the anxieties of the prelates who issued the *Pastoral* of 1843. Divorce is stigmatized in this latter *Pastoral* as a growing social evil and the bishops "are determined to employ the severest authority of the Church against persons guilty of so heinous a crime and to cut them off from her communion." The good effects of the conversions in England through what is known as the Oxford Movement are recognized, and in the following *Pastoral*, that of 1846, the Movement occupies a prominent place. The *Pastoral* of 1849 repeats to some extent the salutary effect of devotion to the Mother of God upon society and religion.

The *Pastoral* of the First Plenary Council of 1852 has a section on the needs of the Church in America, and the faithful are reminded that the bishops and priests are exerting every effort "to found hospitals, establish orphanages, and provide for every want of suffering humanity, which Religion forbids us to neglect." In the longer *Pastoral* of the Second Plenary Council of 1866, the value of a strict appraisal by the civil government of its limitations in the matter of legislation, the authority of the Church in the Sacrament of Marriage, the necessity of a virile Catholic press and of Catholic literature, the effects upon society by an irreligious educational system, the need of Catholic Protectories and Industrial Schools for poor and neglected children, the social evils hidden in sinful amusements, and the great need of approaching the Negro problem with sane zeal—these are some of the topics treated in this remarkable document.

From the viewpoint of social welfare, the *Pastoral* of the Third Plenary Council of 1884 is more ample and more detailed than any previous Charge. We find here, for example, a recognition by our prelates of the effect of the frontier movement in the West and Far West upon the Church. Current philosophies of life which weaken the bond of social unity are described in terms which even the uneducated can understand.

The insinuation of a conflict between Catholic belief and American ideals is dealt with vigorously; and the message given is one that Amercans of all faiths could grasp:

The spirit of American freedom is not one of anarchy or license. It essentially involves love of order, respect for rightful authority, and obedience to just laws.

The influence of Christian education in the formation of American life is treated with generous space, and the body of the *Pastoral* is devoted to the subject of the Christian home. The observance of the Lord's Day is treated from both the social and the religious point of view, and the excellence of Catholic societies and fraternities for social, religious, and beneficial purposes is likewise extolled.

Through all these official messages from our bishops runs the one theme—the paths of duty and of virtue for the Catholic are clearly marked and pointed out, as the *Pastoral* of 1884 says, "not to restrain your freedom, but that you may journey safely, that you may live wisely and virtuously, that you may have happiness, temporal and eternal."

INDEX